Google
Tips & Tricks

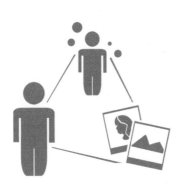

Welcome to Google Tips & Tricks, your ultimate guide to Google's amazing software. Offering a whole host of free applications covering a range of subjects, the internet giant has taken the world by storm, especially since the launch of its Android mobile platform. In this Revised Edition, you'll find all the old favourites covered, such as Gmail, Calendar, Picasa, Maps and more. On top of that, you'll find guides to Google Drive and Google Play, the latest apps to find their way onto desktops and mobile devices. So whether you're looking to improve the way you work, stay social, have some fu creative, you'll find everything you need here.

Google
Tips & Tricks

Imagine Publishing Ltd
Richmond House
33 Richmond Hill
Bournemouth
Dorset BH2 6EZ
☎ +44 (0) 1202 586200
Website: www.imagine-publishing.co.uk

Head of Publishing
Aaron Asadi

Head of Design
Ross Andrews

Production Editor
Jon White

Senior Art Editor
Dani Dixon

Design
Charlie Crooks

Printed by
William Gibbons, 26 Planetary Road, Willenhall, West Midlands, WV13 3XT

Distributed in the UK & Eire by
Imagine Publishing Ltd, www.imagineshop.co.uk. Tel 01202 586200

Distributed in Australia by
Gordon & Gotch, Equinox Centre, 18 Rodborough Road, Frenchs Forest,
NSW 2086. Tel + 61 2 9972 8800

Distributed in the Rest of the World by
Marketforce, Blue Fin Building, 110 Southwark Street, London, SE1 0SU

Part of the

bookazine series

Contents

Unlock the power of the world's most amazing free apps with these expert tips and tricks…

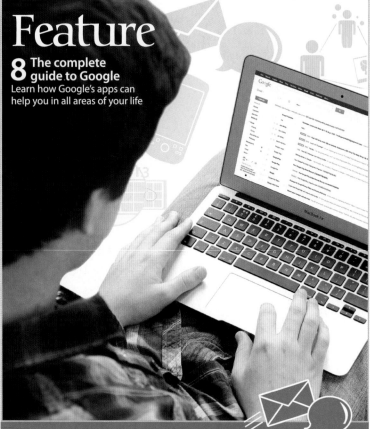

Feature

8 The complete guide to Google
Learn how Google's apps can help you in all areas of your life

Communication

Lifestyle

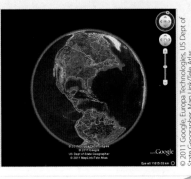

'Courtesy of Dell Inc.'

Productivity

Mobile

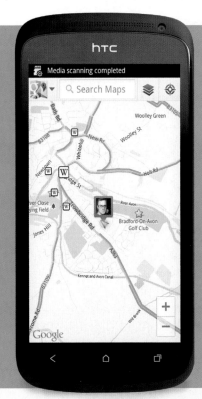

The Complete Guide to GOO

Get to know how Google applications can help every area of your life…

Google has grown from being a simple search engine provider to a purveyor of multiple services in just a decade. The services now offered by Google are wide-ranging, and in many cases ahead of the competition, yet they all have one thing in common: they are free.

As the products are further expanded and intertwined to work with each other, we are quickly reaching the point where many users could use the free Google products for all of their computing needs in place of paid software. The fact that Google has a commanding lead in the field of search means that its associated products will have

a huge potential user base to appeal to, as has been shown by the success of Gmail, which now commands the custom of hundreds of millions of users.

In recent years, some notable acquisitions have served to make the Google empire even bigger, with YouTube and Android being good examples of the company

Google
Tips&Tricks

building acquired platforms to the point that they are now household names. Google offers a huge amount of functionality for free, which when used together can form the backbone of your computing world. Most crucially of all, pretty much all of the services should be compatible with your system, no matter which platform you are using. So what are you waiting for?

"Google offers functionality that can form the backbone of your computing world"

Communication

Keep in touch with the help of Google

Gmail has quickly become one of the most popular email platforms on the planet, and for good reason.

Signing up for a new account takes a minute, and you are immediately given a huge amount of online space, and a superior interface for your trouble. There are some adverts in the main email page, but they are subtly placed and non-intrusive, which creates space for your emailing that rivals the best from Microsoft and other email providers. The benefits of Gmail are clear – not only are you given a large amount of space to work in, but the knowledge that millions of others are using the service means that you can be assured of a quick fix if a technical problem arises. Google is a brand that everyone is aware of, and reliability is at the core of its success, so uptime has been kept to a level few others can match. When you consider that spam filtering is included, there really is no reason not to look to Gmail in place of many paid-for solutions.

Google also provides other communication services, such as Google Talk and associated plug-ins which enable calls to be made over an internet connection for free, and also offers online chats via instant messaging. The service has been integrated into other Google offerings such as Gmail, which now offers the chat functionality within the standard Gmail window. Users can immediately chat to other Google users, and the resulting chat logs are saved to the Gmail account alongside normal emails. It brings instant messaging and voice calling to the one application, and therefore all of your communication needs can be catered for in one place. Video chat is also available, and software versions for a variety of mobile platforms enable you to use the service whenever and wherever you like.

Google also offers a service called Google Voice, which is currently US-only, but is expected to come to other countries in the future. It allows calls to international phone numbers at a much discounted rate, and a unique phone number which some now use to replace their traditional landlines. It has the potential to replace landlines for most people, thanks to the inclusion of voicemail, conference calling, call blocking and numerous other facilities that you would expect from a landline. Crucially, there are a number of services included that landlines are not capable of delivering, such as online archiving of calls, and SMS and email voicemail notifications. The future looks bright.

The Google communication services are already at a level which means that they can be used for almost all communication needs, but as they advance, they could potentially be used by large businesses, and gain a foothold in the wider telecoms and business email markets. For the average user, Google offers a lot of functionality that is independent of the computer they use, and it is hard to ignore so many clever services that are completely free to use.

5 ways to: improve your communication

Keep in touch in a variety of ways without paying a penny

Organising

One major benefit of the Gmail interface is the way in which labels are organised and displayed. When you receive a new email, you can quickly assign a label (category) to it, and it will be available within a folder alongside similarly labelled items. In the main email list, the label is displayed with the correct colour coding. The presentation rivals – and in some cases surpasses – more expensive email clients.

Chat

It is likely that when you are emailing people, they are also online, but email can be a slow form of communication when trying to have a conversation. If a contact is online, you can chat to them straight away from within Gmail using Google Chat. A small box will pop up showing the chat log, and it will even be saved within Gmail for future reference.

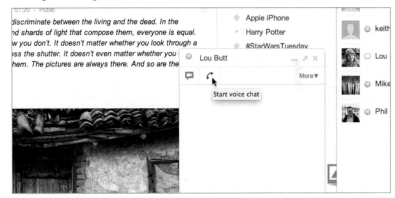

Emailing

Gmail offers a world class email interface, which is available in any browser. Your contacts are stored alongside emails, and even a basic task manager is built into the interface. Each task can have an associated email, and typing the start of a contact's name will offer you the opportunity to email them straight away. Themes let you make the experience personal to you, and the spam protection is almost foolproof.

> "Gmail offers a world class email interface, available in any browser"

Groups

Besides the well-known services, there are many other offerings from Google that can help you communicate with others. Groups is a service that lets you send mailing lists to a specific group of people, discuss events online with the same group, and even share files with each member at the tap of a button. This can be handy for businesses and those with a wide circle of friends.

Speaking

The multitude of online communication services currently available has reduced the amount of time people spend speaking to each other verbally and visually, but Google Voice and Google Talk can redress the balance. The good news is that calls will be much cheaper, or in many cases free, and they are compatible with many other Google services. The call quality can also be enhanced, as digital technology is used to deliver each call.

Video and voice plug-in

Lifestyle

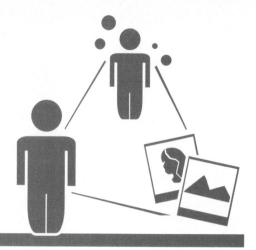

There's a Google app for every part of your life

Google's worldwide presence makes it ideal for those who are looking for services to share information with friends and colleagues, as it is likely that many of them will be using the very same services. Picasa is an online photo-sharing service that lets you upload new images and share them with friends. On top of that, it can be used to edit and manipulate specific effects, and as you would expect from Google, it is completely free.

YouTube is known around the world as the market leader in online video, and there are many ways in which you can utilise the service to show off to friends or reach a wider audience. You can upload videos from a desktop PC, and many smartphones now offer YouTube as a default app with the ability to upload videos directly from the phone. Most websites also use YouTube to host their videos, and every browser is capable of displaying the videos, so it should be available no matter what device you are using. When you have set up a YouTube account, your friends can subscribe to your updates, and will be notified as soon as you post a new video.

If you want to reach a much wider audience, you can set up a blog in Google's Blogger service, which only takes a minute or two to create. Because Google owns the service, new entries are indexed immediately to Google search, and this offers an advantage when trying to get your content read by more people quickly. It's a fairly basic service that will not suit professional bloggers, but will still be ideal for most potential and current bloggers.

Google Circles is Google's answer to Facebook, and enables users to share photos, videos, status messages and almost anything else in real-time. It hasn't reached the scale of Facebook yet, but it does make the social networking experience much quicker and easier to use as you are able to separate your friends list off into separate groups so that everything you post doesn't necessarily have to be seen by everyone.

The social side of Google is further enhanced by Google Latitude, which is a feature of Google Maps. It can display your current location to chosen people, and when a group are meeting up, it can make the entire process much easier.

The list of free services continues with the likes of SketchUp, offering the ability to share 3D models. As you can see, the range of lifestyle services is varied to the point that you may not need to look outside of Google for any of your social needs. Even better, most of these Google services work well with non-Google services such as Facebook and Twitter.

5 ways to: improve your everyday life

All of your social needs can be catered for by Google services

Video

YouTube is one of the most popular services in the world, and setting up an account and sharing your own videos is incredibly simple. You can upload videos from a PC or a smartphone, and you can also subscribe to videos of people you know. It is an all-encompassing service that is perhaps the most social of all, and one that can be used within a circle of friends as much as to follow the famous.

Photos

Photo sharing is hugely popular, and can be a positive force to bring people together. Picasa makes the process as easy as possible, and enables real-time sharing of the photos you take and the photos of others. Add in the ability to edit the photos and a variety of mobile apps to let you share from anywhere, and it could quickly become a favourite service that you use every single day.

The alternative Facebook

Google Circles is a slick social network that allos you to group together specific people into specific circles so that you can share things with certain groups and not others, bypassing the dilemma of whether you want you close family members to read all of your blue rants! Setting up circles is as easy as dragging and dropping and and can post comments and media just as easily as you can in Facebook. What's more, Circles scans your Gmail account for possible friends.

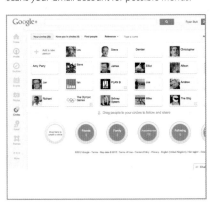

Reading news

Getting your daily dose of news has been made even easier by Google News. It gathers together news stories from 4,500 English-language news sources across the globe, and groups stories together in a very user-friendly way. Putting articles into sections, Google News allows you to personalise the news selection by picking your favourite categories, as well as allowing you to easily share interesting reads with friends and family.

Tell the world

Google's Blogger offers a complete solution for creating your own blog, which you can have up and running in a matter of minutes. The tie-in with Google helps a lot for search indexing and it is completely free. With the knowledge that thousands of blogs are hosted by Google, you can also be assured of the best uptime available, and a continually reliable service.

Productivity

Make your daily tasks much easier with Google's extensive functionality

When you sign up for a free Google account, you are automatically allocated a generous amount of online storage space, which is currently close to 8GB. This is higher than on most competing services, and can be used for emails, photos, documents and almost anything else you would like to store and back-up online.

The Google Drive service alone takes advantage of this space by letting you create, modify and upload all types of files, and even includes the ability to manage your documents in folders. This effectively makes it a worthy alternative to Dropbox and other online storage services, but with the advantage that you can store everything you need in the one place, including your all-important email communications. If you are a power user, and use up your allotted space, you can purchase even more for a very reasonable sum, ie. $5 per year for 20GB. It is scalable, affordable, and extremely reliable.

Other services that can be used within this space include Reader, which will track and present all of the blogs and news feeds you want to follow in real-time, and Finance, which presents business information and interactive charts and customised searches that can be used for specific communities or organisations. It is quite difficult to not find a service from Google that will help you get things done, and because they are comparable to competing software services, it is hard to even consider alternatives at times.

The services on offer are also quite flexible, and can be used in a variety of ways. For example, you can set up a Gmail account to send as a different email address, such as a custom domain, and then set up your custom domain email to auto-forward incoming emails to your Gmail account. This means that you can use a completely unique identity, yet retain the excellent organisational qualities and stability of the Gmail platform. Google Drive accepts

a multitude of file formats and lets you create and export documents in all of the most popular formats as well, so you can do all of your Office document creation through this service and never touch a software solution.

The one downside of most Google solutions is that they require an internet connection to work, and they tend to run in browsers. The browser side can be advantageous, because it allows you to use the services no matter what device you are currently using, but many still prefer the feel of a standalone application. Software like Fluid for Mac OS lets you set up your Google services to work like apps; you can create an icon, and they will show up in their own window just like standard apps, and there are similar solutions available for Windows. There are also plans to make services like Google Drive work offline if required. This will add one more killer feature to an already long list of solutions that really can change the lives of the people using them.

5 ways to: improve your daily tasks

You can do almost anything with Google

Sharing

Google Drive has changed the way you create and share documents. Google Docs has now been incorporated into Drive, meaning from the one screen you can create a document, form, spreadsheet or drawing, and share it with the world. Drive works across devices and platforms, meaning any changes you make can be synced and viewed whenever you next open them up.

Get organised

Google Calendar is more capable than many standalone paid-for solutions thanks to its lightning quick performance and the myriad advanced features that are included. You can set up multiple calendars on different subjects, and go on to synchronise them with mobile devices and your home PC. When you make a change on one device, it will automatically be shown on any other device connected to the same calendar.

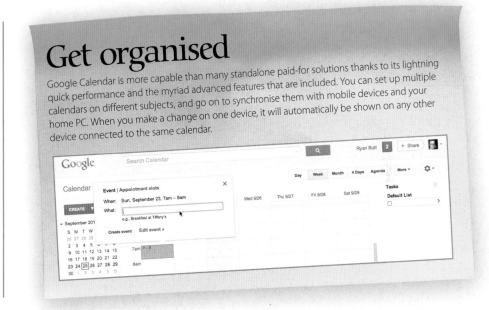

Research

Few would argue against the fact that Google's search tool is the best in the world. It has built a reputation for providing accurate and relevant results by using the information we provide every minute of the day. Not all Google searches are the same, because a search by one person could bring up different results than another person searching the same keywords, because the system will have learnt what you have searched for in the past.

Tasks

A little-known feature of Gmail is the ability to create and manage tasks from within the main interface. This lets you assign emails to tasks easily, and manage everything in the one place. With your contacts also held within Gmail, you may find that this quickly becomes your go-to place for most of your productivity needs, and it certainly is an adequate competitor to Outlook, with the added pro of being free.

Keep up

Google Reader lets you specify news services to follow, and these will be updated in real-time as the news happens. There are many clients available that utilise the service to bring the latest news to mobile phones, PCs and tablets, and it is widely recognised as one of the best news reading clients in the business. The wealth of information this service can collect is astonishing.

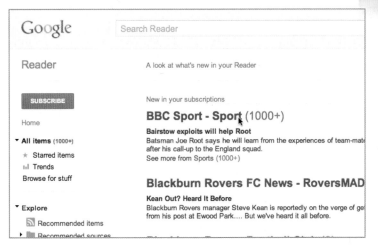

Mobile

Make your life productive while you're on the move with Google's array of mobile applications

Ever since the birth of Android, Google has become a major player in the mobile phone arena, and thrown much time and money at porting its main services to all of the mobile platforms, not just Android. You can literally do anything you like on an Android phone now, and the integration with the main Google services has been accomplished sensitively to recreate the experience and make it as familiar as possible to the Google desktop user. The natural tie-in with Google starts from the moment an Android phone is turned on, and inputting a Google account ID will automatically offer access to mobile Gmail, navigation, the Play Store and countless other offerings. If there is a service that Google hasn't yet ported to mobile, it's likely that a third-party developer has, and possible that they have created an app than can do more with the service.

YouTube was initially a desktop-only service, but the proliferation of faster mobile networks and more sophisticated mobile technology has enabled the service to work perfectly on every Android smartphone. Even the budget Android phones can now offer a viewable experience, and Google has ensured that the service is a core part of the Android operating system. Besides viewing content, you can take videos with a phone camera, and immediately upload them for your friends to see via YouTube. The Google tie-in means that you will receive immediate updates of content that have been previously uploaded by friends.

The ability to create and share content from a mobile phone continues because photos can also be uploaded and shared via a phone, and even documents can be browsed and edited using the mobile Google Drive service, which will enable you to work anywhere. This is particularly useful if you need to urgently change or create a document for work, and will enable you to continue working even when you are away from the office. All of the services come together to let you do almost anything you can do on a desktop via a smartphone.

Because the Google services naturally work online, any changes you make on a mobile will be replicated on any other device you use and vice versa. If you delete an email on a phone, it will be deleted on the server, and thus shown when accessed via a desktop. This is also true of documents that are uploaded or deleted, photos that you upload, and even mobile chats that you undertake. No matter what you do on a Google service and where you do it, everything stays in step so that all of your data is consistent at all times.

On an Android phone, everything from the operating system to the apps in the Play Store derives from Google, and it is true that without all of the services offered by Google, our lives would be a lot less efficient and a lot less interesting. The benefits of Google products are almost too numerous to mention.

5 ways to: improve your mobile life

Google services are just as effective to use when you are out and about

Google apps

Google has created many mobile solutions that work together to recreate the main Google services in mobile form. For example, on an iOS phone you can use almost every service by downloading the free Google app, which also includes the ability to search by text, voice and even photos using a smartphone camera. Most of the Google services are also natively supported on Google Android phones, so you can be using them no matter where you are.

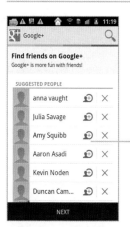

Navigation

Google Maps is well known on all platforms, but the inclusion of Google Navigation on Android smartphones has taken mobile mapping to a whole new level. As usual for Google, the service is free, but in this instance it offers full turn-by-turn navigation, traffic monitoring and a range of other features that make it as good, if not better, than many hardware navigation solutions.

Communicate

Mobile phones are all about communication, and being able to use Google Talk and Google Voice (US-only at this time) from a BlackBerry, iPhone or Android smartphone can save a lot of money on monthly bills. With free text messages and a separate number for the Google Voice service, you will be able to completely change the way you use your mobile, and keep in contact with friends in more ways than ever before.

Blogging on the move

Being able to update a blog on the move can offer many advantages for those who are serious about providing timely content for their readers to view. The Android Blogger app allows real-time updating from an Android phone, with photos and text completely changing the way a blog is managed. It will save time and make the content more interesting, which is more than you would normally expect from a free service.

Thousands of apps

The recently updated Google Play, which is accessible through Android phones and tablets, offers more than 200,000 apps, which cover almost every possible use. Many are free, and even the paid titles are priced very low. From sophisticated multiplayer games to professional productivity solutions, the Play Store offers something for everyone. There are also a host of third-party apps that are designed to work closely with the Google services, which makes the entire Google experience even more impressive.

> "The Play Store now offers something for everyone"

Communic

Expert tips and step-by-step guides to help you communicate using Google apps…

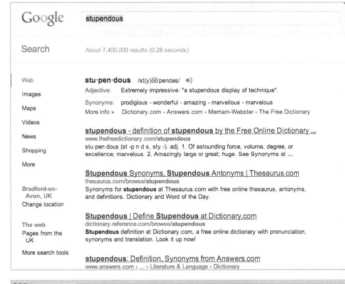

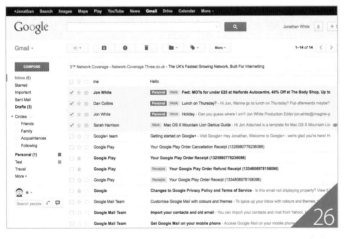

ation

"It is hard to ignore so many extremely clever communication services that are free to use"

Google

Contacts ▾

NEW CONTACT

My Contacts (6)

▾ Circles (4)
   Friends
   Family
   Acquaintances
   Following (4)

Most Contacted

Other Contacts

New Group...

Search people..

☐ Bobby Phelps
☐ Dan Collins
☐ Gavin Thomas
☐ Jack Parsons
☐ Sarah Harrison
☐ Steph White

A guide to Gmail

Everything you need to know about Google's email service

Gmail is an incredibly complex and clever online service that manages to hide all of the trickery behind the process. It's simple to use yet capable enough for the most serious of email users. With many project management-style features and reliability that few other clients can match, it is the perfect email solution for the majority of users.

The huge amount of included space and the way the system works with other Google services, such as Contacts and Tasks, means that it will soon become an integrated service that helps you to deal with the communications you receive. It's hard to find a feature in other email solutions that Gmail does not include, which makes it a worthy rival to its often more expensive competitors.

The presentation is also extremely clean and should help keep you focused on what you need to do every single day.

> ## "It's hard to find a feature in other email solutions that Gmail does not include"

Contacts
Tasks and contacts are fully embedded within the Gmail system and they work together perfectly

Search Mail
Google's world-leading search capabilities are built right into the heart of Gmail

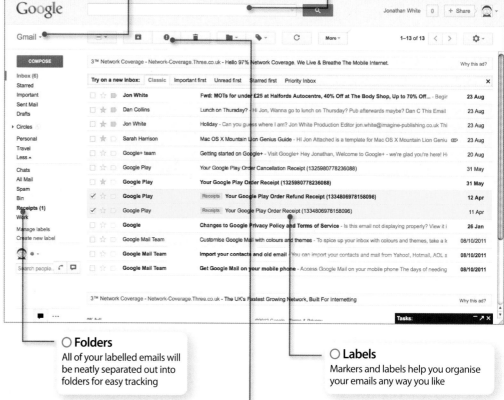

Folders
All of your labelled emails will be neatly separated out into folders for easy tracking

Labels
Markers and labels help you organise your emails any way you like

Report Spam
The spam protection works almost invisibly in the background and will save you lots of time

Priority Inbox
Let Gmail organise your emails

The Priority Inbox feature in Gmail is an extremely clever system that can work out what emails you need to read first. It uses your previous email usage to determine what you want to read first and will organise emails using your historic behaviour. It looks at the emails you reply to, the emails you ignore and the ones that you have historically starred or labelled as important.

In many ways, it replicates the way that Google Search works, because each list of search results does not just depend on the keywords that are searched for, but the user's search history.

Of course, it's near impossible for a computer to fully understand how you prioritise your work, so you can still change the importance of each email by starring them or adding importance markers. The longer you use Priority Inbox, the more accurate it will become because it has more data to work with. In the right hands the feature will be invisible to the user, but one that could have more impact than any other.

Think of Priority Inbox as your very own personal assistant who does all of the hard work for you and lets you get on with communicating with people.

Priority Inbox is easily found in the Settings menu

This is how your prioritised emails will appear

Key features

Personal	☐ ★ ☐	Sarah Harris○	
Travel	☐ ☆ ☐	Google+ tean	
Less ▲			
Chats	☐ ☆ ☐	Google Play	
All Mail	☐ ★ ☐	**Google Play**	
Spam			
Bin	☑ ☆ ☐	**Google Play**	
Receipts (1)	☑ ☆ ☐	Google Play	
Work			

Chat

You can chat to any of your email contacts from within Gmail, which makes the entire experience more personal and more efficient than many other systems. All of your chat logs are automatically saved for future reference and Chat can easily replace email communication for many needs.

Contacts ▾ ☐

NEW CONTACT

My Contacts (6)

Contacts

You can set up a database of contacts from within Gmail itself, and it can be used for everything from composing new emails to having a quick chat. It's integrated into the entire Gmail system and can also be synchronised with smartphones too.

☐ Buy anniversary card
☐ Book table for 7pm
☐ Send email to George
☐ Buy bread & milk
☐ Send budget report
☐ | ❯

Tasks

You can create a task from an email and then have it directly linked to the task, and you can also set due dates and indents if needed. The entire system is housed within a small pop-up box and is as subtle and quick to use as you could hope for.

Settings

General Labels Inbox Accounts and Import Filters Forwarding

Language: Gmail display language: [English (UK)]

Maximum page size: Show [50 ◆] conversations per page
Show [250 ◆] contacts per page

Keyboard shortcuts: ◉ Keyboard shortcuts off
Learn more ○ Keyboard shortcuts on

External content: ◉ Always display external content (suc
○ Ask before displaying external conte

Browser connection: ○ Always use https
Learn more ○ Don't always use https

Conversation View: ◉ Conversation view on
(sets whether emails of the same topic are ○ Conversation view off
grouped together)

Stars: Drag the stars between the lists. The st
star for search, hover your mouse over the

Presets: **1 star** 4 stars all stars

In use: ☆

Not in use: ★ ★ ★ ★

Desktop Notifications: Note: This browser does not support desk
(allows Gmail to display pop-up notifications
on your desktop when new chat and email
messages arrive)
Learn more

Button labels: ◉ Icons

Drafts

▸ Circles

Personal

Travel

Less ▲

Chats

All Mail

Spam

Bin

Receipts (1)

Work

Manage labels

Create new label

Customisations

You can customise the entire look of Gmail so that it suits the way you work. From themes to the number of emails displayed per page, the list of customisation options goes on and on. Throw in the ability to create visual signatures, use desktop notifications and a clever conversational view and it all comes together to create a service that can be completely unique to each individual user.

"It all comes together to create a service that can be completely unique to each individual"

Spam

Gmail's spam protection is recognised as one of the most effective systems in the world. Almost all incoming spam will automatically be sent to the spam folder for you to check and delete if necessary. You can also set up custom filters to ensure that as much spam as possible is removed from your inbox before you even see it. Spam emails could become a thing of the past in Gmail.

Get connected with Google Contacts

Contacts is a feature that's incredibly useful, but it's hidden within the Gmail interface

Google Contacts is good enough to be the only contact manager that most people will ever need. Besides integrating perfectly with Gmail, it can be synchronised with most of the major smartphone platforms so that you have all of your most needed contacts with you all of the time. This lets you amend and add new contacts when you receive them and also call them at the touch of a button. They can be integrated automatically with Facebook and other social networks and even used as points to navigate to with one tap.

You can use Google Contacts for business or pleasure. Groups can be set up for specific companies and photos added to each contact so you will never forget a face again.

Contacts | Get started with Google Contacts

1: Finding Google Contacts

In the main Gmail interface, it may not be obvious where to find Contacts. Well, it's hidden away slightly. Click on the Gmail title in the top-left corner, and a drop-down menu will appear where you can select Contacts or Tasks.

2: Add your first contact

In the left-hand panel you will see a 'New contact' button. Click this to bring up the fields you need to complete to add new contacts. There are many fields to complete such as phone, email, etc, but try to fill in as many as possible.

3: Complete the contact

You can now click the 'Add' button at the bottom to include relevant fields. Everything from relationship to nicknames can be added, and this will make finding the contact a lot easier. The notes field is also useful if you want to add random information about an individual.

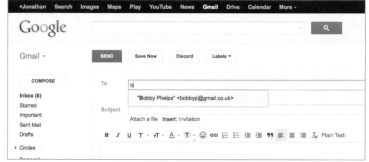

4: Use the contact

Once the contact is set you will be able to use it in many ways. Just typing the start of the person's name will bring up their email address and you can simply click to choose it. Contacts will quickly become the backbone of all of your communications.

Add attachments to your emails

Knowing how to use attachments effectively could make all the difference

When attachments are used correctly, they lift emails to a whole new level. In Gmail you can send attachments of any type up to a limit of 25MB each, which is very generous when you consider that many business email systems are limited to only 10MB. This is useful for long presentations, large documents and complex databases.

There are many things that you can customise within Gmail, such as the ability to upload attachments in the background (so you can continue to work), and you can also choose how you want to deal with incoming attachments. Gmail has very good spam support, so you're also afforded a level of protection to ensure that you're given adequate warning before downloading and opening attachments from people you don't know.

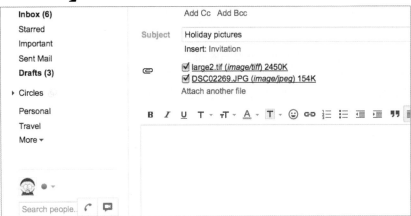

Gmail | Make the most of email attachments

1: Adding an attachment
When you have created the text and contact for an email you want to send, look for 'Attach a file', which should be just below the main subject line. When you click it, a new window will appear that will let you choose which file to attach.

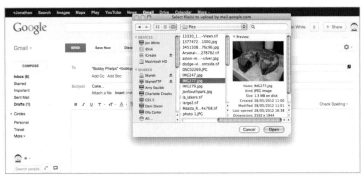

2: Choose the attachment
In the new window you will need to scroll to the file you want to attach to the outgoing email you're about to send. When you have located it, double-click on the file and you'll be returned to the main screen where it will begin to upload as an attachment.

3: Upload the attachment
If the file is large you will see a progress bar that fills up as the file uploads to the Google servers. When it has completed uploading you will be able to send the email. The speed of the process is dependent on your internet connection.

4: Changing settings
In Gmail settings under General, you can scroll to the bottom and change the way attachments are handled. You can choose to have one file upload at a time with no progress bars, or upload multiple files and see their progress in real time.

Filter spam from your email account

Spam can blight any inbox, and despite Google's clever spam detection, the ability
to filter specific emails can give you a spam-free life if you make a little effort

Filters are a feature of Gmail that not many people
actually use. They look complicated at first glance, and
when the system works so well anyway, why bother?
Well, there are many reasons to use filters, and in this
tutorial we will tell you why they are useful, as well as
giving you the tools to get started. With some time spent
creating them, you may find that a lot of your email
organisation can automatically be done for you. As new
emails arrive, they can be labelled or saved to specific categories, and you can
even try to eliminate spam completely from your inbox with some clever tricks.

Understanding the messages that you receive is crucial to setting up the right
filters, and perseverance is key. When you receive emails, and you realise that you
may want them put in a particular place, just set up a filter. The more you set up,
the better the system works, and over time you will have an inbox that is more
or less completely automated. It may feel tiresome to continually set up filters at
first, especially for spam, but it's well worth the effort in the long run.

Gmail | Make life easier with filters

1: Where to start
In Gmail, go to the settings section, and look for
the Filters link at the top of the page. Click the link
and you will see a blank page that has a 'Create a
new filter' link. Click this.

2: Set up a filter
You will now see a new window with some
options available to you. The best way to start is
by setting up a filter for your own email address.
This makes testing easier.

3: The first page
Once you have input your own email address, you
can then click 'Create filter with this search'. This
brings up a new window that lets you choose
exactly what you want to do with incoming emails.

4: Labelling
Click 'Apply the label', and then choose a label from
the drop-down box that subsequently appears.
Once you have done this, click 'Create filter'. You
are now all set to test it.

5: Test it
Now send yourself a test email and wait for it
to arrive in your inbox. You should see that it is
automatically labelled with the tag you chose –
with no manual intervention at all.

6: Detect spam
You can now create a filter for commonly received
spam. We will use the example of 'replica' as a
common word that is often included in spam. Go
back to the filter settings and create a new filter.

Gmail settings
Make sure spam never reaches your inbox

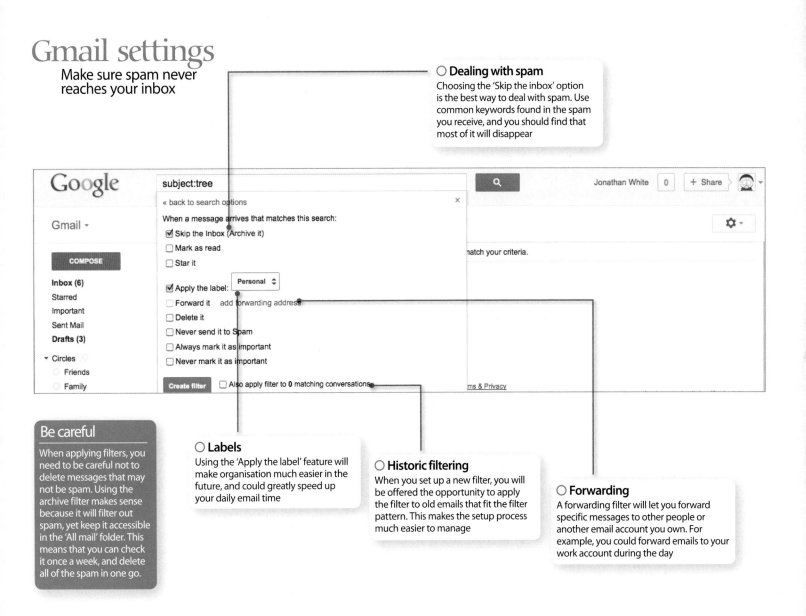

○ **Dealing with spam**
Choosing the 'Skip the inbox' option is the best way to deal with spam. Use common keywords found in the spam you receive, and you should find that most of it will disappear

Be careful
When applying filters, you need to be careful not to delete messages that may not be spam. Using the archive filter makes sense because it will filter out spam, yet keep it accessible in the 'All mail' folder. This means that you can check it once a week, and delete all of the spam in one go.

○ **Labels**
Using the 'Apply the label' feature will make organisation much easier in the future, and could greatly speed up your daily email time

○ **Historic filtering**
When you set up a new filter, you will be offered the opportunity to apply the filter to old emails that fit the filter pattern. This makes the setup process much easier to manage

○ **Forwarding**
A forwarding filter will let you forward specific messages to other people or another email account you own. For example, you could forward emails to your work account during the day

7: The spam filter
Create a new filter, and input the word 'replica' in the 'includes the words' box. This will force the filter to look for any email with the word 'replica' in it.

8: Remove spam
Click 'Create filter with this search', and tick the 'Skip the inbox' field. When an email arrives with the word 'replica', it will never show up in your inbox.

9: Just checking
If you navigate to the 'All Mail' folder, you can check the archived emails from time to time. This is where the filtered messages will be held.

Organise your mailbox in Gmail

Gmail has many functions that can keep your inbox clutter-free and perfectly organised

Email can be a big part of your life, and when the number of incoming messages is high, it makes sense to organise everything as clearly as possible. Gmail makes the process remarkably easy, and does so in a highly visual way. It manages to strike the right balance between complexity and simplicity, with a clear style of presentation that will suit anyone who needs to get everything in perspective.

There are many functions that will help to keep a mailbox in order, and using them sensitively is key to getting things right. It's all too easy to overdo your use of these features and make everything look too cluttered, but with the right approach you can be more organised than ever before. There are labels, stars, folders, filters and countless other tweaks that you can use, but we will concentrate on the main ones to get you started. Gmail is

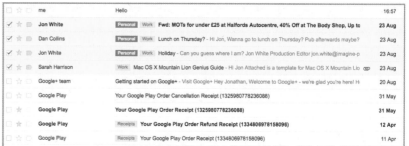

completely free, and it is surprising that it offers more organisational features than many standalone email applications, but we won't complain, and should just enjoy our new-found organised lives. With the right approach, the time you spend dealing with emails could be cut by as much as half.

Gmail | Get your emails organised

1: Labels
A long list of emails can all look alike, so the first thing to do is to create some labels. Head over to the cog icon over on the right-hand side and click Settings. Select the Labels tab across the top.

2: Create a new label
After doing this, look for the 'Create new label' link, and then click it. This will enable you to create your first label, so you can start the organisation process properly.

3: Choose a name
You now need to name the label. Note that if you choose to do so, you can nest the current label under an existing label for filing that requires more complex organisation.

4: Customisations
Once the label has been created, you will see it in the left-hand column. When you hold the mouse over it, you can click the arrow to change the colour of the label. Brighter colours for important emails work well.

5: Stars
A very quick way to remember recent emails that you need to look at is to use the stars option. You will see the outline of a star to the left of each email. Click it to highlight.

6: Don't overdo it
Try to only set up categories and labels in broad subjects. It is all too easy to set up too many categories, which would defeat the object of labelling in the first place.

Tidy your inbox
Use labels to get rid of clutter

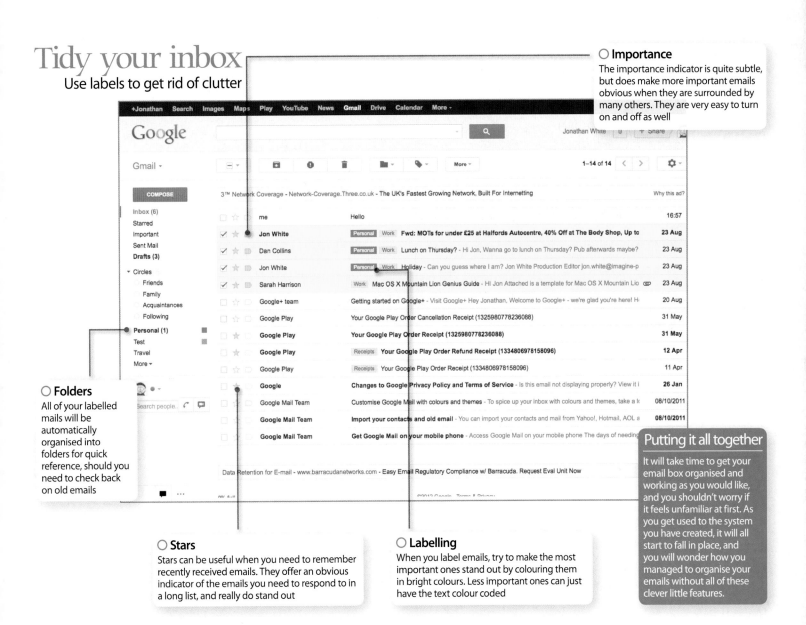

○ Importance
The importance indicator is quite subtle, but does make more important emails obvious when they are surrounded by many others. They are very easy to turn on and off as well

○ Folders
All of your labelled mails will be automatically organised into folders for quick reference, should you need to check back on old emails

Putting it all together
It will take time to get your email box organised and working as you would like, and you shouldn't worry if it feels unfamiliar at first. As you get used to the system you have created, it will all start to fall in place, and you will wonder how you managed to organise your emails without all of these clever little features.

○ Stars
Stars can be useful when you need to remember recently received emails. They offer an obvious indicator of the emails you need to respond to in a long list, and really do stand out

○ Labelling
When you label emails, try to make the most important ones stand out by colouring them in bright colours. Less important ones can just have the text colour coded

7: Searching
Remember that no matter how well you organise, the search facility is always available. Simply type a word, and Gmail will look through your entire inbox for the emails you need.

8: Tasks
If you click 'More' while in your inbox, you can add the email to a task. It will show up as a new task with a link back to the original email for the purpose of quick reference.

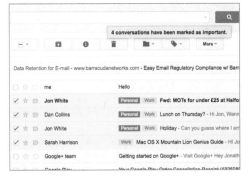

9: Importance
You can click the icon next to the star on each email in order to mark it as important. This will turn the icon yellow. You can also mark email as important through the 'More' drop-down menu.

Learn to use Google Translate

Get to grips with translation, the Google way

There will always be times when you want to read something interesting on the internet or in a letter, but unfortunately you don't understand it because it's in a foreign language. Fortunately, Google offers a translation service that will help you understand any text in a matter of seconds by converting it to the language of your choosing. It can be used for blocks of text or entire webpages and is almost universal in its scope.

There is also a Google Translate app available for iOS and Android smartphones, and the service can even automatically translate webpages in Google Chrome so every page will be perfectly accessible to you. The internet is a big place – as, indeed, the world is – but Google Translate makes it feel a little smaller. It's a wonderful tool that helps bring the world's information directly to you, no matter who wrote it. It's certainly a lot quicker than learning a new language!

> "A wonderful tool that helps bring the world's information to you, no matter who wrote it"

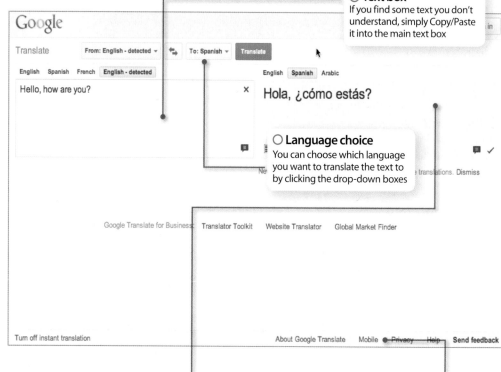

Text box
If you find some text you don't understand, simply Copy/Paste it into the main text box

Language choice
You can choose which language you want to translate the text to by clicking the drop-down boxes

Large selection
You can translate more than 50 languages, which is more than most online translators

Mobile app
An Android app is available that lets you take the smooth translation service with you

Achieve almost-perfect translations   Getting a rough idea…

When you translate text in Google Translate, you need to remember that the system is still a computer and as such no translation will be perfect. Try some example phrases to see how they come up, but you will probably find that some of the text reads strangely at first. The trick is to remember that you will be getting the general meaning and the actual translations of each word so you'll be able to understand the final result.

This is particularly true of the more complex languages which even the best human translators can struggle to understand at times, so keep your expectations reasonable

and you will get a lot out of the service. It is free, extremely quick and does offer accurate translations almost all of the time, which makes it yet another jewel in the ever-growing Google crown.

Common phrases can be more accurately translated

Understanding the Google Dictionary

Do you need a dictionary? Google is here to help

Everyone needs a dictionary from time to time, because there's no individual on the planet who knows the meaning of every single word. Google understands this, and so it offers a small, free service called Google Dictionary, which you can download from the Chrome Store and add it to your Chrome browser to quickly look up the meaning of a word. Google Dictionary used to be a standalone service as part of the Google catalogue of online services, but this was terminated back in 2011 and the system has now been condensed down into the standard Google search engine. To add it, go to the Chrome Store and search for 'Google Dictionary' and you'll be taken to an extension. Click 'Add' and the functionality will be added to your Google search engine.

Now, whenever you need to look up a word, simply type it into the search field in Chrome and the top hit will be a dictionary definition. If you need further insight then options are on hand to provide further info. The system is certainly quicker and simpler than it once was.

"When you need to look up a word, type it into the search field in Chrome"

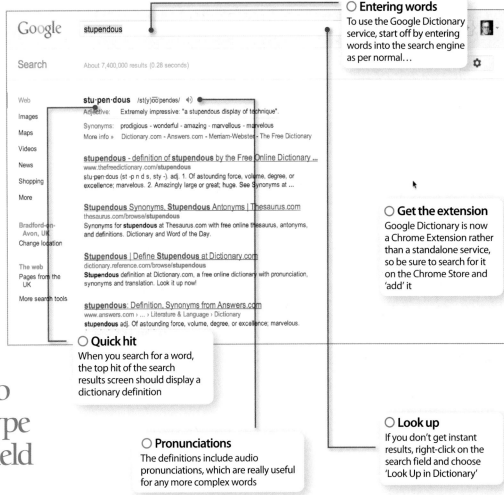

○ **Entering words**
To use the Google Dictionary service, start off by entering words into the search engine as per normal…

○ **Get the extension**
Google Dictionary is now a Chrome Extension rather than a standalone service, so be sure to search for it on the Chrome Store and 'add' it

○ **Quick hit**
When you search for a word, the top hit of the search results screen should display a dictionary definition

○ **Pronunciations**
The definitions include audio pronunciations, which are really useful for any more complex words

○ **Look up**
If you don't get instant results, right-click on the search field and choose 'Look Up in Dictionary'

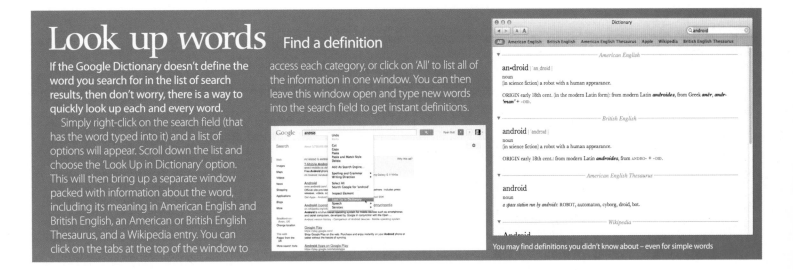

Look up words   Find a definition

If the Google Dictionary doesn't define the word you search for in the list of search results, then don't worry, there is a way to quickly look up each and every word.

Simply right-click on the search field (that has the word typed into it) and a list of options will appear. Scroll down the list and choose the 'Look Up in Dictionary' option. This will then bring up a separate window packed with information about the word, including its meaning in American English and British English, an American or British English Thesaurus, and a Wikipedia entry. You can click on the tabs at the top of the window to

access each category, or click on 'All' to list all of the information in one window. You can then leave this window open and type new words into the search field to get instant definitions.

You may find definitions you didn't know about – even for simple words

Start using Google Talk

Everything you need to know about Google Talk

Google Talk is so much more than just a feature that sits alongside Gmail and the other Google services. It lets you chat with friends and colleagues with one tap, you can share files of any type and size with contacts and you can even make and receive video and voice calls.

If anything, the 'Talk' name does not do it justice because almost every form of communication is covered in this diminutive feature that sits quietly alongside all of the other Google services on screen, yet it somehow helps to make you much more productive and communicated than ever. Google Talk has the potential to bring you closer to the people you know and love, even when you're far away from them, and there are very few services that have that. The fact that Talk is so well integrated into other Google services just makes it even more impressive.

> "Google Talk brings you closer to those you love, even when you're far away"

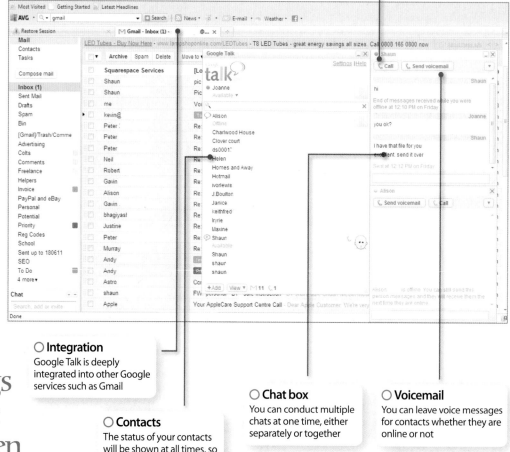

Clarity
Voice calling is easy to initiate and the result is crystal-clear call quality

Integration
Google Talk is deeply integrated into other Google services such as Gmail

Contacts
The status of your contacts will be shown at all times, so you know who is available

Chat box
You can conduct multiple chats at one time, either separately or together

Voicemail
You can leave voice messages for contacts whether they are online or not

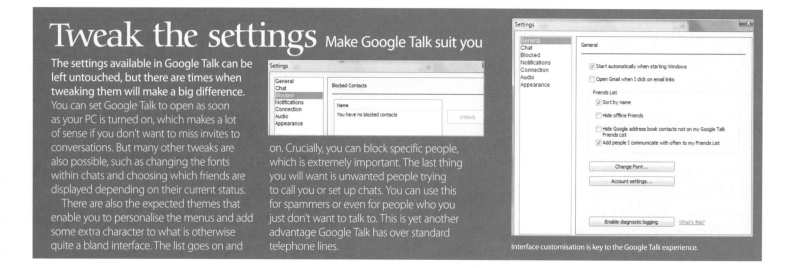

Tweak the settings Make Google Talk suit you

The settings available in Google Talk can be left untouched, but there are times when tweaking them will make a big difference. You can set Google Talk to open as soon as your PC is turned on, which makes a lot of sense if you don't want to miss invites to conversations. But many other tweaks are also possible, such as changing the fonts within chats and choosing which friends are displayed depending on their current status.

There are also the expected themes that enable you to personalise the menus and add some extra character to what is otherwise quite a bland interface. The list goes on and on. Crucially, you can block specific people, which is extremely important. The last thing you will want is unwanted people trying to call you or set up chats. You can use this for spammers or even for people who you just don't want to talk to. This is yet another advantage Google Talk has over standard telephone lines.

Interface customisation is key to the Google Talk experience.

Key features

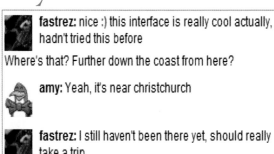

Instant messaging

Instant messaging is one of the least social methods of communication, just behind email, but it can often be the perfect medium when you need to check that someone is okay. All you have to do is tap one button and you can be conversing immediately. The inclusion of smileys also helps add some personality to your conversations.

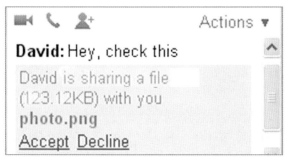

Share media

Files of any type and size can be sent using Google Talk, and this makes it the ideal service for sharing information with others. The process to send a file is so quick and simple that you don't even have to break into the conversation to do it. The files will arrive while you are still talking and can enhance any conversation whether it is for business or pleasure.

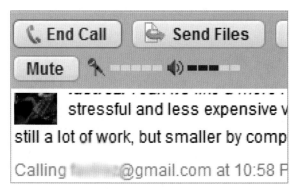

Talk

The voice facility in Google Talk could easily replace a traditional landline thanks to the call quality and ease of use. Only one tap is needed to initiate a call during a conversation and calls between Google Talk users are completely free.

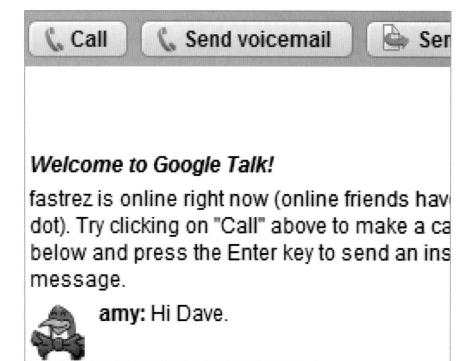

Leave a message

You can leave a voice message for someone whether they are online or not and the facility goes way beyond simple voicemail. Messages will be received in Gmail and the files can be listened to straight away or saved to a PC. You can even email the sender as soon as the message arrives in your inbox, which blurs the communication methods housed in Google Talk almost perfectly. This is what voicemail should have always been like.

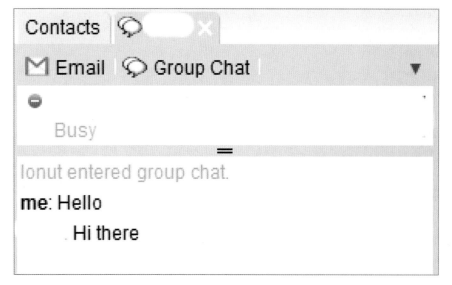

Multiple chats

You can chat to multiple people at once if you so wish by using the Google Chat Gadget. It lets you invite new people into a conversation to create a Group Chat and just requires tapping a button and choosing who to invite. You will find that Group Chats are often more interesting, but that they will sometimes spin off at a tangent. The fact the facility is available is great though and adds a new dimension to communicating using computers.

Make a Google Talk call

Google Talk makes voice calling more convenient, clearer and cheaper. It's easy to set up and you'll be speaking to people in minutes

Google Talk is well known for its ability to speed up communication between friends and colleagues, and is a complete service that brings different forms of communication together in one solution. The Google Talk Gadget can be used from any computer and allows instant messaging, but to use Google Talk for voice outside the US an application needs to be installed, or you can use a plug-in from Google that allows basic video and voice chat from Macs and PCs – go to www.google.com/talk for more information on what software your computer needs. Google Talk has now been subtley woven into

the fabric of Google+. So you can instantly chat with anyone in your circles or enter in email addresses for outside contacts.

To use the feature, click on the 'Chat' menu in the lower-right corner of your Google+ page and this will bring up a list of contacts. Anyone who is currently online and available is marked with a green dot and then you just send an invitation to the person you wish to speak to and, once they accept, you can enjoy free voice or video calls through your computer. With great features like this, surely the days of the humble land line telephone are numbered!

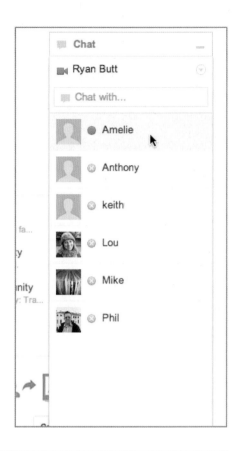

Google Talk | Get in touch using Google Talk

1: Install the software
Go to Google's main Talk page and look for the link to download the Google Talk client. It is only 1.5MB in size so should download in seconds and won't take up too many system resources when it is running. It will start up when the PC is turned on in the future.

2: Setting up
Once the software has installed you will need to sign in with your Google account username. You will see a list of friends populated in the main screen if they are already using Google Talk, and you can invite those who are not using the service.

3: Check the status
The status of your contacts will be shown by small icons next to each name. If it is green you should be able to instant message them straight away to see if they want to have a voice chat. This will ensure they have time to talk.

4: Make the call
All you have to do now is click the 'Call' button to initiate a voice call. You can end the call or send files during the conversation at any time. There are no telephone numbers to dial and it is really quick to use as well.

Leave a message using Google Talk

Google Talk isn't just about talking and instant messaging – voicemail can also be extremely handy

Voicemail has for a long time been a feature of mobile phones and landlines that feels antiquated and inconvenient. You have very little control over how to leave a message and the same is true when you pick up new messages. However, digital services change all of that and Google Talk makes the facility not only useful, but fun to use and very flexible.

You can leave voicemails for people whether they are available or not, and you can also customise the service for your own needs by creating voice memos that only you will hear. The messages are delivered in a similar fashion to email, which makes them easier to listen to and each message can run for a full ten minutes. You can save the message files for prosperity and share them with others should you need to – it all comes together to produce a digital voicemail system that feels like a product from the future. Here we show you how to leave a message and how to retrieve messages left for you.

Google Talk | Leaving a voice message

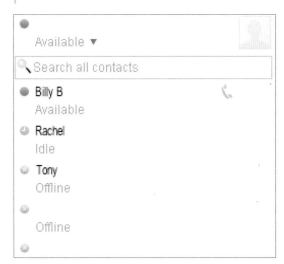

1: Check the status

When you check the statuses of your contacts you will see that some are available and that some are not. Use the icons to determine if you wish to leave a voicemail for them, no matter what their current status is.

2: Open the contact

If you click on the contact you want to reach, you will see two options at the top of the chat box. You could type a quick message in the main text box, but you can also call them or click the 'Send voicemail' button.

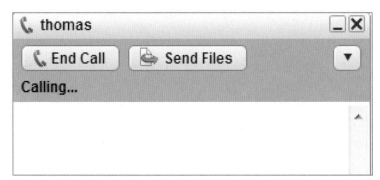

3: Leave the message

The call will now automatically route to the messaging service where you can leave a voicemail up to ten minutes long. At any time you can click the 'End Call' icon at the top to end the message and it feels similar to leaving a message on a normal phone.

4: Retrieve the message

The voicemail will be received into Gmail and the recipient can either play the message immediately or download it to listen to at his or her leisure. They can also reply with an email if they so wish, which merges the two communication methods perfectly.

Share media in Google Talk

Google Talk enables sharing of almost any file type directly to the person you're talking to

When you're having an online conversation with someone, there will be times when you need to refer to something physical. Whether it's a report during a business conversation or a holiday photo to show off how much fun you were having, text on its own is not always enough.

Google Talk lets you send almost any file format you want to the person you're talking to, and the speed at which the facility works makes it ideal for dropping an item into a conversation. As the file is sending, the progress bar will show when it will complete, and you can even carry on chatting during the process. The file size limits are generous, so even longer videos are supported. Google Talk could potentially replace other methods of transferring files such as FTP because it works so quickly, and you can discuss the file in real-time with the person you're sending it to. No more emails back and forth trying to work out what each person means – just a file and a conversation.

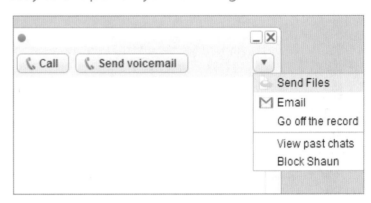

Google Talk | Share media in Google Talk

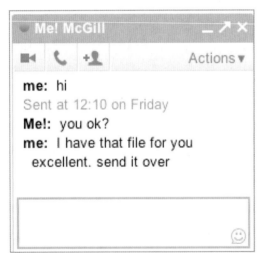

1: Where to start

During a conversation you may find that you need to send a file to someone. Fortunately Google Talk has a solution to hand that is fast and will get the file to the person you are talking to as quickly as possible.

2: What to do

Click the right-hand arrow that sits unobtrusively next to the 'Call' and 'Send Voicemail' options. You will see options for emailing, sending files, viewing past chats etc, and this will likely be a button that you'll find yourself clicking a lot during chats.

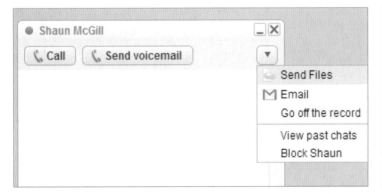

3: Find the file

Clicking 'Send Files' will take you to the usual browse boxes for you to choose the file you want to upload. You can choose large files as well – the only difference is that they will take longer to upload and reach the recipient.

4: It's on the way

As the file is being sent to the recipient, they will see a progress bar showing how much of the file has been delivered. The conversation can continue while the file is being sent and they will be notified when it has reached 100%.

Google Talk

How to share a file with one of
your Google Talk contacts via a
text conversation

○ **Multiple sharing**
You can keep many chats running
at the same time and also share files
with multiple people. Each chat box is
small enough for you to be able to see
what people are saying

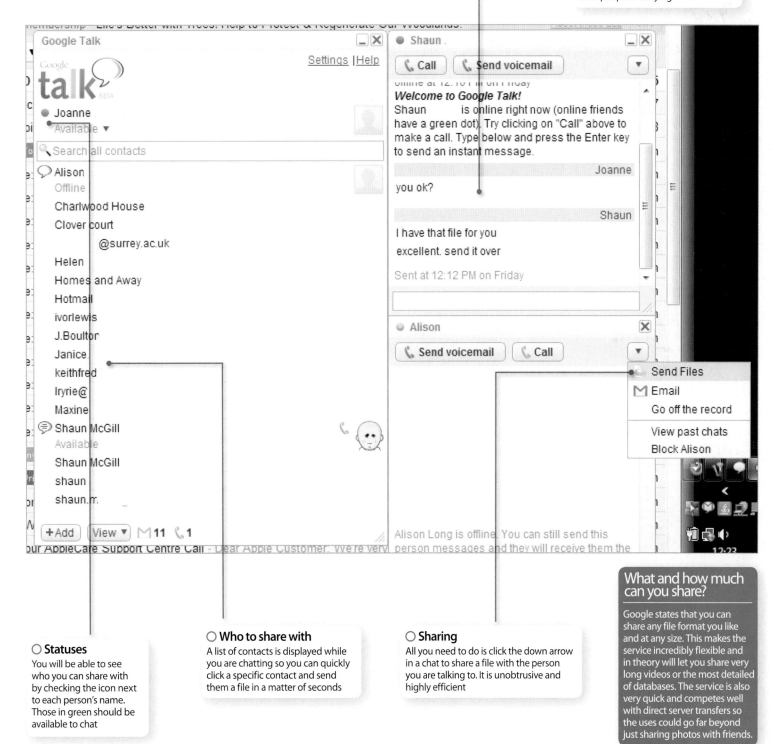

○ **Statuses**
You will be able to see
who you can share with
by checking the icon next
to each person's name.
Those in green should be
available to chat

○ **Who to share with**
A list of contacts is displayed while
you are chatting so you can quickly
click a specific contact and send
them a file in a matter of seconds

○ **Sharing**
All you need to do is click the down arrow
in a chat to share a file with the person
you are talking to. It is unobtrusive and
highly efficient

**What and how much
can you share?**

Google states that you can
share any file format you like
and at any size. This makes the
service incredibly flexible and
in theory will let you share very
long videos or the most detailed
of databases. The service is also
very quick and competes well
with direct server transfers so
the uses could go far beyond
just sharing photos with friends.

Introducing Google+

Get to know Google's answer to Facebook and Twitter

Google+ combines the best bits of Facebook and Twitter and throws in a few unique ideas of its own that make it far more than just another social network.

The innovative Circles feature enables you to sort your friends into distinct groups, restricting what information you share with them. So, for example, you can put your boss into a Colleagues circle, your mum into a Family circle and your friends into a Friends circle and choose to share specific posts with only specific groups. Anyone not in one of those specified groups won't see the updates you don't want them to see. It's a powerful feature that makes Google+ a truly valuable service. Throw in the Hangouts feature, where you can video-chat with up to nine other people; a local search function that uses all the power of Google's search engine; and a beautiful interface, especially for photos, and you've got a service well worth investigating.

> "The best bits of Facebook and Twitter plus a few unique ideas"

○ Filter content
You can filter your timeline to instantly see the posts from your friends or family, or those in other circles you have set up

○ What's on your mind
Post an update or share a photo using the box that appears at the top of the home page. This is an easy way to keep your account up to date

○ Trends
The trending feature, like that in Twitter, shows you what topics people are talking about, giving you a real-time insight into current opinion

○ Posts
Google+ is, of course, nothing without the content from yourself and other users. Your most recent updates and photos are displayed in the main part of the screen

○ New people
Google+ constantly recommends new people you might want to follow, often using your address book to match those that also use the service

Gaming on Plus
Discover social gaming

Google+ is about a lot more that simply sharing stuff. The social site is also a growing hive of gaming. Many of the most popular games you will know about from smartphones, such as *Angry Birds*, are available to be played in the web browser within Google+ itself.

The games are completely faithful reproductions of the ones you have already played and that alone makes it the perfect time-waster. But there is an additional social aspect to the gaming within Google+. The games that people in your circles have played are also displayed on the Games page. In

some games this amounts to nothing more than seeing the high scores of those people, a target for you to try to beat to give you bragging rights over them. In other games, such as *8 Ball Pool*, you get the full multiplayer experience. You can invite your friends to join you in a game, but if they are not available right now, you can be paired up with a random player.

The gaming part of Google+ is one of the unexpected joys of the service, and with the ever-increasing power of computers and the capabilities of web browsers, the quality of games is improving all the time.

Yes, you can play *Angry Birds*, and much more, on Google+

Key features

Events

'Events' is a simple feature you can use to invite people to events you are holding, such as parties or anything else that you want select people to know about. Your invites will show up on their Google+ pages and will also be integrated into the Google Calendar service for all the attendees.

Explore

Google+ is a vibrant location for discussion and posting news and photos on interesting topics. The Explore screen is your window into this. It picks out interesting posts that may or may not be relevant to you and invites you to comment. You can also click on the trends for a real-time view of opinion on a hot topic.

Photos

'Photos' is one of the best features in Google+. It's easy to use – you can upload pictures directly from an Android device or iPhone – and has a fantastic interface for viewing and commenting on your own and others images.

Circles

The idea behind Circles is what separates Google+ from other social networks. Anybody can choose to follow you, and when they do they will see all your posts and photos that are marked as viewable by All. By default that is every post, but on a case by case basis you can choose to make a post only viewable by a particular circle. Drag a person into that circle to give them access to that content.

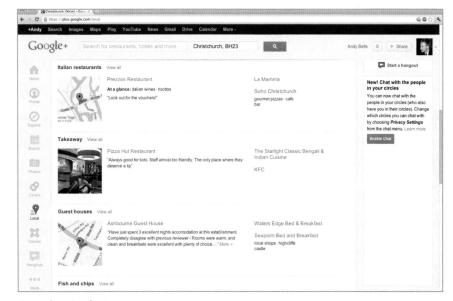

Local search

As you would expect, Google+ makes full use of Google's search engine expertise, with a powerful local search function. This shows you what is going on in your nearby area, who is posting, and highlights any interesting places to go. You can also check in at certain locations and rate businesses and restaurants you go to.

Stay social with Circles

Everything you need to know to understand Circles

When you first join Google+, chances are you'll be confused and overwhelmed. Circles, the Google+ social networking tool, won't help matters, since you'll be tempted to very loosely segregate your friends, family and other online pals into only a handful of groups.

By specifying what you post to certain circles, you are basically limiting it so that only those who are attached to that group will be able to view it. Unlike Facebook and Twitter, this means that you don't need to worry quite so much about having your post being made visible to all your followers. If you want to discuss something private with a selection of your closest friends, then you can, and no one will ever see the post unless you attach it to that group. Conversely, you can still set posts to be 'public', meaning everyone on Google+ will have the opportunity to view it, regardless of whether they're in a circle or not.

"Unlike Facebook and Twitter, you don't need to worry so much about your posts being visible"

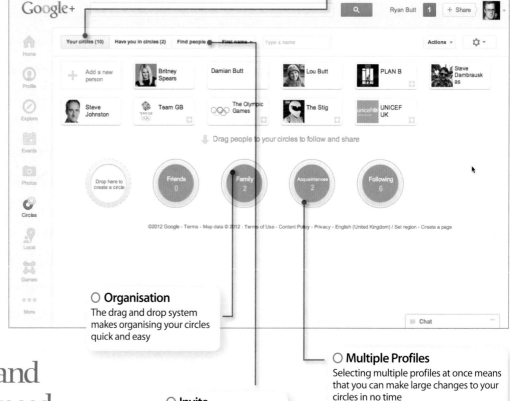

○ Circles
You can even specify a circle of followers to appear in the top section, for when you want to filter through larger circles

○ Organisation
The drag and drop system makes organising your circles quick and easy

○ Invite
'Find and invite' means that you can add new people to your stream in no time

○ Multiple Profiles
Selecting multiple profiles at once means that you can make large changes to your circles in no time

Use the Suggestions
Help fill out your stream

On the right-hand side of the main stream page, you will noticed the 'Suggestions' menu. These are people who are part of your extended circles; in other words, those that have been added to the circles of your own followers. As you've probably seen with Facebook, the chances are that you may know some of these people, and would want to add them. Google+ wants you to fill out your feed as much as possible, and providing that you keep your circles tidy, this should never prove to be too much of an issue. Hover over the image of any of these suggestions to find out a little more about them, or click on them in order to search their profile and posts in closer detail. If you're satisfied that Google has suggested someone that you think you might appreciate following, then simply click the 'Add to circles' button, and choose one or more circles that you think they would fit into. You can even create a new circle from this menu. Alternatively, if you've decided that the suggestion is not for you, then once again hover over the image and click the little 'X' that appears to the right of it. Upon doing this, their icon will vanish, and will subsequently be replaced with yet another suggestion.

Listen to the Google+ Suggestions to find new people to follow…

Key features

Multiple circles

People can be added to multiple circles. For example, if you know a friend of yours is really into films and TV – but loathes videogames – they will be content sitting in your circles titled 'Friends', 'Films' and 'TV'. When you post something suited to those subjects, they will see the post.

Sharing

If you've seen a post that you know your friends will really appreciate, click the 'Share' button to repost it. Doing so will enable you to specify certain circles, so there's no need to worry about others seeing something private.

Add a little interest

Circles isn't just about your nearest, dearest, and other people from the far-flung corners of your social circles, you can follow public figures, sports clubs and other organisations too. Click on the 'Fun & Interesting' box and see what's out there.

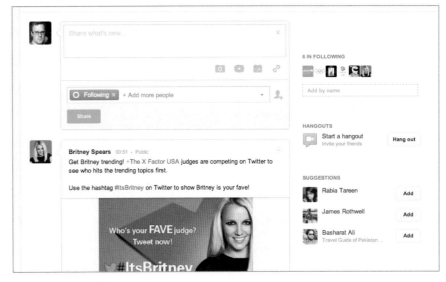

Limited viewing

Your main stream is the feed of all the people in your circles and their related posts, regardless of subject matter or their relation to you. With circles, however, you can choose to view just the posts of a specific circle, meaning that you can better digest the comments and shared media of a certain group. If you only want to keep track of what your friends are doing, then clicking on their circle in the left menu will filter out only their content.

"You can choose to view just the posts of a specific group"

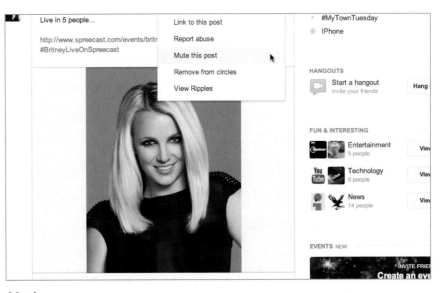

Muting posts

Since each new entry into your stream is its own mini-thread, often conversation can begin, and not just stop. If this happens, whether you're privy to it or not, it can quickly overtake your entire stream. By muting the post, you can opt out, choosing to no longer see the post or receive notifications of new comments into it. Additionally, you can always block the poster should this sort of thing happen far too often.

How to organise your circles

Set up your circles to get the best from Google+ and to keep your streams under control

Circles are key to an enjoyable Google+ experience. When you first join the social network, you may be overwhelmed with exactly where to go, what to do and how to do it. It may resemble Facebook and Twitter in design and features, but without first organising your circles you may not last long enough to discover the intricacies that separate it from the two behemoths of social media.

Creating the right circles is important to better managing your stream, and while it might be tempting to bundle everyone into the 'Following' circle, it'll be far more efficient to segregate your friends, family and online acquaintances into their respective feeds. For the effective Google+ user, however, it's even better to attach people to specific circles regarding their personal interests or relevance to you, enabling posts to have a more direct impact to the right people.

Google+ Circles | Use Circles efficiently

1: Head to the circles
Listed down the side of the Google+ page are a series of categories. Click on the 'Circles' section, which is between 'Photos' and 'Local'.

2: Creating a circle
Create a new list by clicking the far-left circle with 'Drop here to create a new circle' on it. Type the name of the circle into the text bar.

3: Adding to the circle
Click 'Add a new person' and type the name of the person you want to add. Left-click their profile to add them to the circle.

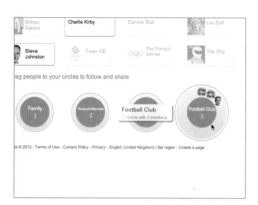

4: Saving the circle
Once you've added all the people you want, click 'Create Circle'. Once done, the circle will appear alongside your existing circles at the bottom.

5: Deleting a circle
If you want to remove a circle, select a circle from the group at the bottom and then right-click and choose 'Delete circle' option from the list.

6: Moving between circles
Click on a circle and a selection of followers will appear. Drag their icons to move them to another circle. This will also keep them in their current circle.

Delving into Circles

The Circles interface explained

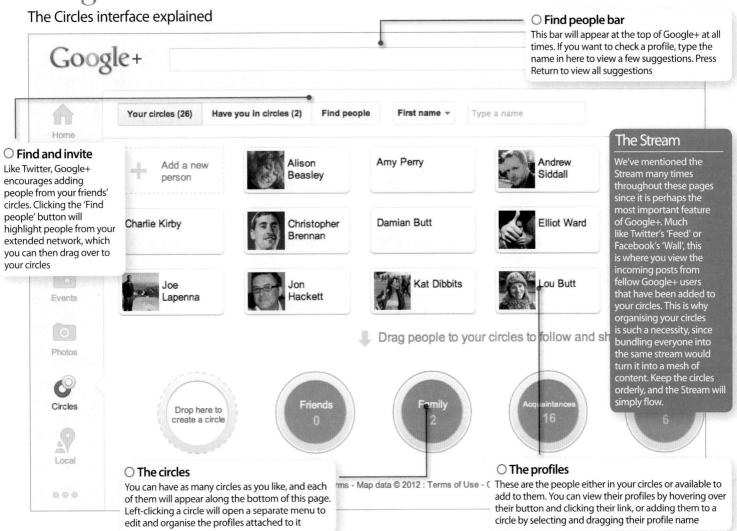

○ **Find people bar**
This bar will appear at the top of Google+ at all times. If you want to check a profile, type the name in here to view a few suggestions. Press Return to view all suggestions

○ **Find and invite**
Like Twitter, Google+ encourages adding people from your friends' circles. Clicking the 'Find people' button will highlight people from your extended network, which you can then drag over to your circles

The Stream
We've mentioned the Stream many times throughout these pages since it is perhaps the most important feature of Google+. Much like Twitter's 'Feed' or Facebook's 'Wall', this is where you view the incoming posts from fellow Google+ users that have been added to your circles. This is why organising your circles is such a necessity, since bundling everyone into the same stream would turn it into a mesh of content. Keep the circles orderly, and the Stream will simply flow.

○ **The circles**
You can have as many circles as you like, and each of them will appear along the bottom of this page. Left-clicking a circle will open a separate menu to edit and organise the profiles attached to it

○ **The profiles**
These are the people either in your circles or available to add to them. You can view their profiles by hovering over their button and clicking their link, or adding them to a circle by selecting and dragging their profile name

7: Removing someone from a circle
When you open a circle, all of the people inside will appear on screen. Simply click on the 'X' next to a person's name to remove them from the circle.

8: View circle Streams
Hover over a circle, then right-click and choose the 'View Stream for this circle' link. You can now see what folk in that particular circle are posting.

9: Viewing a circle
Back in your personal stream, a bar at the top will display your circles. Click any of these to view posts from people only in that circle.

A guide to Google+ Hangouts

Video conferencing with thousands of people

Considering the many uses of Hangouts, it seems bizarre that Google isn't making a song and dance about it. Unlike most video conferencing tools, Google+ Hangouts don't require specific software or a trail of invites, passwords and usernames. All you need is your Google+ account, and someone to host a hangout. The service enables you to use your computer's webcam to chat with your friends, though just a headset or microphone will be enough. There's even the option to use text chat for those who don't have any of the necessary equipment. We've already seen a range of uses for the tool, from business meetings and news reports to live videocasts, that can have direct interaction from its followers. There's even YouTube streaming, so you can share the latest videos while – quite literally – hanging out with your friends.

○ View
Once a hangout is complete you can view the participants in a Google+ post afterwards

○ Invite
You can invite your own friends and Circles to any hangout, providing the host allows it

"All you need is a Google+ account, and someone to host a hangout"

○ Mute
Muting the video and sound is only a click away, with another click re-enabling it

○ Observe
As long as a hangout is active, you will be able to pop in and out to see what is going on

○ Webcam
You don't need a webcam, but most modern devices come with them built-in; you might as well use it

Start your own videocast

Videocasts have been around for a few years, but they just don't have the staying power of the multitude of podcasts that litter the internet. Both downloads, in fact, often require specific editing software in order to tie it all together seamlessly and professionally. If you've ever considered yourself to be something of an entertainer, but don't have the luxury of an expensive camera or recording equipment, then Hangouts could well offer you the perfect solution. Google+ is built to cultivate this kind of growing breed of internet user, and with a healthy spread of Google+ followers, absolutely anyone can possess the capacity to create a brand-new videocast. With the inclusion of YouTube videos, too, you could even decorate a videocast with a healthy selection of related content, either to keep your watchers amused, or to offer context to something that you're discussing. With the immediacy that the Hangouts service provides, it would be a surprise if these sort of live videocasts didn't instantly become popular. The options are endless, and with the videocast constantly growing both in popularity and functionality, you can be certain that many more will turn up in the near future, too.

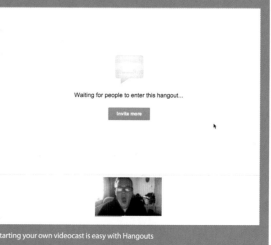

Starting your own videocast is easy with Hangouts

Hangout's features

Automatic video switching

Google+ will automatically detect who is speaking. Providing there aren't multiple voices at once, Hangouts can pick up and switch to the stream of whoever is talking. The service is trying to get you hanging out with your friends digitally, and with a feature like this it works much like a standard conversation.

Video previews

Considering the number of people that could enter a hangout, it's really quite impressive to see a video preview of everyone. Since you could use the software on a phone or laptop, you could find yourself using the service in some pretty unique locations indeed.

YouTube streaming

Being able to link to, view and watch YouTube with your friends makes sharing videos all the more immediate, while you and your friends can enjoy it together. If you're a YouTube video creator, you could even use it to debut your latest creation.

Muting

Having the option to mute sound is important for any video conferencing software, especially during more official uses. Google+ will enable you to mute and unmute both sound and video during a hangout – as well as mute your own microphone – at the touch of a button. These are handily accessible along the bottom of the Hangout window, so you won't need to look too hard when messing with settings like you have to do with most software.

"Being able to mute sound is important for video conferencing"

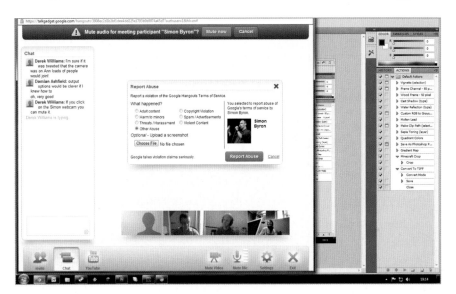

Reporting abuse

While you may invite specific people to a hangout, ranging from whole Circles to certain individuals, that doesn't stop others from inviting whoever they please. That's where the 'Report Abuse' button comes in, enabling users to report anyone they feel is in some way causing problems, at which point Google will step in to see the necessary actions are taken in order to deal with the abuse. Perhaps not an exciting feature, but an important one nonetheless.

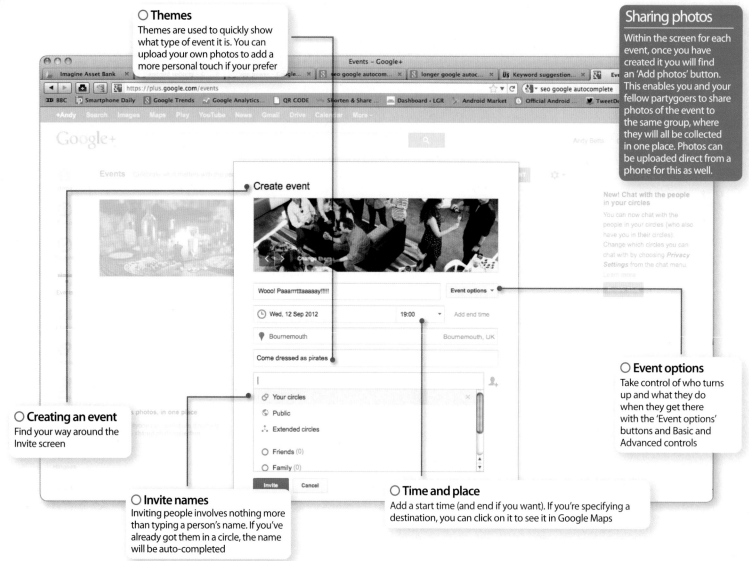

Themes
Themes are used to quickly show what type of event it is. You can upload your own photos to add a more personal touch if your prefer

Sharing photos
Within the screen for each event, once you have created it you will find an 'Add photos' button. This enables you and your fellow partygoers to share photos of the event to the same group, where they will all be collected in one place. Photos can be uploaded direct from a phone for this as well.

Create event

Creating an event
Find your way around the Invite screen

Invite names
Inviting people involves nothing more than typing a person's name. If you've already got them in a circle, the name will be auto-completed

Time and place
Add a start time (and end if you want). If you're specifying a destination, you can click on it to see it in Google Maps

Event options
Take control of who turns up and what they do when they get there with the 'Event options' buttons and Basic and Advanced controls

Send out invites with Google+ Events

Organising a party? Events in Google+ is the quickest way to ensure that everyone gets an invite

Unlike other social networks, Google+ does not limit itself to friendships in the virtual world. While the service is a fantastic way of getting back in touch with people or meeting new ones with shared interests, it also includes one major feature for your real-world friends too: Events.

Google+ Events is the easiest way of organising real-world events and ensuring that everyone you want to be at your event gets an invitation. Whether you are planning a major birthday celebration or simply want to meet up with a few friends for a drink after work, Events can handle the entire process. There's no need to send separate invitations, and your invitees can view the invitation on a calendar as well to ensure there are no scheduling mix-ups to deal with. Best of all, the service does not limit itself to Google+ users alone and you can invite anyone you like simply by adding their email address.

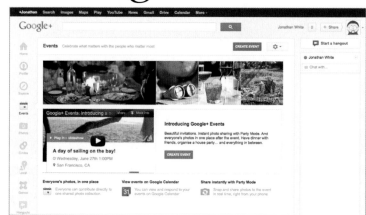

Google+ Events | Send out invites for events

1: Find events
Events is integrated into the full Google+ service on the desktop. Locate this part of the app by clicking on the Events icon in the left-hand column.

2: Create event
There's a quick overview of the service to help you, but you can dive straight on it by clicking the red Create Event button to start planning your party.

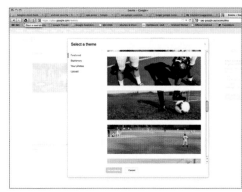

3: Choose theme
You need to choose a theme for your invite. There are dozens available in a wide number of styles so you should find one to suit. Or add your own photo.

4: Event options
Click 'Event options'. You might want to deselect the 'Guests can invite other people' option. Under Advanced, you can also make the event online only.

5: Other details
Fill in all the other details for your event, including a title for it. Pick a date and add any other information that you feel is necessary, such as dress code.

6: Invite some people
Click the 'Add person' icon to the right of the invite box. You can invite Google+ friends by clicking on their names, or type an email address and click Add.

7: Send the invite
With all that accomplished, you are now ready to send the invite. Simply click the Invite button and the job will be done.

8: View on the calendar
Your Events page will show the status of the event and enable you to invite more people. Click 'Check my calendar' to see the event within your schedule.

9: Accept an invitation
Those receiving an invite will see it on their Google+ Home screen. Just click Yes, No or Maybe to reply, and you can also add a comment for the organiser.

Lifestyle

We explore the applications that help to enhance your life, with in-depth guides and advice

A German girl showing the rule of thirds for image compo... **54**

52

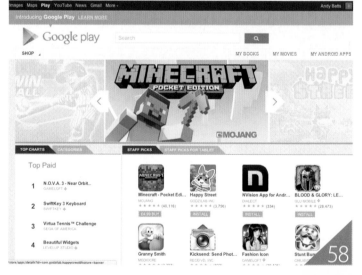

58

"All of your social
needs can be catered
for by Google"

Get to grips with Picasa

An overview of this powerful online image software

Picasa is an eye-opening image-editing manipulation and display tool and is a valuable yet free addition to your collection of software applications. A simple download and install process can be performed from the web itself, and you can select to have an icon on your desktop after installation is completed.

More internet-connected than many other more basic 'picture viewer'-type applications, Picasa is easy to use and very intuitive – built as it is with familiar Windows-style drop-down menus and straightforward clickable button controls on the screen.

Picasa has been designed to develop and extend your creative abilities so that you start doing things with images that you might not have previously considered. Many of the options are heavily automated, meaning the user can simply sit back and leave the software to control much of what happens on the screen. Above all, it's fun to use, and there's more to discover than you might at first think – so let's dive in.

> "Picasa has been designed to develop and extend your creative abilities"

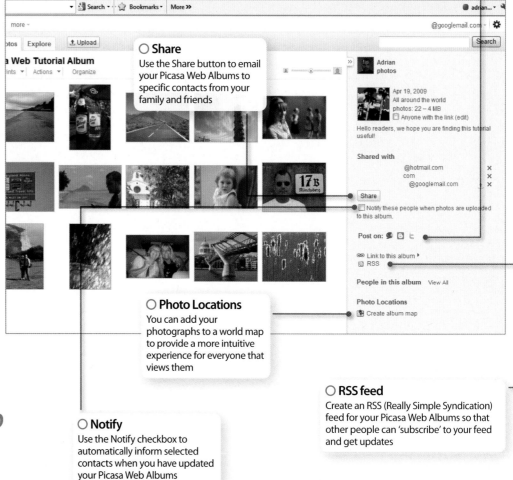

○ Social networking
Picasa is web-connected from the ground up. Share your images on Twitter straight from your albums

○ Share
Use the Share button to email your Picasa Web Albums to specific contacts from your family and friends

○ Photo Locations
You can add your photographs to a world map to provide a more intuitive experience for everyone that views them

○ Notify
Use the Notify checkbox to automatically inform selected contacts when you have updated your Picasa Web Albums

○ RSS feed
Create an RSS (Really Simple Syndication) feed for your Picasa Web Albums so that other people can 'subscribe' to your feed and get updates

---

How to add tags in Picasa
Add an extra layer of info to your uploaded pictures

Once you have uploaded albums of your photos to your Picasa account, it's possible to add people tags in order to name and shame friends and family who happen to be in them.

This process is quick and easy and is well worth doing as it adds an element of fun when sharing your photos and also presents an extra layer of reference when others are viewing your photos.

To get started, simply navigate your way to the particular photo that you wish to add a tag to, the click on the 'Show/Hide People' button, which is the first of the four icons on

the bottom right-hand side. The sidebar on the right will now open up the People panel. It will automatically detect faces for you to tag, so you can just type in their name in the 'Add name' field. Alternatively, click on the person to tag and type in their name there. Hit Return and a new window will appear. Select 'New Person' and add in any details such as their nickname and email address, then click OK. In this window you can also sync to Web Albums.

Now when you or your friends hover their cursor over the image the tagged person's name will appear so everyone will know who the stars of your pictures are.

Tagging people is a fun way of sharing information with friends

Picasa's core features

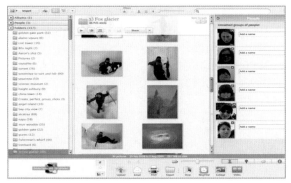

Use Picasa Albums

Once you have installed Picasa, your attention will be drawn to the Folders list on the left of the screen. This is your control panel for navigating around Picasa's core features. After you've gone through the 'Upload from my computer' option during Picasa's set-up function, you'll be able to access Folders straight away.

Create a slideshow

Creating slideshows is easy in Picasa; just click the green Play button and away you go. You can chose which transition will be used to go between photos, rotate and zoom in on images from within the slideshow, set the display time and more.

Edit your shots

When you move on to edit your photos, the original images in their original locations on your computer are not touched until you decide to save your changes. Picasa will also create a new version of your photo with the changes and edits applied.

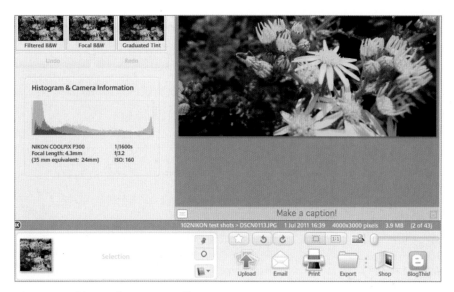

Get your Picasa images online

Once you've selected all of the photos and images you want to share online, click the Upload button in the Photo Tray. You can find this marked with a green arrow icon at the bottom of the screen. Picasa is designed to be closely linked to what a user does online and is intended to form part of Google's central family, which includes Gmail, Google Drive, News and Maps.

"Picasa's closely linked to what a user does online and forms part of Google's central family"

Get yourself on Gmail

By signing in to your Gmail account for Picasa Web Albums you can enable a world of online image sharing. Just enter the normal name and password you use for accessing Gmail. If you don't have an account it takes just minutes to sign up for free. Once you start looking at the breadth of other services offered by Google, you might be surprised to find that there is a whole lot more than just email available. It's free too, so why not make the most of it?

Organise your photos in Picasa

With Picasa's Folders pane you can easily organise and group your shots into albums

Once you have installed Picasa, your attention will naturally be drawn to the Folders list on the left of the screen. This is your control panel for navigating around Picasa's core features. After you have gone through the 'Upload from my computer' option during Picasa's setup you will be able to access Folders straight away. By scrolling down your Folder list you can view all photos displayed by Picasa.

It is important to remember that by installing Picasa, you have handed over control of your computer's image library. This means that changes you make to folders in Picasa affect the corresponding folders on your computer's hard drive. In this tutorial we show you how to take your photos from your folders and organise them into Picasa Albums.

Picasa | Using albums in Picasa

1: Starting a new album
Select the photos you have chosen to go in your album and drag them to the Selection panel at the bottom-left corner of your screen.

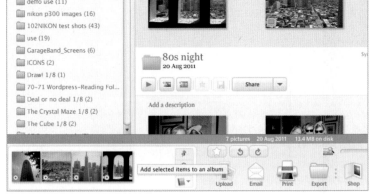

2: Add to album
Now click the 'Add selected items to an album' button found in the Selection panel to add your selected pictures to the album.

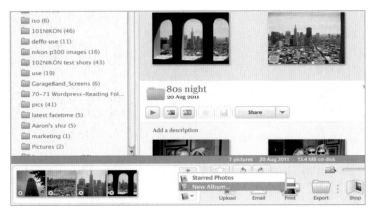

3: Create album
Click the blue New Album button – this will group these selected shots into their own album. But first a new window will pop up.

4: Album properties
Here you'll be given the opportunity to detail the album's properties. You can name and date the album at this point, among other things.

Find your way around albums
The folders interface makes organisation easy

○ **Search Picasa**
Picasa's Search function enables you to simply enter a word or term (the results narrow as you type) and the application will show all possible matching search term options

○ **Folders**
A list of all the folders you have built is shown on the left-hand side of the screen. What you do to the images in these folders is reflected in your computer's own folders which store your images

○ **Press to play**
Picasa's green Play button starts slideshows of your albums. If you've added music (select the 'Use Music for Slideshow and Movie presentations' option in Album Preferences) you'll hear it as soon as the images start to roll

○ **Selection panel**
The blue icon adds selected items in the selection panel to an album, the red circle clears items from the selection panel and the green pin marker is used to hold images

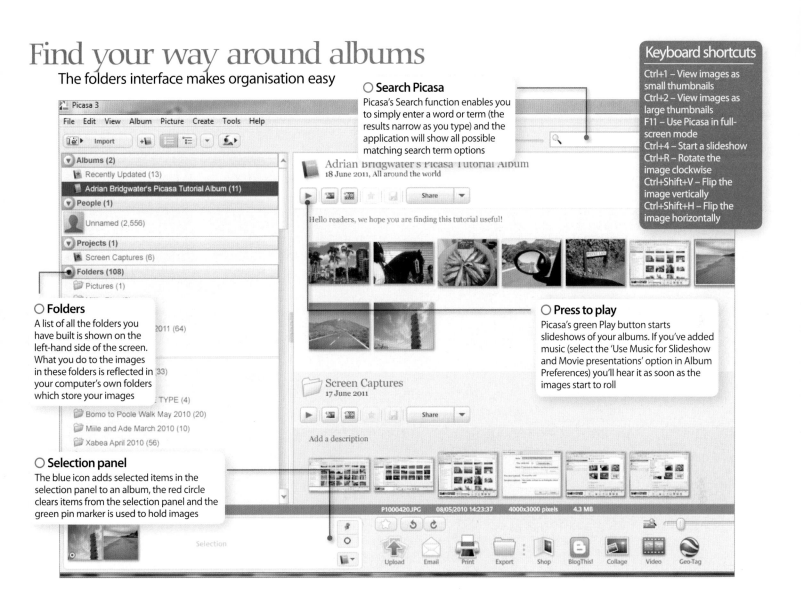

5: Editing album properties
You can change your album properties at any time by double-clicking the name of the album or right-clicking and selecting Edit Album Description.

6: Add more images
To add more images to this album, move them to the Selection panel, click the 'Add selected…' button again but this time click on your album name.

Edit your Picasa images

Picasa has a whole range of one-click fixes and tools to help you edit your images

As you probably already know by now, Google's Picasa is a great way to view and organise your images in a fun and intuitive manner with lots of easy-to-use options. It's important to realise, though, that Picasa is just a viewing and control window – it does not actually store your images for you; the hard disk on your computer continues to look after that job.

After you've organised your images and created folders, you can also use Picasa to edit your shots. The controls are simple and you can add a variety of easy to implement fixes and creative effects. The following tutorial shows you how to use the interface to edit your photos and make them the best they can be.

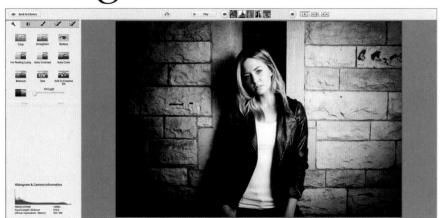

Picasa | Editing and tuning images in Picasa

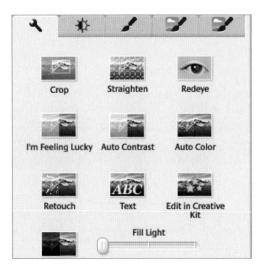

1: Basic Fixes

This is Picasa's first editing control panel where you can perform functions including cropping, image straightening, red-eye reduction, auto contrast and auto colour functions. You can also try out the I'm Feeling Lucky option to try Picasa's all-in-one lighting and contrast fix.

2: Tuning

You can use the sliders in the Tuning tool to adjust the colour and lighting. Fill Light adds light to foregrounds in images with bright backgrounds. Highlights amplifies the bright spots of an image to make the whites more vibrant. Shadows darkens shadows where needed. Colour Temperature provides more image 'warmth'.

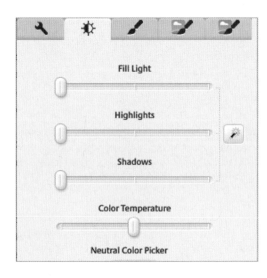

3: Effects

Always fun to play with, Picasa's effects buttons allow you to apply tints, colour saturations, sepia tones, black and white effects and even soft focus and film grain effects.

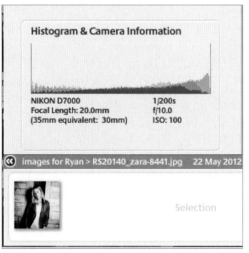

4: Switching between controls

You may want to switch between the three different image-editing tabs, or you may wish to get back to the Library itself. Your Back to Library button is located above the three main tabs. There is also a 'hide tabs' function shown as '<<', located in the blue bar below your image histogram information.

The key Picasa editing tools
The photo interface is easy to navigate your way around

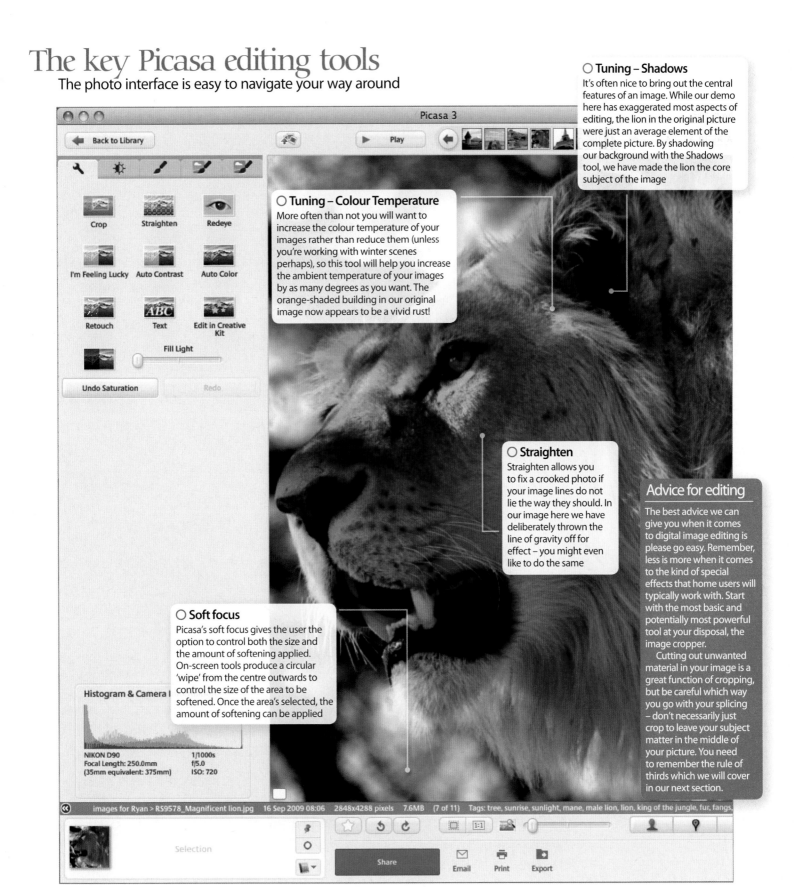

○ Tuning – Shadows

It's often nice to bring out the central features of an image. While our demo here has exaggerated most aspects of editing, the lion in the original picture were just an average element of the complete picture. By shadowing our background with the Shadows tool, we have made the lion the core subject of the image

○ Tuning – Colour Temperature

More often than not you will want to increase the colour temperature of your images rather than reduce them (unless you're working with winter scenes perhaps), so this tool will help you increase the ambient temperature of your images by as many degrees as you want. The orange-shaded building in our original image now appears to be a vivid rust!

○ Straighten

Straighten allows you to fix a crooked photo if your image lines do not lie the way they should. In our image here we have deliberately thrown the line of gravity off for effect – you might even like to do the same

Advice for editing

The best advice we can give you when it comes to digital image editing is please go easy. Remember, less is more when it comes to the kind of special effects that home users will typically work with. Start with the most basic and potentially most powerful tool at your disposal, the image cropper.

Cutting out unwanted material in your image is a great function of cropping, but be careful which way you go with your splicing – don't necessarily just crop to leave your subject matter in the middle of your picture. You need to remember the rule of thirds which we will cover in our next section.

○ Soft focus

Picasa's soft focus gives the user the option to control both the size and the amount of softening applied. On-screen tools produce a circular 'wipe' from the centre outwards to control the size of the area to be softened. Once the area's selected, the amount of softening can be applied

○ Make a collage
Picasa will automatically make a collage for you. Go to your Albums, click the 'Create' menu, and select 'Picture Collage'. Your collage will be fully editable

Collage styles
You can choose from six different styles of collage using the top drop-down menu on the Settings tab:
Picture pile: this is your default setting, and this collage looks like a pile of scattered pictures.
Grid: selected photos are arranged into regular rows and columns.
Mosaic: Picasa fits images into the page. Unlike the 'Grid' collage, the pictures are not aligned into neat rows and columns.
Contact sheet: Photos are arranged together tidily as thumbnails.
Multiple exposure: Your photos are superimposed over one another.

○ Move collage images
You can click individual images inside your collage to move them around – use the arrow tool shown on this image to tip photos up or down, and even delete the images that you decide you don't want

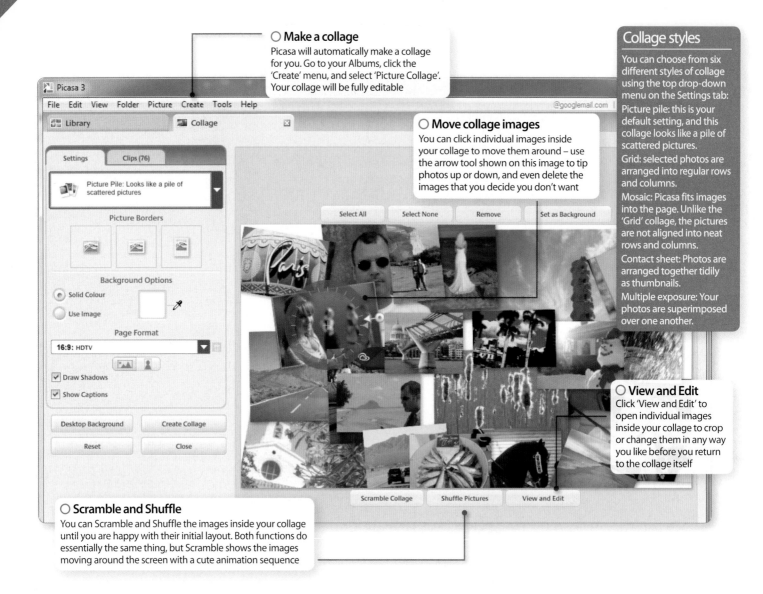

○ View and Edit
Click 'View and Edit' to open individual images inside your collage to crop or change them in any way you like before you return to the collage itself

○ Scramble and Shuffle
You can Scramble and Shuffle the images inside your collage until you are happy with their initial layout. Both functions do essentially the same thing, but Scramble shows the images moving around the screen with a cute animation sequence

Explore Picasa's extra features

If you want to unlock the power of some great extra features, then a new area of creativity awaits…

Picasa provides users with a layered approach to its services and options. While novices may be happy to use the core functions to file, upload and share images, more confident users may wish to explore Picasa's extended functions. In truth, many users will find Picasa to be well designed, and may want to explore more.

If you are keen on discovering more, the way to approach this with Picasa is to look at the drop-down-menu structure, and realise how similar the options are to software applications that you may already use. Starting with 'File', 'Edit' and 'View', Picasa's other options are 'Picture', 'Create', 'Tools' and 'Help' – not too dissimilar from Microsoft Word.

In this tutorial, we will take you through two of the key extra features of Picasa – creating a slideshow, complete with captions and transitions, and making a photo collage of all your favourite shots.

Picasa | Create a slideshow in Picasa

1: Viewing a slideshow

Viewing a slideshow is simple; all you do is click the green play button, which is located inside any folder. After doing this, the slideshow will play continuously until you hit Escape to stop it (esc).

2: Adding captions

You can add captions to your slideshow images. Just double click the image in library view when the slideshow is not playing. Click on the grey line just below the image to get a typing cursor, and enter your wording.

3: Playing a captioned image

When the image plays, the caption will show up on the screen, and then remain there for approximately three seconds before it starts to dissolve, and then eventually disappear.

4: Turning captions off

Hit the spacebar while the slideshow is playing in order to bring up the slideshow options menu. Click the green tick/checkmark icon in order to turn the captions on or off.

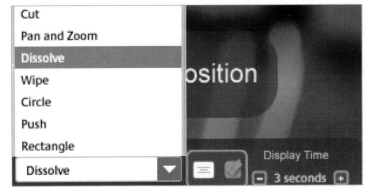

5: Changing screen 'wipe'

You can change the 'wipe' that Picasa slideshow uses to transition between images. Experiment with the different options to see which one you prefer – we have a preference for the default Dissolve setting.

6: Change the Display Time

You can hit the 'Plus' and 'Minus' tabs, which are located in the bottom right of the slideshow option pane, in order to increase or decrease the length of time that each image displays for.

○ Slideshow

The slideshow option is a nice way of sitting back and enjoying your picture views. Hit F11 to go into full screen mode during playback. Hit Esc to stop playback, which will be continual

Composition

The rule of thirds is a photographer's composition rule which states that any scene should be thought of as being made up of nine equal squares. Any points of interest, like the horizon or a flower, should rest on the lines that divide the squares. It creates a more dynamic picture.

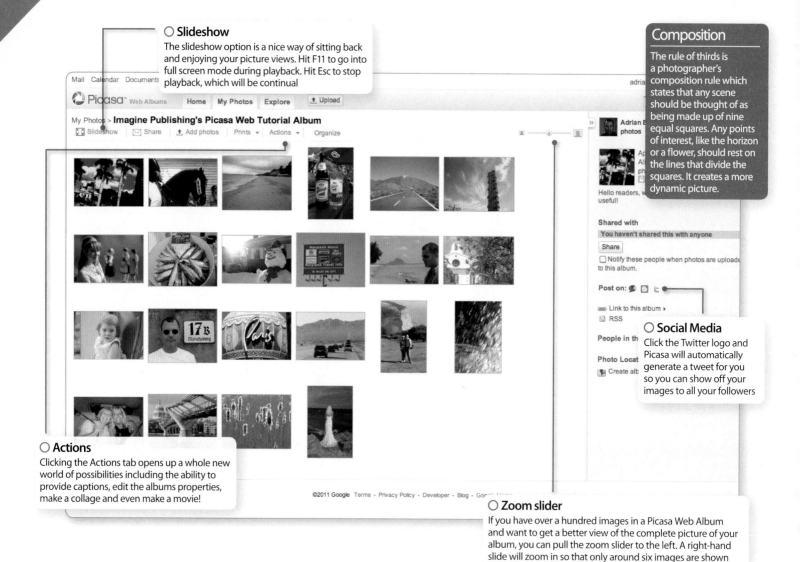

○ Social Media

Click the Twitter logo and Picasa will automatically generate a tweet for you so you can show off your images to all your followers

○ Actions

Clicking the Actions tab opens up a whole new world of possibilities including the ability to provide captions, edit the albums properties, make a collage and even make a movie!

○ Zoom slider

If you have over a hundred images in a Picasa Web Album and want to get a better view of the complete picture of your album, you can pull the zoom slider to the left. A right-hand slide will zoom in so that only around six images are shown

Share images with Web Albums

Picasa has a great way of connecting your images to others across the internet

We all enjoy sharing our images with people that we know and love. With nearly all our friends connected via the internet all over the world these days, it's a great way of bringing a little more colour to our online existence. Of course for some people it's just a great way of showing off what amazing photography skills they might happen to possess.

Picasa's Web Albums function is as simple to use as email itself – it is a simple yet powerful tool for selecting and uploading images to albums that will exist online. All you need to have to start with is a Gmail account, and this is simple to sign up for if you don't already own one.

The following tutorial will guide you on a step-by-step journey as you select and upload pictures. You can then share your images with everyone you know by simply sharing a link to your albums.

1: Select your photos
Click on each image you want to share while holding down the Cmd/Ctrl key. If you hold Shift instead, Picasa will select all photos in a group.

2: Time to Upload
Once you've selected the photos you want to share, click 'Upload' in the Photo Tray. It's marked with a green arrow icon at the bottom of the screen.

3: Sign in to Google
Sign in to your Gmail account for Picasa Web Albums. Just enter the normal name and password you use for accessing Gmail. Click 'Sign in'.

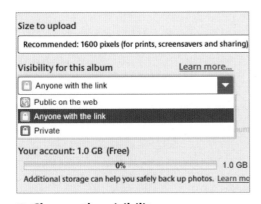

4: Click New
You can select to send images to one of your existing online albums or click the New button (top right) to create a new one.

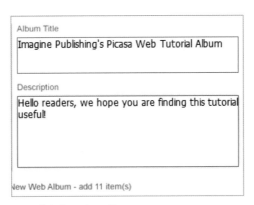

5: Add the details
Click under 'Album Title' and 'Description'. You might like to include date and location details here relating to when and where you took the photos.

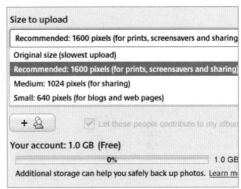

6: Pick the upload sizes
This is where you choose your preferred upload size. You should just go with Picasa's recommendations unless you have a poor connection.

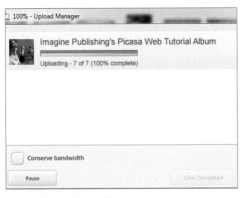

7: Choose the visibility
Choose your album's visibility level. This option enables you to let anyone with the link to your images view them, or make them public/private.

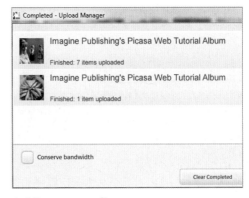

8: Upload the album
Click the Upload button. Picasa's Upload Manager will appear and show you the status of the upload. Its speed will vary with your connection.

9: View your album
You can view your album from this point onwards. To do this you can click the 'View Online' option that is presented at the end of uploading.

A guide to Google Play

Google Play is the one-stop shop for multimedia and apps

Google Play is Google's own store for selling apps for Android devices, as well as multimedia content – including books and movies – that's available on a whole range of platforms. The importance of the service to Google cannot be overstated, and it now takes pride of place on the Google toolbar. Go to any Google page and there you will find it at the top of the screen, alongside the more familiar services such as Search, Maps and Images.

Google Play ties directly into your Google account, so through the service you can access all the apps you've downloaded to an Android device; on any browser that you log in with, you can access movies you've paid to rent; and within the Google Books app (for desktop, Android, iPhone or iPad), you can read any of your purchased books. Play also connects to your Google Wallet account and you can buy hardware through the site – the popular Nexus 7 tablet is available here, and more devices are expected to be added in the future.

"Play connects to your Google Wallet and you can also buy hardware"

◯ Google account
Google Play is fully integrated with your Google account, including services such as Maps, Gmail and Google+. All can be accessed through the toolbar at the top of the screen

◯ The shops
You can buy apps, movies, books and devices, all via the links on the left of the screen. It's a great way to browse for new stuff as well

◯ Search
This is a Google product, of course, so you would expect a powerful search engine to be involved, and it is at the heart of the service

◯ Your content
The shortcuts to your content show everything you have bought and downloaded through Google Play. Want to watch one of your movies? Just click here!

◯ Recommended for you
As you start using the service, Google Play builds up a profile of the things you like and starts to recommend new content for you. It's a very handy feature

---

Orders and settings Take control of your account

One of the best things about using Google Play on a desktop computer rather than the app on an Android phone or tablet is the way it enables you to dig deeper and really take control of your account. Clicking the 'My Orders and Settings' link at the bottom of the screen takes you into a relatively unknown part of the service that you can use to manage your account. The first screen is the Orders screen, which lists every single item you have ever bought or downloaded through Google Play.

You can view the status or your orders here, such as shipping information when buying a device, or how long your movie rentals have

left to run. You can also request support, for example if you buy an app that doesn't work and you need to request a refund. The second screen, Settings, shows all the Android devices tied to your account. This is a useful feature if you have a phone and a tablet, or if you are juggling multiple devices in one household all tied to the same account.

It's also a good idea to remove the devices you no longer have, to avoid your account becoming too cluttered with information. You can also set your email preferences here, configuring which emails you will receive from Google Play.

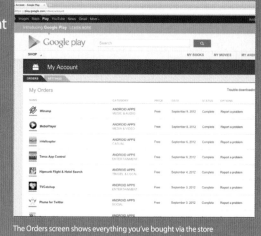

The Orders screen shows everything you've bought via the store

Key features

Android apps

Although Android devices all come with the Google Play store app pre-installed, Google Play in a desktop web browser represents the easiest way to find new apps and download them to your device. Make sure you are logged into the same account as on your phone and you can download apps with a single click.

Books

Google Play Books can be purchased and downloaded to any device on which you have got the Play Books app installed. This not only includes desktop and Android devices, as you would expect, but also iOS devices such as the iPhone and iPad. This platform-independence ensures you can also keep your books with you.

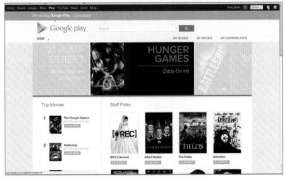

Movies

The availability of movies depends on which country you're based in. In the US you can buy movies and TV shows to view on the desktop or an Android device, but in other territories content is more limited.

Devices

A relatively new addition to Google Play is the Devices section. From here you can buy hardware from Google, such as the Nexus 7 tablet. This ties in to your Google Wallet account so you can buy with just a couple of clicks and the charge will automatically go onto the credit card you've got tied to your account. Other devices in the Nexus range can also be bought through Play, with the range being refreshed annually.

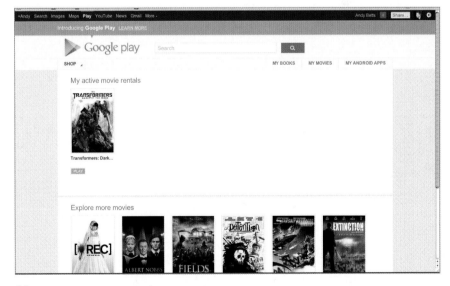

Manage your account

Perhaps the best feature of Google Play on a desktop is the ability to manage your account. It consolidates everything you have bought or downloaded via the service and makes it available to you to view and manage through a single screen. Clicking the My Android Apps button, for example, enables you to install or uninstall apps remotely on your Android phone or tablet.

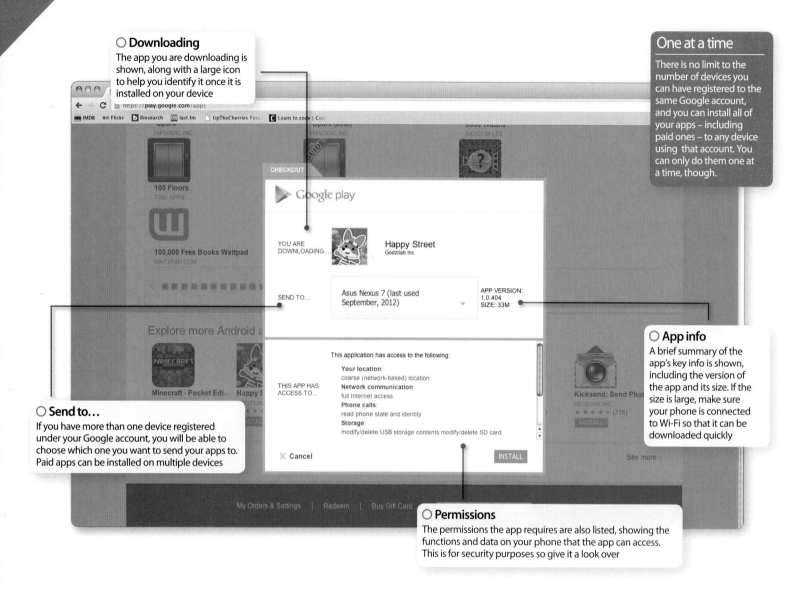

○ **Downloading**
The app you are downloading is shown, along with a large icon to help you identify it once it is installed on your device

○ **Send to...**
If you have more than one device registered under your Google account, you will be able to choose which one you want to send your apps to. Paid apps can be installed on multiple devices

One at a time
There is no limit to the number of devices you can have registered to the same Google account, and you can install all of your apps – including paid ones – to any device using that account. You can only do them one at a time, though.

○ **App info**
A brief summary of the app's key info is shown, including the version of the app and its size. If the size is large, make sure your phone is connected to Wi-Fi so that it can be downloaded quickly

○ **Permissions**
The permissions the app requires are also listed, showing the functions and data on your phone that the app can access. This is for security purposes so give it a look over

Download apps via your desktop

The quickest way to download Google Play apps or content to an Android device is via the web

Every Android phone and tablet comes with access to Google Play, a series of stores where you can buy apps, movies or books directly on the device. It's an incredibly convenient system, giving you access to a whole world of new content no matter where you are. Yet it isn't the quickest way of getting apps onto your device.

If you want to install several apps at a time, perhaps if you have reset your phone or want to find the best out of a collection of similar apps, the best way to do it is via your desktop web browser.

You log into your Google account, the same one you use on your Android device, access the Play Store in the browser and can remotely buy or download apps.

Simply clicking on them in the desktop browser will automatically, and somewhat magically, make them appear on your Android device, ready for you to use. Read on for the details.

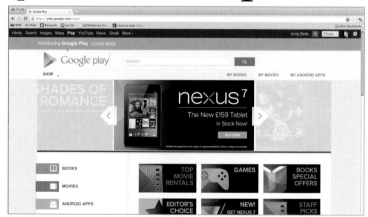

Google Play | Download via a desktop web browser

1: Log in
Go to **play.google.com** in your desktop web browser. If you aren't already logged in, do so now by clicking the Sign In button at the top right.

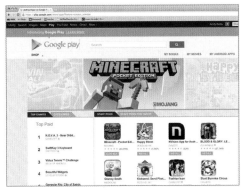

2: Browse the store
Start browsing the Play Store. You can install books, movies and apps in the same way. We're going to be doing apps, so click the 'Android apps' button.

3: Choose an app
You can browse apps by categories, most popular, or search for specific apps by name or keyword. Click on an app when you find one.

4: Check compatibility
When you view the app's page in your browser, a message will appear on the left telling you whether or not the app is compatible with your device.

5: Install the app
If the app is free, just hit the Install button to install it. If it's paid, you will see the price and must click that to commence the purchase process.

6: Choose the device
By default you'll only have one device available to install to. If you have multiple devices, choose the one you want to send the app to.

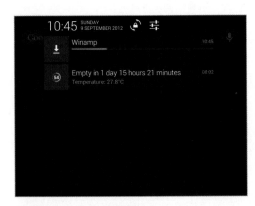

7: Check your device
Click Install to complete the process. Now switch to your Android device to see the app downloading. You can continue installing other apps during this.

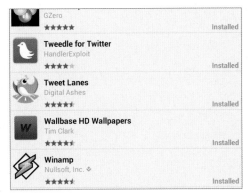

8: Locate the app
On your device, open the app drawer, find the app you've remotely downloaded and launch it. It'll also be in your on-device Play Store list of installed apps.

9: Uninstall remotely
Click the My Android Apps button (near the top) on the desktop and you can view all your installed apps. Click the trash can icon to uninstall them.

Introducing Google News

The virtual online dynamic newspaper from Google

As we witness the proliferation of tablet computers and sophisticated smartphones, more and more people are turning to the web for their news than ever before. Google clearly saw this trend developing and has spent the last few years refining its very impressive online news site. Built from a combination of 4,500 English-language news sources worldwide, the website works by grouping stories together in much the same way that you would see in a newspaper's various sections.

Google says that, traditionally, people looking for news would pick up a print publication (or its online version) that they know and trust and start looking for headlines that interest them. "We do things a little differently," says Google. So Google News sets out to give readers more personalisation options to get the news delivered the way they want it. Several publishers' links are shown for each story, so the reader gets more choice and can control his or her reading at every click.

> "Google News gives readers the chance to get the news delivered the way they want it"

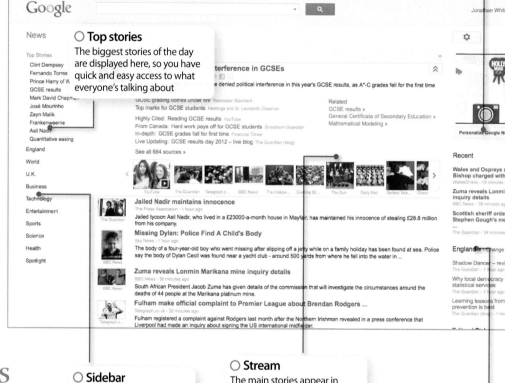

Viewing videos
Watch the news you're interested in

The Google News service offers a great way for people to read about what's going on in the world, from a range of different sources from around the globe. However, it also offers the ability to watch news reports from a number of news channels.

A large number of the top stories will have videos you can watch, either displayed as popular videos in the top-right of the page, or indicated by 'play' arrows on the image browser. These reports can very in length, from quick snippets of news to in-depth features discussing the issue at hand. The videos themselves can come from a number of different sources, from major US networks to videos that have been uploaded to YouTube.

When clicking on a video to watch, it'll open in a pop-up window. This will offer the usual controls such as 'play' and 'pause', but you'll also be able to get more information about the video, share it directly from this window and 'like' it. On top of all this, you can also watch the video in full-screen mode, change the video quality, turn on captions and even set a reminder to watch the video later. These extra video features add to the impressive array of options that Google News offers anyone wanting to keep up to date.

There are plenty of news-worthy videos available, as well as stories

Key features

Image news search

It might be a cliché, but a picture really is worth a thousand words. Google's image-driven news search option is a great way of getting a 'feel' for news on a certain subject before you read it. The image links themselves are sorted by relevance to your search, but you can change this to sort by date if you wish.

Links

The main news stories on Google News will provide you with a link, and this link will take you to a compendium page with more links, images and even videos relating to the news story that you are interested in.

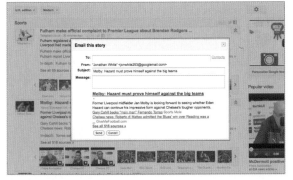

Share the news

You can email news links to your friends if you want to flag up an item of interest to them. After typing in your recipient's email address directly on the page, you can also send them a special message to give them an extra reason to read your news link.

News Spotlight

Part of Google's most recent update to its News service, Spotlight is an area that presents an assortment of articles of what is known as 'lasting interest', as opposed to quick updates or breaking news. Spotlight has moved from the bottom of the News homepage to now be located right in the side column. You can also find the Spotlight service in the Section menu.

> "Google's image-driven search option is a great way of getting a 'feel' for news on a certain subject"

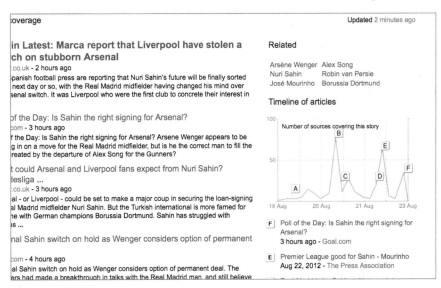

Timeline of articles

Google News provides a timeline service for major news stories so you can see how they are breaking across the world's news resources. Shown as 'Number of articles' on the vertical axis against the day and date on the horizontal axis (broken into ten-hour blocks), this option gives the reader the chance to see how a story has grown over time and whether or not coverage is still peaking.

Customise and filter Google News

How to personalise your Google News so you see the stories that matter most to you

Google News is designed to save you time trawling endless sources for the stories that are most applicable to you. With an interface that is fully customisable, Google News enables you to filter by categories based on your own personal tastes and interests.

If you favour football results over *X Factor* results then you can add a section for the latest sports stories and drag it to the top of your page, relegating entertainment news to the bottom. It's so easy to manage and organise that you can get an instant news fix just by glancing over the page, before clicking on stories for more in-depth reports. You can even change countries to gather stories by region and unlock features that are specific to certain nations – such as 'News for you', accessible from the US site.

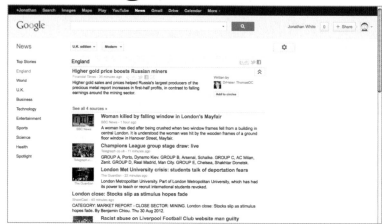

Google News | Set up your news desk

1: Catch top stories
By default your Google News browser will display the most popular news at the top of the page, giving you a taster of the biggest stories.

2: Change the view
The News page will be displayed in a 'Modern' style. If you want to change how stories appear, select the drop-down menu and choose a different option.

3: Local stories
By entering in your town, city or postcode you will be able to add an additional feed of stories that are applicable to your chosen area.

4: Changing area
By clicking on the drop-down at the top you will be able to change your country and get access to the stories from that region.

5: In real-time
Some stories will offer you the option to view them in real-time. Click this option and the page will automatically update as soon as news comes in.

6: News by section
Also on the left-hand side of the screen is a list of news categories that you can click on to jump to that particular area of news – such as Business.

Setting up Google News
The many features of Google's news service

○ Settings
By clicking on the cog icon in the top-right corner of the screen you can alter your settings and personalise the way News works for you

○ Search engine
Being Google, a search engine obviously features heavily on the page. Here you can enter keywords to search for in the 'News' pages or broaden your hunt to the web in general

Advanced search
If inputting keywords into the search doesn't uncover the stories you want then you can click on the 'Advanced news search' link to specify more intricate aspects. By utilising this search you can specify dates, exact sources, locations, authors and look for precise words or phrases, leaving no stone unturned.

○ Video
Some stories will offer videos for you to watch. Popular videos related to the story will be displayed here

○ Sharing
If there's a story you like, find interesting, or think others will appreciate, there are a number of ways to share it. You can do so via Google+, Twitter or Facebook

---

7: Make it personal
Over on the right-hand side of the page, you have the ability to personalise your News experience. Here you can select the subjects you're interested in.

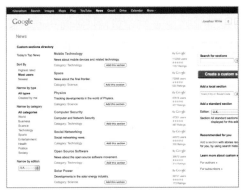

8: Advanced options
Click the Advanced option and you can personalise your news even further. You can add more specific sections so the news is more tailored to your tastes.

9: Custom section
Click the 'Create a custom section' button and you can compile your own section, built around the specifications you set.

Learn to use Blogger

Everything that you need to know about Blogger

Blogger is Google's free tool for creating blogs. It can be found on the web at http://www.blogger.com. As you are probably aware, you can use blogs for everything, from updating your friends and family on things about your life, to giving your own advice, discussing your political views, or relating your experience regarding a topic of interest. Perhaps you have a passion for a hobby that you want the world to know about? Either way, Blogger is a great tool to do all of this.

Best of all, you will be pleased to hear that it's free. Although it's undeniable that there are far more fancy blog tools out there, few – if any – match Blogger for its user-friendly interface, and for the amount of tools that you get for no money whatsoever.

> "You can use blogs for anything, from keeping your friends and family up to date, to giving out advice"

○ **Options menu**
Click on this drop down menu to jump to various sections, including 'Overview', 'Stats' and your 'Settings'

○ **Create new blog**
The dashboard will display all of your active blogs and you can create a new one by clicking on the 'New Blog' option

○ **Reading list**
The 'Reading List' section allows you to follow other blogs that are of interest to you

○ **Settings**
Click on the 'Settings' option and you'll be able edit all facets of your blog, including enabling the option to update your posts via email from your phone

○ **Blog stats**
Get a quick update on how many people are reading and following your blogs by clicking on the 'Stats' option

Using the stats in Blogger

To open up your statistics page, you need to log in to your dashboard. Next to each blog will be a drop-down menu, click on this to access various options. Inside the 'Stats' section, you will see a set of option tabs that will allow you to see how many page views there have been from now, or from the very first day your blog went live. This is a very handy feature, and if managed right can be the difference between a successful blog and a… well… not so successful blog. How you define 'successful' may be different to how someone else defines it. But the point is, if your blog isn't being read, then you can see by your stats, and

this will allow you to make some adjustments and figure out why that is the case. Go to 'Overview' to check your updates.

The 'Stats' page allows you to quickly see how many people read your blog

Blogger's best bits

Setting up your blog

Setting up a Blogger account takes just a few easy steps. You can sign in using an existing Google account (or create a new one) and then give yourself a profile name, assign a photo and then you're done. When you have a profile set up, click on the 'New Blog' button to start writing.

Easy editing

Once your blog is set up, Blogger has a basic editor. Most blogging tools do not have robust HTML editors, and the ones that do often require Java or other plug-ins. You could also do advanced editing with HTML.

Emailing your posts

You can optionally configure Blogger within the settings page with a secret email address, so you can email your posts to your blog. This is handy for making updates on the fly or updating from your mobile/Cell phone, or other mobile devices.

Free hosting of your blog

Blogger will host your blog for free on blogspot.com. You can also use Blogger to automatically FTP (file transfer) your blog posts to your own web space. But you need to make sure that you have the correct server settings from your internet service provider, otherwise you may experience unpredictable results.

> ## "Blogger will host your blog for free on blogspot.com. Make sure you have the right server settings"

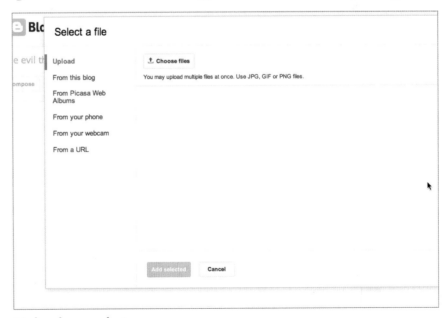

Upload your photos

Blogger will let you upload pictures/photos from your desktop and post them to your blog. You can choose the basic layout and size of your images, and they'll be uploaded to Blogger's server space, so you don't have to host the pictures on a different website.

Create your first blog post in Blogger

Adding posts in Blogger is quick and easy. Simply style them by using the built-in WYSIWYG editor

Adding blog posts in Blogger is neither hard nor slow – the ease of use is one of the best things about it. Normally the posts you write are quite short and are written directly and conversationally, but obviously you can make them as long as you want and as often as you like – and with added styling and images.

The styling of your posts can be controlled easily by the built-in editor (WYSIWYG, 'what you see is what you get') and can be written either in code view (HTML) or normal text view, which is called 'Compose' and is very similar to how you would work in a Microsoft Word document. The built-in editor will enable you to add in images and video as well as complete formatting of your posts.

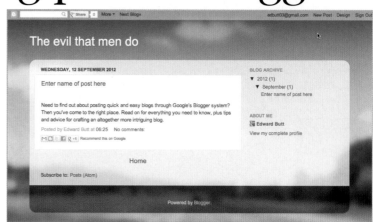

Blogger | Make your first blog

1: New post entry
Log in to Blogger and open your dashboard. In the Manage Blog section you'll see an orange button that says 'New Post'. Click it.

2: Posting page
Once in the Posting page you will be able to add in a title for your blog. Once this post entry has been published that title will become clickable.

3: HTML or Compose
You have the choice whether or not to use the text editor in HTML mode or Compose mode. Anyone with knowledge of HTML would benefit here.

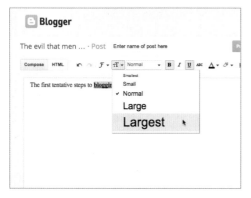

4: The text editor
The built-in text editor is a nice tool. It has the ability to upload images and video for you to insert into your posts, as well as many other formatting options.

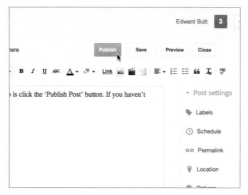

5: Publishing your posts
Once you're happy with your post, all you need to do is click the 'Publish' button. If you haven't got time to finish it, then click 'Save'.

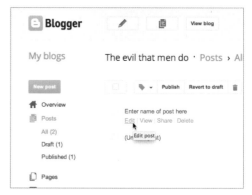

6: Once published
Once published, you will be given the option of either viewing your post, changing it with an 'Edit' option or create a brand new post altogether.

Posting with Blogger
The blog entry screen is easy to use

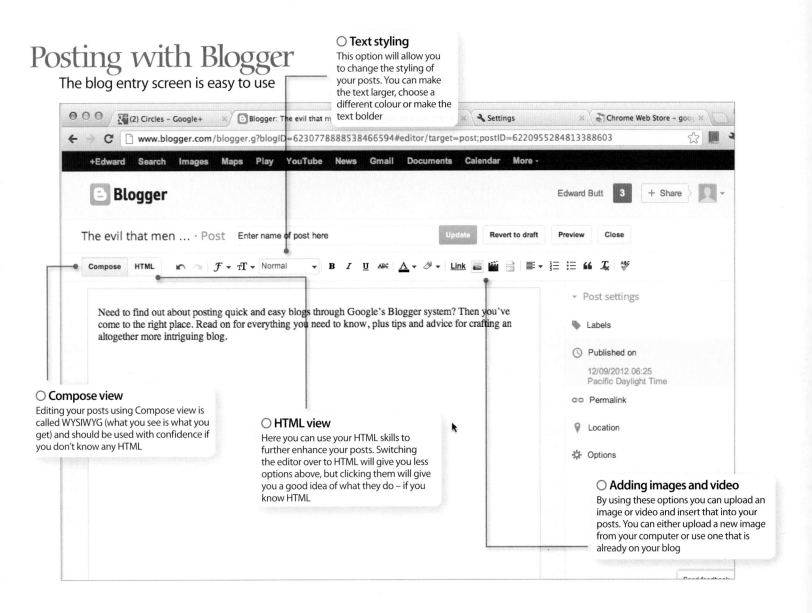

○ **Text styling**
This option will allow you to change the styling of your posts. You can make the text larger, choose a different colour or make the text bolder

○ **Compose view**
Editing your posts using Compose view is called WYSIWYG (what you see is what you get) and should be used with confidence if you don't know any HTML

○ **HTML view**
Here you can use your HTML skills to further enhance your posts. Switching the editor over to HTML will give you less options above, but clicking them will give you a good idea of what they do – if you know HTML

○ **Adding images and video**
By using these options you can upload an image or video and insert that into your posts. You can either upload a new image from your computer or use one that is already on your blog

7: Editing your existing posts
From within your Dashboard you can choose to edit your posts, and this will take you to a new page, which will enable you to see/edit all previous posts.

8: Publish multiple posts
Still inside the editing page we can check all of your posts that we edited and then click 'Publish'. This will publish all posts at once.

9: Post labels
Another nice feature is the ability to label your posts. Doing so will allow you to locate a specific post when needed by using the Labels bar to the left.

Create custom blog designs

The Template Designer brings amazingly beautiful and professional blog designs to Blogger blogs

When you first open an account with Blogger, you will be presented with its default template and theme. However, this is not enough for the creative person, and being able to create your own custom templates without the technical know-how is something that Blogger does best. There is a feature called 'Template Designer' that allows you to choose and customise a template.

Once you try out the Blogger Template Designer, you get access to 15 brand-new templates. You can easily change the layout with one click to one, two, and three-column layouts for each template, with complete control over the size and arrangement of the columns. So in this tutorial we will take a good look at how to create a customised Blogger template.

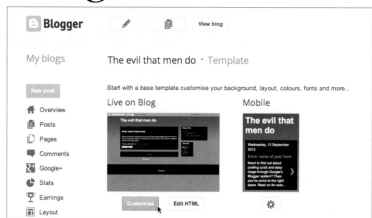

Blogger | Make a customised template

1: Where to find Template Designer
Log in to your Dashboard and you will see a list of categories down the left-hand side of the screen, one of which is called 'Template'. Click on this.

2: How templates work
When crafting a blog, you can start off with a base template and then customise your background, layout, colours, fonts and more.

3: Templates and themes
You'll also see you have a wide range of templates to choose from, each with several different themes. Click on one to preview it with your blog.

4: Start customising
While your theme is bring previewed, click on the 'Customise' button underneath the display window to start making that theme your own.

5: Background options
You will notice a sidebar menu to the left that will allow you to view templates, change the backgrounds, adjusts widths and change the layout.

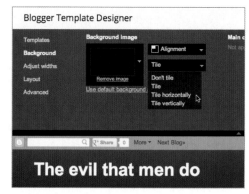

6: Changing the background
By clicking the background link, you get given some options. You can change the background image, align it and tile it, among other things.

Make your blog unique
The Template Designer has a wealth of options

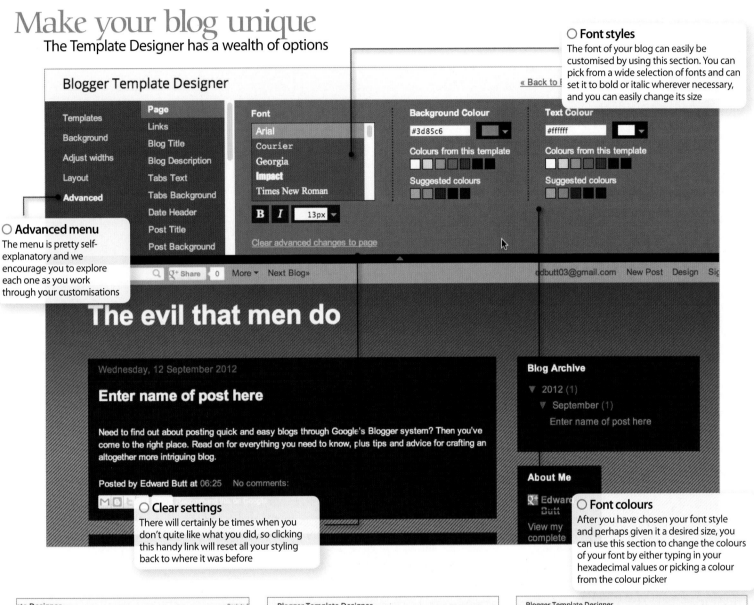

○ **Font styles**
The font of your blog can easily be customised by using this section. You can pick from a wide selection of fonts and can set it to bold or italic wherever necessary, and you can easily change its size

○ **Advanced menu**
The menu is pretty self-explanatory and we encourage you to explore each one as you work through your customisations

○ **Clear settings**
There will certainly be times when you don't quite like what you did, so clicking this handy link will reset all your styling back to where it was before

○ **Font colours**
After you have chosen your font style and perhaps given it a desired size, you can use this section to change the colours of your font by either typing in your hexadecimal values or picking a colour from the colour picker

7: Adjusting the widths
Clicking on the 'Adjust Width' option in the sidebar will allow to you do just that – adjust the overall width of your template using the sliders provided.

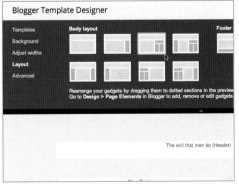

8: Changing the layout
Changing the layout of your template is very easy. Just click on one and click the 'Apply To Blog' button up on the top right.

9: Advanced option
The Advanced option enables you to take full control of how your theme will look, like changing the style of all your text, for example.

Use Blogger's drag-and-drop system

Blogger's simple drag-and-drop system lets you easily add and arrange page elements

With Blogger, where you want your elements to appear on your page is now totally under your control. Rearranging your blog's content is as easy as using your mouse to drag-and-drop individual page elements to wherever you desire. What you have is the parts that make up the blog people will view. These parts are called page elements and can be easily placed (dragged) into certain places. To move these page elements around all you do is move your mouse cursor over an element until it changes from a white arrow into a black dragging tool. Then drag it to the place your desire.

In this tutorial we will show you how to make the most of these drag-and-drop elements to make your site exactly how you want it to be, as well as show you how to add gadgets.

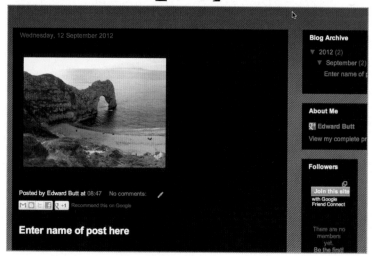

Blogger | Drag-and-drop page elements

1: Accessing the layout option
If you haven't already done so, log in to Blogger and open up your dashboard. To the left of the screen is a list of options, one of which is 'Layout'. Click on this to get started playing with the layout of your blog.

2: Editing a page element
At the corner of each page element you will find a tab called 'Edit'. Clicking this will open up a new page and enable you to make even more changes to your blog's style. Here you can also change its navigation style.

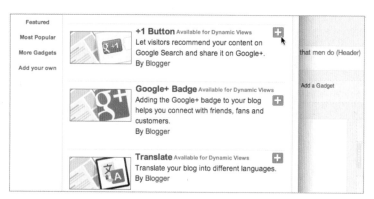

3: Adding a gadget
You can also add new elements to your blog called 'Gadgets'. Clicking the Add Gadget tab will again open up a new window and allow you to add all kinds of cool features like blog stats, popular posts and a search box to name a few.

4: Dragging and dropping
Hovering over any of the highlighted areas, you will notice your mouse cursor change from your normal white arrow to a black arrow to let you know that this can be dragged anywhere inside the dotted areas.

Customise your blog

The areas you can change using drag and drop

○ **Favicon**
At the very top left of our page we can edit our favicon. By clicking 'Edit' we can locate and upload a new favicon

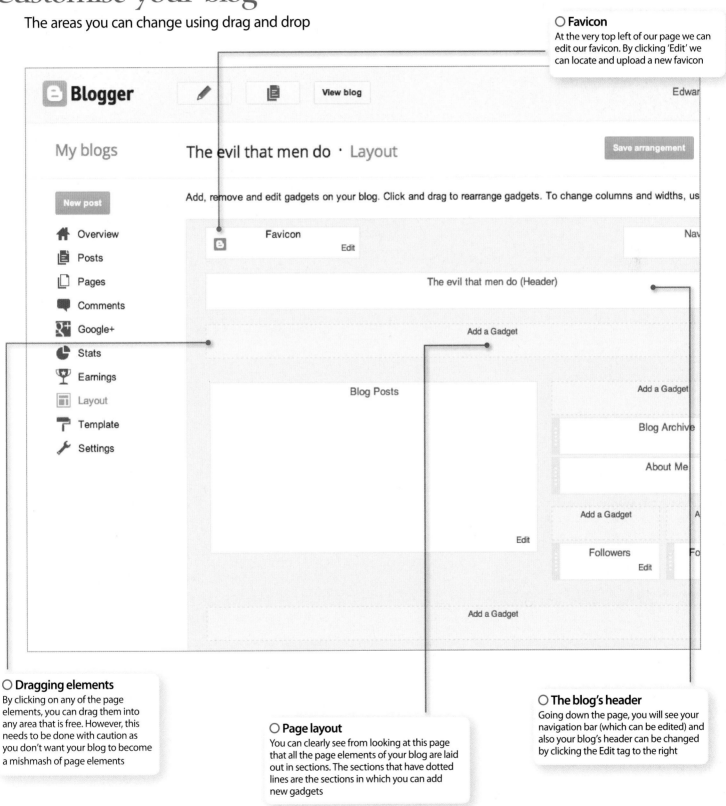

○ **Dragging elements**
By clicking on any of the page elements, you can drag them into any area that is free. However, this needs to be done with caution as you don't want your blog to become a mishmash of page elements

○ **Page layout**
You can clearly see from looking at this page that all the page elements of your blog are laid out in sections. The sections that have dotted lines are the sections in which you can add new gadgets

○ **The blog's header**
Going down the page, you will see your navigation bar (which can be edited) and also your blog's header can be changed by clicking the Edit tag to the right

Upload images to your blog posts or pages

How to get pictures on your blog

Managing a blog will mean adding plenty of posts whenever you feel the need, whether it's your hobby or just a topic of interest. Either way, you will need to know how to add images to your posts to make them more enjoyable to read. And, as usual, Blogger makes this a piece of cake, and we'll show you how easy it is in four easy steps.

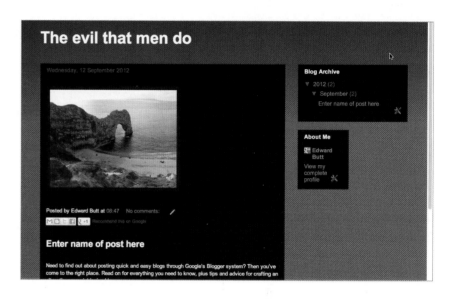

Blogger | Add an image to your posts

1: The posting page
Log into to your Dashboard and click the 'New Post' button. Once in the posting page you will see the text editor bar at the top of the text window.

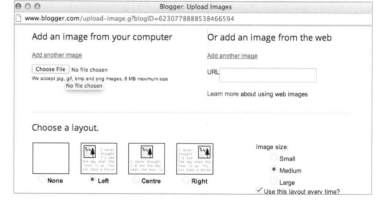

2: The Image Uploader
Clicking the little image icon on the text editor in 'HTML' mode will bring up the Image Uploader. Here you can click 'Browse' and locate your image.

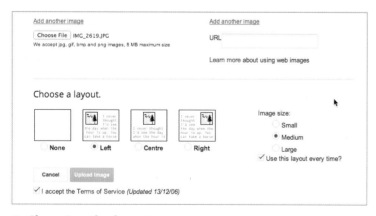

3: Choosing the layout
Next, choose where on the page you would like your uploaded image to sit. You'll have a choice of none, left, centre or right.

4: Upload the image
Click 'Upload image' and you'll see a page telling you it's uploading. Click 'Done' and you'll be taken back to the text editor with your image uploaded.

Manage your comments in Blogger

Having a blog means getting post comments – here's how to manage them

Anyone who runs a blog – professional or personal – will get reader comments on most of their posts. It's one of the fundamentals of having a blog. People who read your posts will no doubt want to either thank you for such an informative article or observation, or they might want to offer their own opinion, whatever that may be.

Either way, as a blogger, you need to know how to manage those comments and choose which ones to keep or which ones to delete. In Blogger you can choose a couple of different ways of removing your comments, and you also have the options of managing you spam folder. In the next four steps, we'll show you just how easy it is…

Blogger | Managing comments in Blogger

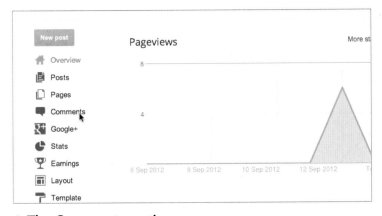

1: The Comments section
Log in to your Dashboard and click the 'Comments' link to the left. Once on the Comments page, the first thing you will see is, unsurprisingly, your comments.

2: Published or spam
You have two places where your comments are stored – Published or Spam. We advise occasionally checking your spam folder for any legitimate comments.

3: Deleting the content
You can remove comments by clicking 'Remove content' and Blogger will let your visitors know it was removed.

4: Deleting a comment
Deleting a comment will get rid of it altogether. Click the comment you want removed and click the 'Delete' button.

Get to grips with Google Sites

Sites enables anyone to create a team-oriented site where multiple people can collaborate

Google Sites is great for anyone who wants to create a collaborative website for multiple users. This could be a company intranet for sharing information, a classroom site for teachers and students, or a fan club.

All the information is stored securely online on 10GB of storage space in one place. You can make your site public or private and choose who can edit your site. Getting started is very easy – it's just a case of clicking a button. There are also a number of features and options on offer, like templates that can be customised, a rich-text editor and, for each Google Apps account, you can integrate with other Google services. You can embed gadgets, calendars, spreadsheets, presentations, photo slideshows and videos.

You can invite people to collaborate with you – and the best thing about Google Sites is it's free to everyone. All you need is an internet connection and an idea!

> "There are a number of features and options on offer, like templates that can be customised"

Create a page
Up on the top right you can create a new page by click the 'Create Page' button

Edit
Click the pencil icon in order to edit a range of your site's features

More actions
This feature will open up many other options to help manage or customise your pages

Public or private
You can choose to share your site with the world, or keep it a little more private and choose who can see it

---

Recent posts

To start with, choose Insert>Recent posts. Choose the page you would like to Show Posts from using the drop-down menu. Choose the post length, number of posts to display, then add an intro post to your announcement and decide if you'd like to include a border and a title. Click Save. You'll be able to edit these choices in the Properties area of the box.

You will also be able to align the text box and choose to have Text Wrap on or off. Under Properties, you change the post length, number of posts to display, add an intro post to your announcements, and decide if you'd

Create an announcements page

like to include a border and a title. As with all Inserts, you will not be able to see what your users will see until you save your page.

Post length:
Short snippet
Include thumbnail of first image in post
Number of posts to display: 5

Add an intro post to your announcements

Display:
✓ Include border around Recent announcements
✓ Include title: Recent Announcements

Cancel

John Doe Voted MVP Of Last Game
draft saved at 4:03 AM

Insert Format Table Layout

Normal   10 pt   B I U A· ·

Home
Announcements
Roster and Stats
Schedules
Match Stats
Photo Gallery
Team Sponsors
Team Information
Contact Us

A-Team sinks Marshfield
posted Nov 13, 2009 4:17 PM by Edward Butt

Image One

Well done to the BTYFC Under 18s team who ran out convincing last pre-season friendly match away to Marshfield Town on Sunday. Ryan Mackie and a calm finish from Tom Kilgalon secured a well-of their first league match away to FC Caine this weekend.

Player of the Week

Image One

Add files

Comments

975

Add comment

Announcements are a handy way to keep all collaborators up to date

Key features

Site creation

It doesn't get much any easier than this. You go to **https://sites.google.com** and click the red 'Create' button on the left. You then choose a template, perhaps a theme, and give your site a name, which will automatically process a unique URL for you. Once you're happy, just press the 'Create Site' button.

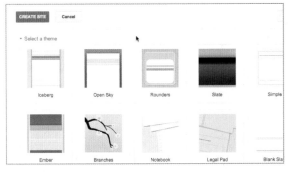

Template themes

When you've found the right template to use and you're happy with the whole layout, you may think of changing the colour scheme. Themes will enable you to accomplish this. There are as many themes to choose from as there are templates, and they can be easily applied with just a click of the mouse.

Share with who?

Once you have the layout, theme and content added, it's time to think about who will be able to see your site. Will it be made public or will it be private? Clicking on the 'More' tab that sits at the top of the page will open up a list of options. Choose 'Sharing and Permissions' to determine who can view it.

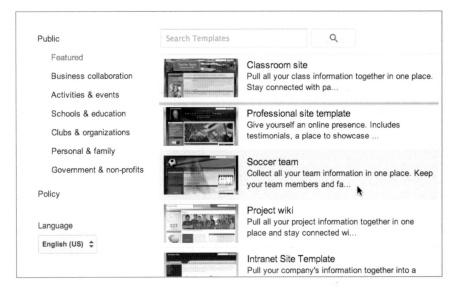

Free templates

There is, without doubt, one main reason why so many people use Google Sites – it's free! Everyone has a budget, so not everyone can afford the cost of designing and developing a content-managed website. So being free is certainly a great reason to start using Google Sites. And it goes without saying that the templates Google offer are also free and you can pick from a whole gallery of templates.

"There is, without doubt, one main reason why so many people use Google Sites – it's free!"

Easy editing

Editing your site's content is a breeze in Google Sites. One you've picked your template and your theme you will certainly want to add content to it as and when. When you're logged in, you can click a button that says 'Edit page' and this will open up a nice little editor at the very top of your page, enabling you to tweak your site.

Change your site's layout

In this tutorial we will learn how to customise our site's layout in four easy steps

Making your website individual to you is really important, as it's the only way it will stand out from the millions of other sites on the web. Pay attention to typography, image use, layout and more and your site will be unique and looking good. With Google Sites, you can easily change the overall appearance of your website by editing your site's layout, themes, colours and fonts.

You have several layout options to choose from in Google Sites, which we will have a look at here, as well as the ability to add new elements to the page and move them around. At a click of a button we can easily move our sidebar over to the right if needed, or we can simply change the dimensions of the header or footer. To change any of these is very easy as we show you in this simple four-step tutorial.

Google Sites | Change the layout

1: More actions panel
Log in to your Google account and open up your front page in your browser. Now press the 'M' key on your keyboard to open up the More actions panel and scroll down and select 'Edit site layout'.

2: Go to 'Edit Site'
The new-look Google Site editing facility provides a basic toolbar at the top of the page. Here you can move various pieces of page furniture around and tweak various aspects of your page.

3: Site appearance page
Now, from the 'More' options menu, choose the 'Manage Site' option and you'll be able to start changing the aspects and dimensions of your headers, sidebars, and more. Click on the 'Change' or 'Edit' links to start making changes.

4: Change site layout
You'll be presented with a nice pop-up form giving you a bunch of options. All we need to do here is change the sidebar's position over to the right. Then click OK and then Save changes.

Customise your site layout

Making changes to the way your
website looks is easy in Google Sites

○ **Save, preview or cancel**
By clicking the preview button you will
be able to preview changes before you
commit to them by clicking Save. As
always, the cancel button will get rid of
all changes

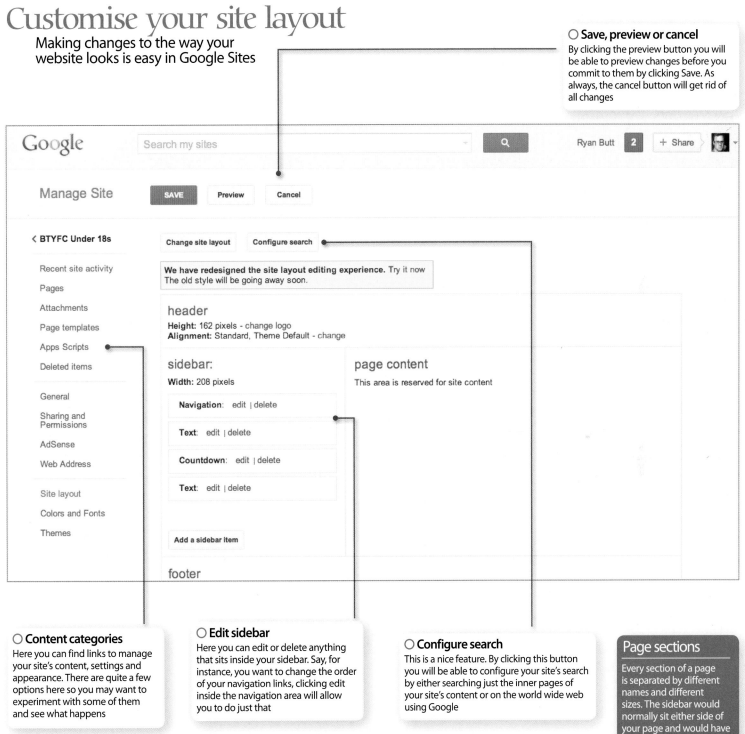

Google   Search my sites   🔍   Ryan Butt 2   + Share

Manage Site   **SAVE**   Preview   Cancel

‹ BTYFC Under 18s   Change site layout   Configure search

Recent site activity
Pages   We have redesigned the site layout editing experience. Try it now
Attachments   The old style will be going away soon.
Page templates
                         header
Apps Scripts   **Height:** 162 pixels - change logo
Deleted items   **Alignment:** Standard, Theme Default - change

General   **sidebar:**   **page content**
Sharing and   **Width:** 208 pixels   This area is reserved for site content
Permissions
AdSense   **Navigation:**   edit | delete
Web Address
                           Text: edit | delete
Site layout
Colors and Fonts   **Countdown:**   edit | delete
Themes
                           Text: edit | delete

                           Add a sidebar item

                         footer

○ **Content categories**
Here you can find links to manage
your site's content, settings and
appearance. There are quite a few
options here so you may want to
experiment with some of them
and see what happens

○ **Edit sidebar**
Here you can edit or delete anything
that sits inside your sidebar. Say, for
instance, you want to change the order
of your navigation links, clicking edit
inside the navigation area will allow
you to do just that

○ **Configure search**
This is a nice feature. By clicking this button
you will be able to configure your site's search
by either searching just the inner pages of
your site's content or on the world wide web
using Google

Page sections
Every section of a page
is separated by different
names and different
sizes. The sidebar would
normally sit either side of
your page and would have
a fixed height and width.
Then your header is always
at the top of your page and
the footer will always be
positioned at the bottom
of your page. All, however,
have fixed dimensions that
can be changed if desired.

*"Say you want to change the order of your
navigation links, then clicking edit inside the
navigation area will allow you to do just that"*

Change fonts on your Google site

It's easy to change the fonts and style of your Google website

With Google Sites, you can easily change the overall appearance of your website by editing your site's layout, themes, colours and fonts.

In this tutorial we will explore how you can change the fonts on your Google site, which can be a very handy skill to have, even though it's so easy to achieve. Changing the style of fonts is normally something that is left to the professional web designers of this world, and is controlled by something known as cascading styles sheets (CSS). However, logging into the Manage Site section of your Google site will enable you to be just as creative as any web designer can get and you won't need any CSS or any other technical know-how.

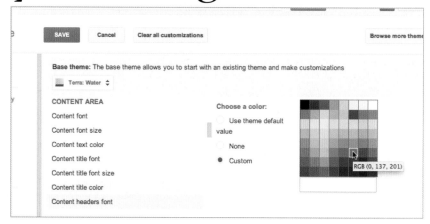

Google Sites | Changing fonts on your Google site

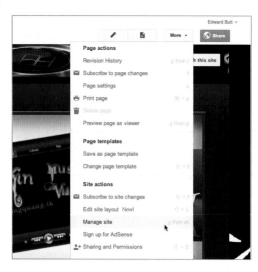

1: Getting started
Log in to your Google Sites account and open up your front page in your browser. Press the 'M' key on your keyboard to open up your 'More Actions' panel. Then scroll down to the 'Manage Site' link and click that.

2: Manage site section
Now inside the Manage Site section, you'll notice a few things. You will see a main area that allows you to see how and when things have been changed. But what we're after is the 'Colours and Fonts' link in the side bar. Click that and continue on.

3: Choosing the font style
When you come on to the Colours and Fonts page, you will see a scrolling area with different categories. All we want to do here is change the style of our font. So click on a category from the list that features fonts and then under 'Choose a font', click on the 'Custom' option and then pick a font from the drop-down menu.

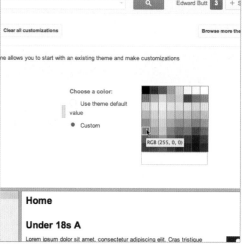

4: Change the colour
Now we can scroll down and choose 'Content text colour'. By default it will be set to use the theme's default colour. But we want to change it to our own colour – a lovely red! So select custom and you will see a colour picker appear on the right. All we need to do now is click on the colour that we wish to use.

Using Google Sites' General Settings

The General Settings page gives us some very useful features

With Google Sites, you can easily manage and change the overall appearance of your site. By using the options within the Site Appearance category under 'More actions' and 'Manage site' you are able to edit your site's layout, themes, colours and fonts. However, going to the General page under Site Settings, you are given some very handy options indeed – options we will explore throughout this tutorial. These options include how you can add a description of your site to help with search engine optimisation (SEO) as well as the option to allow your site to be optimised for mobile devices. And, if you have Google Analytics set up, you can easily add in your property ID to enable it. So let's take a better look at these handy options.

Google Sites | Explore General Settings

1: Getting started
Log into your Google Sites account and open up your front page in your browser. Press the 'M' key on your keyboard to open up your More Actions panel. Then scroll down to the 'Manage site' link and click that.

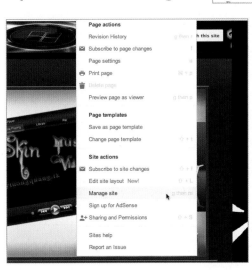

2: Manage site section
Now inside the Manage Site section, you will notice some site categories in the left sidebar menu. Inside the 'Site settings' category about halfway down, you should see the option 'General'. Click that and continue.

3: Site storage and description
In here you can change your site's name and add a description of your site to help search engines find it. You will also notice an indicator of how much storage your site has. If you're uploading large files on a regular basis, then this will serve you well.

4: Analytics and mobile adjustments
If you have signed up for Google Analytics you can add in your property ID here. Scrolling down further you'll see a tick box that will automatically adjust your site for mobile devices. Once you're happy with all your changes, you can then click the red 'Save' button located at the top of the page.

Share your website in Google Sites

Google Sites gives you the option of how you want your site to be seen

Google Sites is a great service for anyone who wants to create a collaborative website for multiple users, and having the ability to make your site accessible to whoever you like is without doubt one of the best things about it.

Imagine if you ran a football club website like our demonstration here and you have chairmen, coaches and committee members all having the potential to be your helpers. Another example would be a school project that you and a few others are working on. Google Sites gives your schoolmates the ability to collaborate with you and then when you're done you can make your project public for all your teachers and classmates to see – it is such a great tool. And, in this tutorial, we will see just how easy it is.

Google Sites | Share your website

1: Site permissions
Setting the site permissions for your website couldn't be simpler. To share a website in Google Sites, go to the 'More actions' menu (or press 'M' on your keyboard) and click 'Sharing and Permissions'.

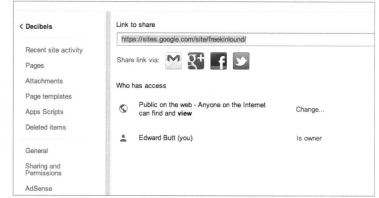

2: To share or not to share
Firstly you will see the link that you will be sharing and then who can see and use your site. Clicking the 'Change' link on the right will allow you to set it to either 'Public', 'Anyone with the link' and 'Private'. You have complete control here.

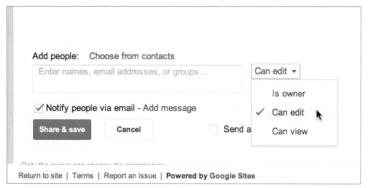

3: Adding people
Now you can add people who you would like to have access to your Google site by typing in their email address in the box provided. You can then set how much they can do, are they the owner, can they edit or can they just view it.

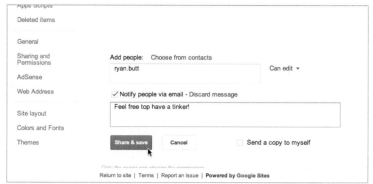

4: Share and save
With the people now added, you can send them an optional comment, so when they receive their invite they know why and what for. Then just for a nice reminder, you can choose to send yourself an email by clicking the tick box.

The Sharing Settings

All you need to share your site
with your friends

○ **Public on the web**
Choosing the public settings, you will
give everyone who uses the internet
the ability to find and use your site
without needing to sign in

Google

Search my sites

Manage Site

< **Decibels**

Recent site activity

Pages

Attachments

Page templates

Apps Scripts

Deleted items

General

Sharing and
Permissions

AdSense

Visibility options:

🌐 **Public on the web**
Anyone on the Internet can find and access. No sign-in required.

👤 **Anyone with the link**
Anyone who has the link can access. No sign-in required.

🔒 **Private**
Only people explicitly granted permission can access. Sign-in required.

[Save] [Cancel]

○ **Anyone with a link**
Choosing to set it to 'Anyone with
a link' will allow just those people
access who have the link. This will
not be public

○ **Cancel**
If you decide you don't want to
change your sharing settings,
just click Cancel to back out

○ **Private**
With your Google site set to 'Private',
the people who have a link to your site
will need to sign up to access it

*"With your Google site set to 'Private', the
people who have a link to your site will
need to sign up in order to access it"*

Work with Google Analytics

Gain more insight into your incoming website traffic for free

If you own a website or blog, the chances are that you're keen to find out how well it performs in terms of visitors. Google Analytics is a free tool that can be easily installed to many platforms and provides information that goes far beyond simple visitor counts. In fact, Google Analytics boasts over 80 different reports that can be used to analyse the trends and habits of your website traffic.

Beyond the simple stats of actual hits to your site, Google Analytics can provide information on which individual pages are pulling in visitors, and which are sending them elsewhere. It can also tell you how much time people are spending on your site before they move on and even what search terms are leading internet users to your domain.

Google Analytics provides this information via interactive graphs and pie charts while results can be polled from various periods of time. All of which is packed into an easy-to-navigate interface.

> "Google Analytics provides information that goes far beyond visitor counts"

○ Pick your time scale
The date window in the top right of the interface provides a flexible way of scanning results over a custom selected period of time

○ Choose your report
The panel on the left-hand side contains the many types of reports that can be applied. Each tab contains an extra section of choices within

○ The results section
With a search type chosen, the relevant results are displayed via a graph here. Moving the mouse over a section highlights information for that period

○ Export your information
The available results aren't limited to the website – they can be easily exported via email or to CSV, Excel or PDF formats via these buttons

○ Standard & custom reporting
While there is plenty of information to plough through on Google Analytics, it's also possible to generate your own reports tailored to your own needs

So many browsers Cater for different browsers

When creating content for your site, it's important to know how people are accessing it. With so many different kinds of devices and web browsers, it's important to make sure that your web presence appears at its best no matter what platform is being used.

Google Analytics can assist with this by tracking the details of the devices and web browsers that are used by the visitors to your website. Different browsers have varying capabilities and knowing what your users are able to access means that you can tailor your content to make it accessible to as many people as possible. For example, if your

website is dependent on Flash content, it's worth knowing how may iOS-based users may not be able to access it. Google Analytics is capable of breaking down your visitor data into what browsers are accessing your sites, what platforms are being used, even down to the screen sizes and colour depths that are displaying your content.

This is done by logging into the Google Analytic website and clicking on the Technology tab on the left-hand side of the screen. This opens up an extra tab labelled 'Browser & OS'; selecting this brings up the details of the recently used browsers.

Find out which browsers and systems visitors are using

Key features

Easy installation

Once you've set up a Google Analytics account, installation is as simple as copying and pasting text. Firstly, set up a profile on Google Analytics, then add your website details to it. The Analytics interface will generate a code that can then be added (by simply copying and pasting) to the template of your blog/website theme.

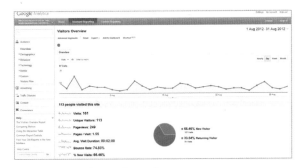

Easy-to-navigate interface

One of Google Analytics's winning features is how it packs so much detailed information into an easy-to-navigate interface. Tabs are located along the top and side of the screen; click these to navigate detailed breakdowns of the available data. These sections then break down into further detailed reports. You can really drill down into the data to find what you need.

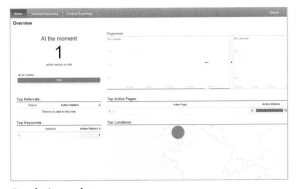

Real-time data

Google Analytics also provides a real-time results section, with info on the real-time visitors to your site, their location and where they came from to get to your domain. It can also pinpoint what content is currently getting the most attention.

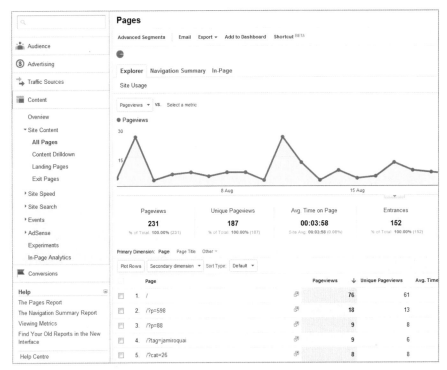

Website performance checker

Google Analytics is capable of comparing the individual pages of your website to help you keep track of which parts of your website perform the best. The dedicated Content section contains a number of links that provide key information on what content keeps the interest of your visitors. It can display which parts of your site are 'landing pages' for your visitors; ie where people are entering your site. Conversely, it can also highlight the pages where your visitors leave.

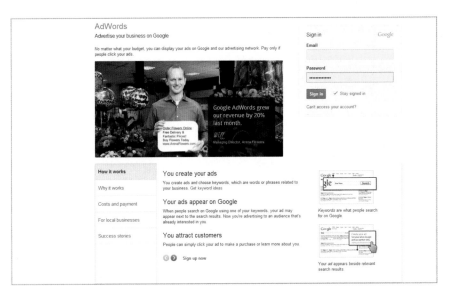

The power of adverts

Google AdWords is an advertising programme run by Google, enabling bloggers, web authors and businesses to create adverts. These then appear on Google search results pages when related search terms are entered into Google. These adverts and their prime location placing can help attract users and generate traffic. It's possible to connect AdWords to an Analytics account and analyse the results under the relevant tabs.

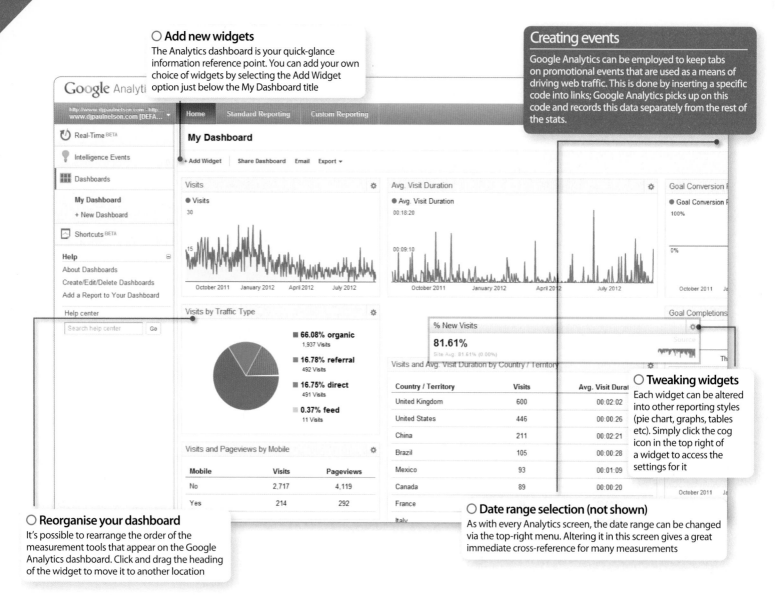

○ **Add new widgets**
The Analytics dashboard is your quick-glance information reference point. You can add your own choice of widgets by selecting the Add Widget option just below the My Dashboard title

Creating events
Google Analytics can be employed to keep tabs on promotional events that are used as a means of driving web traffic. This is done by inserting a specific code into links; Google Analytics picks up on this code and records this data separately from the rest of the stats.

○ **Tweaking widgets**
Each widget can be altered into other reporting styles (pie chart, graphs, tables etc). Simply click the cog icon in the top right of a widget to access the settings for it

○ **Reorganise your dashboard**
It's possible to rearrange the order of the measurement tools that appear on the Google Analytics dashboard. Click and drag the heading of the widget to move it to another location

○ **Date range selection (not shown)**
As with every Analytics screen, the date range can be changed via the top-right menu. Altering it in this screen gives a great immediate cross-reference for many measurements

Analyse data with Google Analytics

Navigating Google Analytics is easy enough; the real trick is using the info to improve your website

While the information provided by Google Analytics may prove interesting to peruse, it pays to understand how that information can be used to tailor your website. Google Analytics is excellent for showing where the strengths and weaknesses lie in your website or blog.

Google Analytics can tell you how many unique visitors your site is getting, give you an idea of how many pages users visit before heading off elsewhere and much more. It can also give an insight into social networks and how they feed traffic to your website. It's even capable of pinpointing the areas of your website that are getting the most clicks. Armed with this information, it's possible to build on the strengths and remove the weaknesses of your website or blog.

Over the next few steps we'll look at how to find this information within the interface and what the different variables can mean for your website.

Google Analytics | What the data means

1: Viewing your traffic

The Audience>Overview tab gives a top-level view of incoming traffic. The vertical axis shows the total number of views on each day.

2: Comparing your visits

Above the graph, click 'Select a metric' and choose one. This adds an overlaid comparison between the total visits and what you selected.

3: Using the information

The visitor totals can be compared with their habits (bounce rate, visit lengths, page views, unique visitors). This shows how well your content engages.

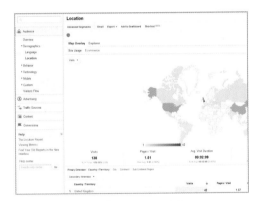

4: Location & demographics

Demographics>Location lets you zoom right in on how your site performs in certain areas. Content can then be adjusted to suit those particular markets.

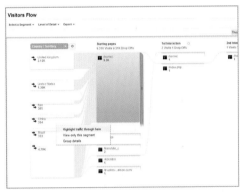

5: The visitors journey

To view the traffic flow through your site, click Visitors Flow. This shows where users drop in and out of your site. Click on sections for more insight.

6: Traffic Sources

Traffic Sources highlights where your visitors are coming from (blogs, website, social networks etc) and what search terms relate to your site's content.

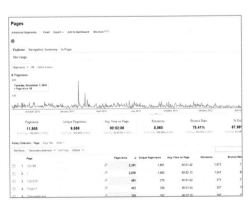

7: Your site content

Similar to Visitors Flow, the Site Content tab shows how individual pages of your site are performing. Here, however, the information is far more detailed.

8: Custom reports

If specific factors are of interest to you, they can be made the focus of your own custom reports via the Custom Reporting section of the dashboard.

9: In-Page Analytics

In-Page Analytics shows exactly which sections are being clicked the most. It's excellent for seeing which specific areas are pulling the most user focus.

A guide to Google Wallet

Turn your desktop computer into a wallet and save time

One of the great things about using the digital realm to purchase online products is the ease and swiftness of the entire payment process. Once you have input your information, transactions are reduced to pressing a button or two. Google Wallet is a supreme example of this philosophy as it not only stores your payment information but also your transaction history so that you can monitor what you have spent and where.

You can even peruse new offers to tempt you in the future. One of the major assets of this service is that all of your transactions can be synced to the cloud. This means that, no matter how many credit/debit cards you may have in your wallet, Google Wallet will take care of the lot under one digital umbrella. At the moment, UK users can use Google's Wallet service via computer-only, but it won't be long before you'll be able to download the mobile app too, to expand payment possibilities.

> ## "Transactions are reduced to pressing a button or two"

○ Payment Methods
Your current credit/debit cards are listed here. Your credit card, for example, will include the ability to edit details and delete the card

Google

Wallet

Transactions
Payment Methods
My Seller Reviews
Subscriptions
Devices

Transactions

DATE	DESCRIPTION
May 21	Online purchases **Word Solver**
May 21	Online purchases **Sound Touch**
May 21	Online purchases **Knots 3D**
May 21	Online purchases **GoldenDict**
May 21	Online purchases **Akinator the Genie**
May 21	Online purchases **Akinator the Genie**
May 21	Online purchases **Vegetable Garden**
May 21	Online purchases **Kids Animals (Children 3 to 9)**
May 21	Online purchases **When I Get Bigger**
May 21	Online purchases **SkySafari**
May 19	Online purchases **Scribd Reader Pro**
May 19	Online purchases **One Fish Two Fish - Dr. Seuss**

○ Devices
One for the future as far as the UK user is concerned. When the mobile version of Wallet appears, your mobile sources will be listed here

○ My Seller Reviews
As the title implies, if you sell any item to someone direct, they then have the opportunity to comment upon the purchase and detail their experience

○ Transactions
This section provides a full list of all of your transactions completed while using Google Wallet, including a description and the date purchased

○ Subscriptions
If you pay for subscriptions, they will be detailed within this section. Keep an eye on how long is left in your current agreement

Personal details
Input your basic contact information

Google Wallet securely stores your credit card information in your Google account so you don't have to enter your billing and shipping information each time you shop online. One of the most important areas that makes this app run smoothly is the Settings. Clicking on it im the top right-hand corner of the screen brings up two tabs.

Firstly select the General tab, choose your language from the long list, then click on notifications if you want to see special offers plus news of service updates. The other boxes are pretty straightforward: your name, address and phone number. The intriguing part of

the Settings is the next tab, the Billing And Delivery Addresses. Click on this and initially it will be blank, asking you to add a New Address. Click on the red box to input your address details and, upon completion, note the Set As Default box. If you have just the one address listed, this box will remain active. If you add a second address, then you can choose which address will be your default.

This will be your primary address to send posted items to and to use as the billing address. Other addresses can also be used as delivery addresses. Note that a map of the address will appear next to each.

General	Billing and delivery addresses

NEW ADDRESS

Country/Region	United Kingdom (GB)
Name	
Street address	
Town/City	
County	LINCS
Postcode	
Phone	

☑ Set as default

Save   Cancel

You can enter more than one address for delivery and billing

Key features

New Credit Card

Card Number		VISA MASTERCARD AMEX DISCOVER
Expiry	1 ⇕ 2012 ⇕ CVC	
Address	Paul Rigby -1 Greestone Place,Lincoln LINCS LN... ⇕
	☑ Set as default
	Save Cancel

Payment

The basic element of the Google Wallet app is the credit/ debit card, the most popular method of paying for products. Within the Payment Method section you can add as many cards or other payment methods as you wish and then title them for particular people, events or services.

Google

Wallet   [ADD CARD OR ACCOUNT ▼]

My Wallet Devices

Transactions
Payment Methods
My Seller Reviews
Subscriptions
Devices

Mobile

'In the works' as far as UK users are concerned, we can look forward to Google Wallet being on our mobile phones in the near future. You will be able to access a NFC terminal at the till, in the same way that you might pay with a contactless debit card.

Contact White Urchin Ventures, Inc

Or you can send an email by filling out the form below.

To: White Urchin Ventures, Inc <whiteurchin@gmail.com>
From: <paulrigby9876@gmail.com>
Subject: Choose request type ▼
Message:

☑ Send me a copy of this email   Send email

Contact

When you have bought an item, you can contact the supplier if, for example, you have yet to receive the product and have been waiting a long time for it or you want to cancel your order or, indeed, if the item has arrived but was damaged.

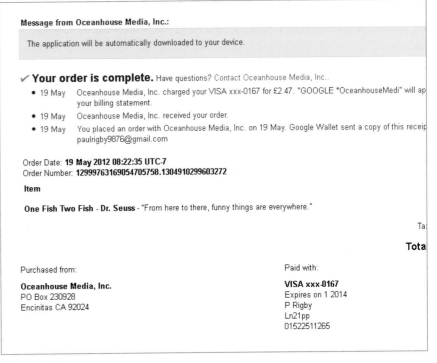

Message from Oceanhouse Media, Inc.:

The application will be automatically downloaded to your device.

✓ **Your order is complete.** Have questions? Contact Oceanhouse Media, Inc..

- 19 May   Oceanhouse Media, Inc. charged your VISA xxx-0167 for £2.47. "GOOGLE *OceanhouseMedi" will ap your billing statement.
- 19 May   Oceanhouse Media, Inc. received your order.
- 19 May   You placed an order with Oceanhouse Media, Inc. on 19 May. Google Wallet sent a copy of this receip paulrigby9876@gmail.com

Order Date: **19 May 2012 08:22:35 UTC-7**
Order Number: **12999763169054705758.1304910299603272**

Item

One Fish Two Fish - Dr. Seuss - "From here to there, funny things are everywhere."

Ta

Tota

Purchased from:

Oceanhouse Media, Inc.
PO Box 230928
Encinitas CA 92024

Paid with:

VISA xxx-0167
Expires on 1 2014
P Rigby
Ln21pp
01522511265

Transactions

When you enter the transactions section, you will see a list of all of your purchases. If you click on one them, you will enter a fully detailed brief of what you ordered and when, how the payment was made and the details of the payment source, the order date and order number, plus who it was purchased from. If it was an app, this might be the first time that the app company details have been made fully available.

⊗ **Your order has been cancelled.** Have questions? Contact White Urchin Ventures, Inc.

- 21 May   Google has cancelled your order. **You won't be charged.** Reason: Customer request to cancel
- 21 May   White Urchin Ventures, Inc received your order.
- 21 May   You placed an order with White Urchin Ventures, Inc on 21 May. Google Wallet sent a copy of this receipt to paulrigby9876@gmail.com

Order Date: **21 May 2012 10:26:57 UTC-7**
Order Number: **12999763169054705758.1376229317339635**

Item	Price
Word Solver - Beat your friends at Scrabble and Words with Friends with this handy cheat!	£1.27
	Total: £1.27
	(includes VAT £0.00)

Purchased from:

White Urchin Ventures, Inc
8085 Skyline Boulevard
Oakland CA 94611

Paid with:

VISA xxx-0167
Expires on 1 2014
P Rigby
Ln21pp
01522511265

Cancelled

Speaking of apps, the details of each transaction even extend to those purchases that were transacted but were subsequently rejected by you. As you may know, you can 'try out' an app for a short amount of time and, if you don't like it, you can – as it were – send it back from where it came. That cancelled transaction will be listed within Wallet too. This item forms a reassuring record and shows that your money was returned to you.

Read with Google Books

How to view, preview and order with Google Books

Google Books, which now forms part of the Google Play Store, is an easy way to find and discover books by entering specific keywords that relate to the title of a book you are after. So if you have heard of a particular book and enter words that relate to the content into the search engine, then Google will deliver a series of books whose contents match your search items. Likewise, if you enter keywords that relate to a particular subject then the search engine will provide a variety of possibilities based on your tastes and interests.

By clicking on a book you will then be able to see basic information about the publication in question and perhaps get to read preview pages to get a hands-on idea if it is something you would like to purchase. If you're happy with your find and decide to purchase a book then you can do this quickly and conveniently through the Google Play Book Store too and get all of your digital downloads delivered to any device so that you can enjoy reading anywhere.

> ## "By clicking on a book you'll see basic info about the publication in question"

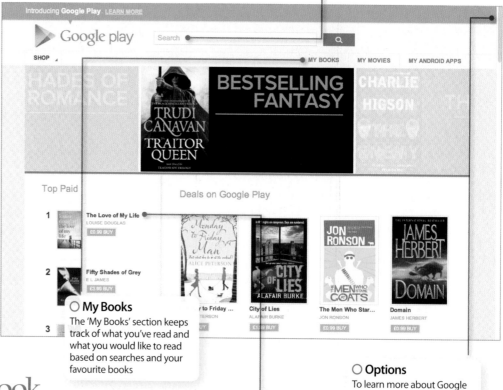

Search bar
Use the search engine to find specific books, or click on 'Advanced Book Search' to search for authors, sentences or topics and ISBN numbers

My Books
The 'My Books' section keeps track of what you've read and what you would like to read based on searches and your favourite books

Topics
The homepage is crammed full of topics to get you started, such as 'Classics', 'Trending Topics' (what other people are reading) and 'Magazines'

Options
To learn more about Google Books and its services, click on the cog icon in the top-right corner (just out of shot here)

Take it to the next level
How to read books on any device, at any time

As well as reading books on the web through your computer, you can download the Google Play Books app for your mobile device and read them on the move. And you can access all of your eBooks wirelessly no matter where you are thanks to your entire library being stored in a digital cloud. What's more, as Google Play Books is compatible with Android, iPhone, iPad and most eReaders, you can start reading a book on one device and then continue where you left off on another.

Although you can't browse the store through the app, all of the books that you download through the service will be instantly synced to your device as soon as you log into your Google account and can then be read on your device. Most eBooks come with flowing text or original scanned pages, or both. Books with flowing text provide the user with greater control over their reading experience, such as the ability to adjust the font size, line space and paragraph alignment.

Designed for easy accessibility, Google Play Books is offering stiff competition to its established eReader rivals such as iBooks and Kindle – but it's certainly good news for the consumer of digital literature with plenty of variety and great deals on offer.

We hope the Google eBook store will come to more territories in the near future

Key features

Search the bookstore

By entering titles, authors or keywords into the search engine, Google Books will provide a list of possibilities. You can also enter entire sentences, specify languages, publishers, subjects, publication dates, ISBN and ISSN numbers to find what you want. Seemingly no stone is left unturned in Google Books' mission to find the books that matter the most to you.

Get yourself some recommendations

If you don't know where to start and need a little prompting to start your book search, then there are a series of subjects listed in a column on the Google Books home screen. Click on a subject and you will be provided with pages full of the most popular books. Information such as author, year of publication and the number of pages can be obtained at-a-glance.

Preview books

By clicking on the cover of a book you'll be treated to a nice zoomed-in view, and you can then scroll down to obtain details about the publisher, year of publication and ISBN numbers. In some cases you can then scroll down further to read exerts from the book to help you get an instant impression as to the style and content and gauge if it is something you would like to purchase or borrow from a library.

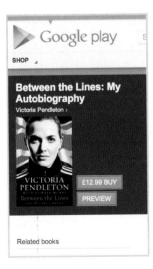

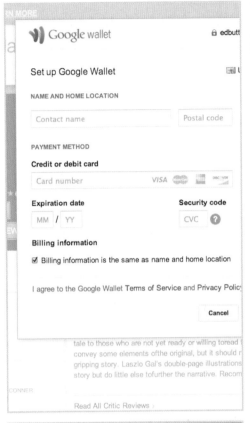

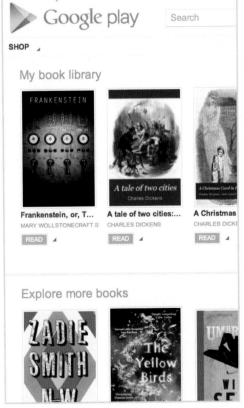

Your personal library

If you like what you see based on your searches then you can click on the title of book to open the info page and then click on the price to buy it. Once the transaction is complete, your book will be added to your personal library. If you are buying a book, as opposed to downloading a free digital publication, you will need to set up your Google Wallet to go ahead with the transaction. You will be guided through this simple process on screen.

"If you like what you see based on your searches then you can click on the 'Add to My Library' link in the left-hand column"

Accessing your library

Downloaded books can be read on the web or through the Google Play Books app on your mobile device. To access the books that you have purchased through the web, click on the 'My Books' link at the top of the page to see your library, then simply click on the 'Read' button next to a book to open it up in your web browser and start reading through your computer.

Search with Google+ Sparks

All the new details on Google's latest web-sharing function

The Google+ Sparks feature is a way of keeping the internet streaming to your Google+ account, covering any number of themes that you might wish to monitor. These won't actually filter through to your main Google+ stream – you will always need to access them through the buttons on the side tab – but they're handy for keeping up to date on your very favourite subject matters. But if you have used Sparks in the past then the system has changed slightly and now you can access Sparks in an altogether more casual way. You do it simply by entering keyword searches in the Google+ search engine. Make your subjects topic-specific (for example, 'videogames' as opposed to just 'games') and you will be presented with a list of Sparks that relate to your favoured topic, and that topic only. Once you have completed your search, click on the 'Everything' menu and choose 'Sparks'.

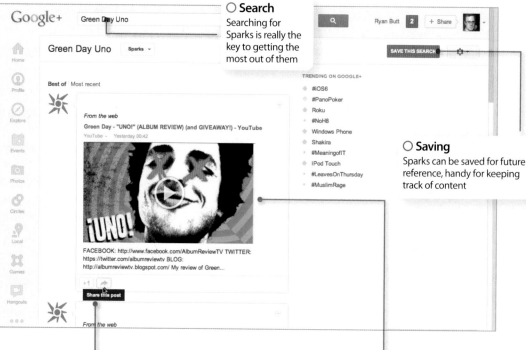

○ **Search**
Searching for Sparks is really the key to getting the most out of them

○ **Saving**
Sparks can be saved for future reference, handy for keeping track of content

○ **Sharing**
Sparks enable you to share any content you found interesting. It's the only way it can be done, without using the link directly

○ **Images**
You won't get any pretty pictures to illustrate your own Sparks, which is a shame

> "Sparks are a way of keeping the internet streaming into your Google+ account"

How to use Sparks
Search specifically

Sparks will only be as helpful as you make them. Of course, you could just leave them and you won't even know they existed, but where's the use in that?

To start using Sparks, enter keywords into the Google+ search field and then click on the blue magnifying glass icon. The content displayed in your stream will then change in relation to the topic that you searched for and the topic itself will form a header at the top of the page. Next, click on the 'Everything' menu next to the topic header and then you will see a menu item called 'Sparks', click on this. You will then be presented with a list of

'Sparks', little news nuggets that relate to your search. It's a neat way to cast a net over topics that interest you and snare a varied selection of content for you to digest. And if you don't have time to read through all of the relayed content the that present moment in time, then you can click on the 'Save This Search' button in the top-right corner of the screen and all of the content that you have collected will be stored for future reference. This is just one of the many free services available through Google+ that, though somewhat subtle, will revolutionise the way you use the internet and ensure mindless trawling is a thing of the past.

Sparks is especially adept at sourcing entertainment information

Key features

Broad subjects

To start using Sparks, you should search for a particular subject, whether it's films, books, gardening or abseiling. Then Google+ will search the web for any of the latest web coverage surrounding those search terms and list them as they would appear in your stream. It's a great way to cut through the chaff and read only the topics you're interested in.

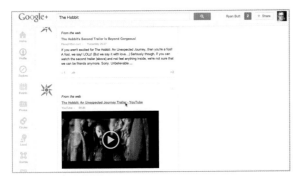

A new RSS feed

While the majority of sites use an RSS feed to keep its readers up to date, Sparks can be used to avoid the text-only news feeds that RSS uses, and instead offer large snippets and links to the full thing. Simply search for one of your favourite sites and all its latest content will be there to see.

Be specific

Despite Google's suggested Sparks telling you otherwise, the truth is being vague in your search will often result in an abundance of unrelated content. Since Sparks searches for the terms used, rather than the subject matter, it can often result in unwanted sites. Searching 'games', for example, will return sports sites, when perhaps you wanted information on videogames.

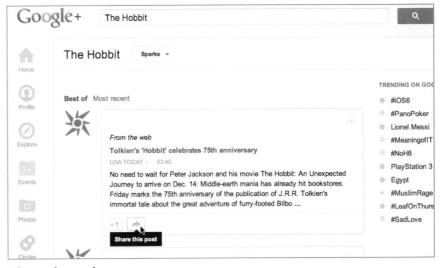

Share the web

While the majority of the web has embraced the '+1' button (a way of showing which things you think are cool), as of yet it doesn't really do anything, other than adding the site to your profile of +1s. Sparks means you can browse the sites and subjects you normally would through Google, then share those links directly with people in Circles. This is only possible through Sparks, since the option to share content cannot (yet, at least) be implemented across the web.

"Only the latest news appears, so if nothing is found then there's nothing new to find"

Timely responses

Sparks, just like Google+, are all about the here and now. Unlike a standard Google search, a Spark search won't return all related content, regardless of when it was posted. Only the latest news and information will appear in a Spark search, so if nothing is found then there's nothing new to find. This is great for when you want something specific, but not so much when a popular subject is regularly discussed on the internet.

Productivi

From searching to navigation and so much more, these are the apps to make your life run smoothly

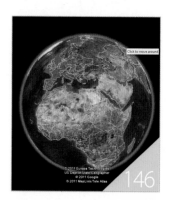

ty 2013

"Google has a long list of solutions that can change the lives of those using them"

126

140

150

Tap into the power of Google Search

Quick and relevant results from a search engine powerhouse

Google Search is without doubt the most popular of the online search engines available. Its exceptional functionality, searching capabilities and ease of use inspire and convey confidence when you need to get quick and relevant search results for a particular query.

The search engine is designed to appeal to everyone from casual online browsers to professional researchers, and although the majority of people use the behemoth to search the web for keywords, images or videos, Google Search lets you do much more than this.

For example, it can be used to search for books, blogs, maps and a whole lot more besides. The search engine's Advanced Search features are exceptionally innovative and let you narrow a search to particular file types or information that appears in selected sites or domains. Some Boolean operators are supported and you can even personalise the search settings to suit your individual preferences.

> "It's designed to appeal to everyone, from casual browsers to professional researchers"

Apps
If you're logged into your Google account, you can access other Google apps directly from here

Search bar
Enter your search query, hit the Google Search button and results will appear

Personalised
Being logged in to your account gives you extra options to share and more

Feeling lucky
The 'I'm Feeling Lucky' button is famous for delivering random results

Define your search Add more search power

Google Search includes a number of advanced features, and the following tips are designed to help you make the most of your searches. To exclude a word, simply put a minus sign (-) immediately before it, but bear in mind that it shouldn't be preceded by a space. For example, type the query 'Apple -iPhone' and Google will search for the word 'Apple' but exclude references to the word 'iPhone'.

Another useful tip is to familiarise yourself with the 'OR' Boolean operator. Google's default behaviour is to consider all the words in the search box. Use the OR operator (note

that you must type OR in uppercase) and you specify that you are searching for either of one or more words. For example, the search term 'Apple iPad OR iPhone' will return results about either one of the two devices. Note that the 'AND' operator isn't required in Google Search.

On a final note, Google automatically employs synonyms and sometimes these can be a little intrusive. Type a plus sign (+) immediately before a word (no space) if you want to search for an exact term. Alternatively, putting quotation marks around the word does the same thing.

Key features

Keeping it simple

Google Search ticks all the right boxes for most people. The service is easy to use and even a basic search can yield results. Searching is simple: just type whatever comes to mind in the search box, hit the Search button and Google will quickly trawl the web for content that's relevant to your search.

Advanced searching

A basic search is useful, but an advanced search often yields better results. For instance, you can search for exact words or phrases and even opt to exclude unwanted words. You can also search for PDFs, RTF documents or Microsoft Office files that contain your keyword(s).

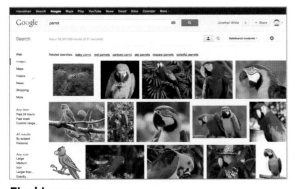

Find images

All the popular search engines feature image searching functionality and Google is no different. A basic image search will often be enough, but if isn't, an advanced search can be used to refine your hunt for pictures.

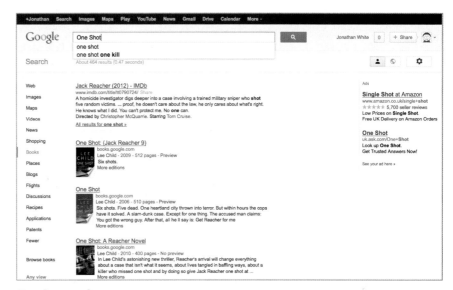

Book search

The primary purpose of Google Search is to hunt for text in webpages and the ability to be able to search for books that contain keyword(s) is a feature that is often overlooked by everyone except academics, researchers and good old-fashioned bookworms. Book Search works just like web search, and the database is growing by the day. You can even search for and then download public-domain and out-of-copyright material to the desktop in PDF format.

> "You can search for exact words or phrases and even opt to exclude unwanted words"

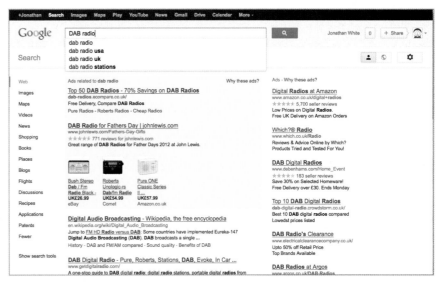

Search results

Performing a search usually reveals four elements that separate Google from other popular search engines: speed, accuracy, objectivity, and ease of use. The order of search results is based (at least in part) on a priority ranking system called PageRank, which assigns a numerical weighting to each element of a hyperlinked set of documents and lists search results in order of relative importance. In short, you will usually find the most relevant hits on the first results page.

Use Google's Advanced Search

To really make the most of your Google search you should try an Advanced Search

The majority of information that you require is available on the internet, and as long as you have the knowledge and patience required to perform a search, relevant information will almost certainly be found eventually.

However, a simple Google Search will often yield too many irrelevant results to wade through, and therein lies the importance of being proficient and specific when searching. If you are struggling with an overwhelming number of search results, use Google's Advanced Search function to narrow the results down by searching for exact words or phrases. You can also choose to exclude unwanted words or to display only results in a certain language. You can also search specific documents or websites for your specific query.

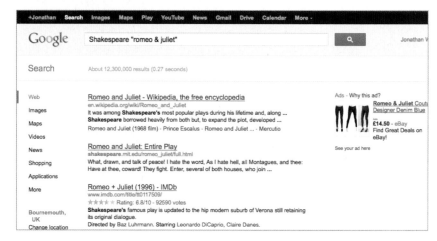

Google Search | Introducing Google's Advanced Search feature

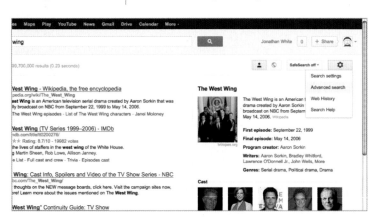

1: Start an Advanced Search
A basic Google search will often inundate you with results. For something more specific, click the cog icon and select 'Advanced search' from the menu.

2: Define search terms
Choose an exact wording or phrase and you will see the number of search results dramatically decrease, increasing the search's relevance.

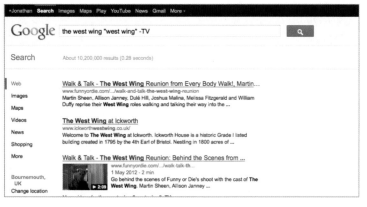

3: Narrow the search
If you still have too many results, try adding in some unwanted words. Google will make sure any results with the unwanted word(s) in do not appear.

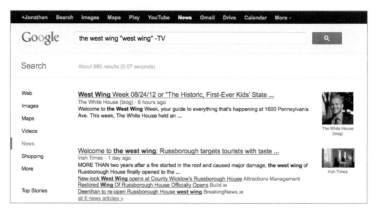

4: Stay up to date
The search terms may be more relevant, but you may want more up-to-date results. Select 'News' from the sidebar to see results from the last 24 hours.

Personalise your Google search

Tweak the Google search settings to suit your personal requirements

Google Search is one of the most comprehensive and feature-packed search engines available. However, tweak the settings to suit your preferences and your search results could be improved. Google's interface enables you to personalise the search settings and choose the language(s) that you wish search results to be returned in, among many other things. You can also configure Google's SafeSearch settings, which is handy if children also have access to your desktop computer.

SafeSearch blocks any pages that contain explicit content. You can elect to use strict filtering (which filters explicit text and images) or moderate filtering (which filters just explicit images). Alternatively, you can opt to not filter your search results at all.

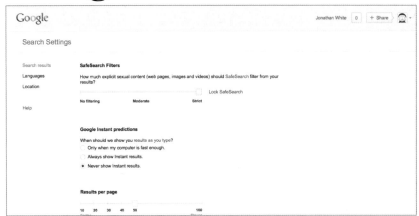

Google Search | Personalise your search settings

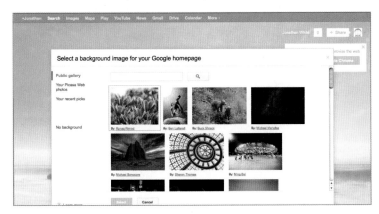

1: Select a background image
Click 'Change Background Image' on the bottom of the main search screen and select an image from the Public Gallery, your computer or Picasa Web Photos.

2: Search Settings
Now click the cog (options) icon at the top right of the main Google screen and select 'Search settings' from the drop-down menu that appears.

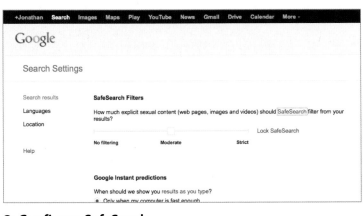

3: Configure SafeSeach
Configure the global settings to suit and then choose a SafeSearch option. Click Lock SafeSearch and strict filtering will be applied to all searches.

4: Google Instant
Now choose if you want to enable Google Instant. This handy enhancement predicts what you are searching for and returns results as you type.

Explore the benefits of Web History

Search and view pages you have visited in the past with Google Web History

When you sign up and create a Google account you are given the choice to enable a little-known feature called Google Web History. If you use the Google search engine regularly, then Web History may well prove very useful as it enables you to view and search across webpages that you've visited in the past, including all your Google searches.

In short, this means that you don't have to hunt high and low for things you've seen and liked in the past. And when you are signed in to your Google account, Web History will provide you with more personalised search results based on what you have searched for in the past and which sites you have visited.

Google Search | Get started with Web History

1: Sign in
To access Web History, click the cog (options) icon at the top right of the main Google screen and select Web History.

2: Web History
You'll now see a record of your search history and a calendar. Your Web History is stored on Google's servers so you can view and manage it from any computer.

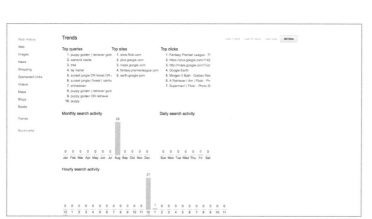

3: Trends and bookmarks
Click the Trends link and you can view lots of information, including top searches and your most frequently visited sites.

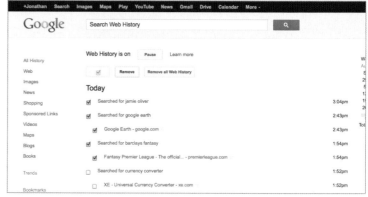

4: Privacy is important
You can delete individual items by selecting them and clicking Remove, or erase your whole history by clicking 'Remove all Web History'.

Search the web for digital images

Google Search offers the discerning user an advanced set of image searching tools

You can explore the web in an entirely new way by beginning your search with an image. All the popular search engines let you perform an image search, but Google offers the most comprehensive image search on the web. Once you have familiarised yourself with the myriad features on offer, you can use the service to quickly and easily find images.

You can opt to perform a basic search simply by typing keywords into the search box or tap into the power of the advanced feature set on offer. For example, you can opt to return just images that are extra-large or even determine your preferred aspect ratio (tall, square, wide or panoramic).

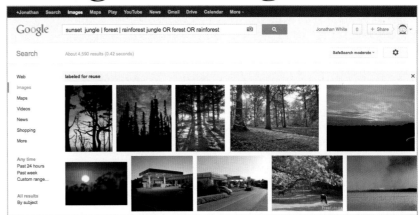

Google Search | How to perform an advanced image search

1: Start with a basic search
Navigate to **www.google.com** and then click Images. Type what you want in the search box and hit Search.

2: Refine search criteria
It's time to refine the search criteria. Click the cog icon and select 'Advanced search' and then configure the search to suit your personal preferences.

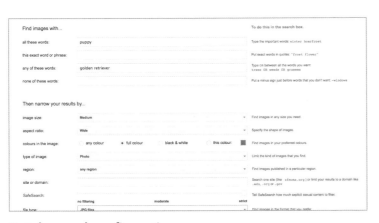

3: Advanced configuration
Click Advanced Search again and configure the appropriate settings, like if you want only a colour picture, to hone the search further.

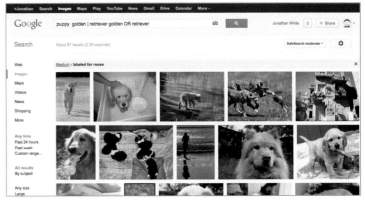

4: Usage Rights
The results will be better. In the Usage Rights field, choose 'Labelled for Reuse' and the results will include images with a licence that lets you copy them.

Browse with Google Chrome

Chrome has all you need to make the most of the web

Your web browser is arguably one of the most important software applications on your computer. When you are reading the latest news, streaming video, engaged in chat or checking your bank account details, you will usually be doing so from a browser.

Chrome has a number of features designed to enhance your browsing experience. For example, it takes no time to boot up webpages, and even complex web applications load and run like lightning. Not only that, but the interface is well organised, uncluttered and intuitive. Chrome also supports the concept of tabbed browsing, and a neat touch is the ability to be able to drag tabs from the browser to create new windows, or to rearrange them yourself to suit your internet browsing preferences.

As a bonus, Chrome's security is second to none, so you can browse safe in the knowledge that the risk of phishing or malware attack is markedly reduced.

> "You can browse safe in the knowledge that the risk of a malware attack is markedly reduced"

Tabs
Tabbed browsing is supported. If one tab crashes or freezes, the others are unaffected

Themes
Customise Chrome with a range of themes, web apps and browser extensions

Search
Use the omnibox to type both web addresses and search terms

Efficient
Chrome is built squarely with simplicity and efficiency in mind. Make no mistake though – it's fast!

Security
Online browsing is safe and secure, courtesy of a range of built-in security features

---

Manage your privacy

Incognito mode ensures your privacy while browsing

There are times when we all like to browse in private. For example, you may need to buy a surprise gift for a loved one yet share the same computer. Incognito mode ensures that neither website visits nor downloads are recorded in your browsing or download histories. In addition, any cookies generated while in Incognito mode are automatically erased after the Incognito window is closed.

Incognito mode is extremely useful, not least of all because it offers you an easy way to browse the web privately and without the need to keep changing your privacy settings either during or between browsing sessions. For example, you can have 'normal' and incognito sessions running at the same time in different windows. One will record your browsing activity and the other won't.

And if that's not enough, you can customise a number of privacy settings for your browser from the 'Under the Bonnet' section of Chrome's options. These give you full control over the types of browsing data that you wish to delete. Even if you have opted not to run a session in Incognito mode, you can still clear your browsing history at any time.

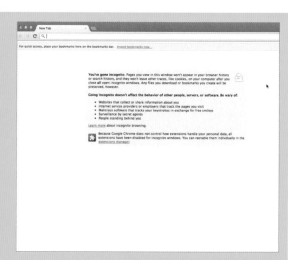

Key features

Ease of use

Boot up Google Chrome and the first thing you will see is a polished, uncluttered interface. Everything is where it should be, and simplicity is the key to the browser's efficiency. A combined search and address bar (also called the omnibox) means that it is easy to seamlessly search and navigate the web from one place.

Translation capabilities

Chrome is the first browser to incorporate 'machine translation' in the browser itself, without the need for additional plug-ins or extensions. If the language the webpage you are viewing does not match the language configured in your Google Chrome settings, the browser will automatically ask if you want to translate the content into your preferred language.

Stable and secure

Chrome has been developed with the concept of secure browsing in mind. If you visit a site suspected of being a security risk, you will get a warning message. Chrome's also built to be stable. If one tab freezes or crashes, the others are unaffected.

> "Everything is where it should be, and simplicity is the key to the browser's efficiency"

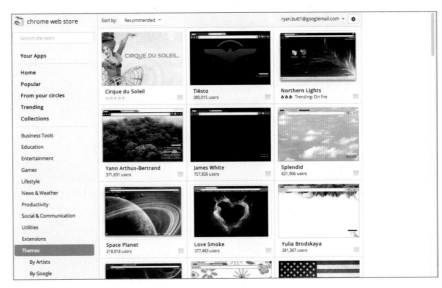

Online marketplace

The Chrome Web Store is an online marketplace where you can discover web apps, extensions and themes developed especially for Google Chrome. Use it to enhance the functionality of your browser by adding features and changing its look.

Customisation options

Chrome has a number of advanced and very powerful features, and these include a range of personalisation options. For example, you can customise the browser with a range of interesting and often visually stunning backdrops called themes. These change the skin of Google Chrome and give the browser more style and flair. You can find special themes developed by Google and a number of international artists in the Themes Gallery in the Chrome Web Store.

Explore Chrome's search bar

Google Chrome's search box makes for an effortless browsing experience

Chrome's browser window is streamlined and clutter-free – it's clear from the moment you boot up the browser that simplicity is a key feature. All the functions are within easy reach and one of the most innovative is what Google has termed the 'omnibox'. Unlike other browsers, Chrome's address bar lets you type both web addresses and search terms. As a bonus, you can even drag text or a link from anywhere on a webpage that you are viewing and place it directly in the search box.

The omnibox makes it easy to search as it provides intelligent suggestions as you type. This makes it a breeze to revisit a recently viewed webpage if you have forgotten the URL.

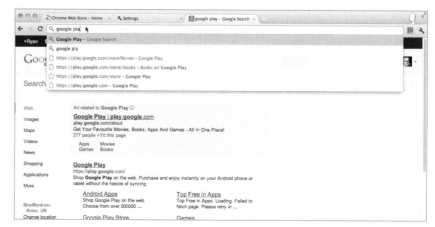

Google Chrome | Get started with Chrome's omnibox

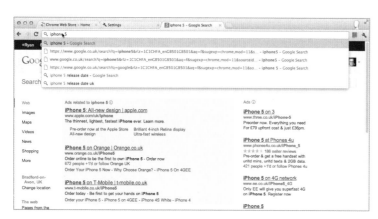

1: Enter a search query
Type a search term in the address bar, press Enter and you'll see results from Google. Enable the 'Instant' feature and search results will appear as you type.

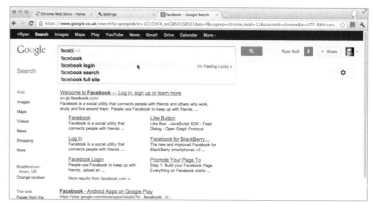

2: Search within a site
Type the web address of the site you wish to search and then press Tab. Now enter your query and Chrome will use the site's search engine to get results.

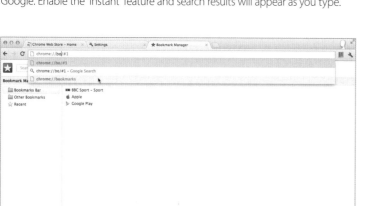

3: Search bookmarks
Start typing in the address bar and you are also shown matches from your bookmarks. A prediction service helps you complete URLs and search terms.

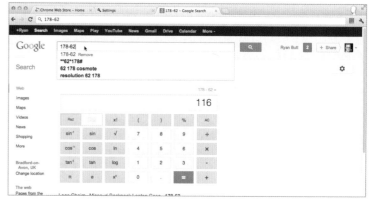

4: Perform calculations
Chrome's omnibox also doubles as a calculator. Rather than load up your computer's calculator, just type your mathematical query into the box.

Create a shortcut icon for Gmail

Google Chrome lets you create application shortcuts for websites you visit regularly

Google's Chrome web browser brings a whole raft of impressive features to the table, each of which is designed to enhance your browsing experience. If you're running Google Chrome on a Windows PC you can create application shortcuts to websites you visit regularly, or for apps that you have installed from the Chrome Web Store. These shortcuts can be placed on your PC's desktop, in the Start menu or on the taskbar for quick and easy access.

If you have a Gmail account, create a shortcut icon on the desktop and another on the taskbar and you will no longer need to boot up Chrome in order to access your email account.

Google Chrome | Create application shortcuts for Gmail

1: Log in to your account
Before you can create a desktop shortcut, open Chrome and type **mail.google. com** in the address bar. Now sign into your Gmail account.

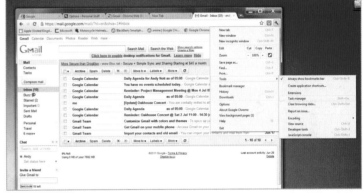

2: Gmail account screen
You will now see your Gmail account screen. Click the spanner icon at the top of your browser and select 'Tools' and then 'Create Application Shortcuts'.

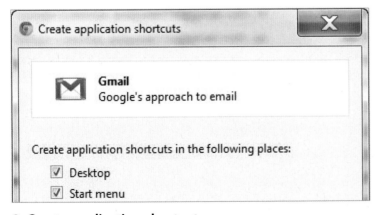

3: Create application shortcuts
You'll be given the opportunity to create shortcuts to Gmail on the desktop and in the Start menu. Check all the boxes and then click 'Create'.

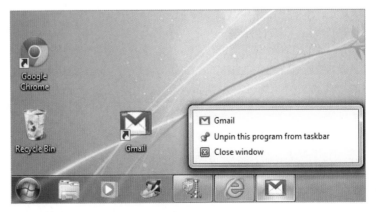

4: Desktop shortcuts created!
Close Google Chrome, take a look at your desktop and you will now see a new Gmail shortcut icon. Click it to launch your Gmail account.

Personalise your browser
Visit the Chrome Web Store and you will find some great ways to personalise your browser. This theme has been created to reflect the joy of spring

Reset the default theme
Because the process is fully automated, downloading and installing new themes is a breeze. But what if you no longer want to use any of the themes you've tried? No problem. You can reinstall the default Google Chrome theme at any time. Just go back to the Chrome Preferences page and, under the 'Appearance' section, click on the 'Reset to default theme' button.

New Tab   New Tab

BBC Sport – Sport   Apple   Google Play   Inbox (19,865) – ry

Google   BBC Sport – Sport   Apple   Google Sites

Sign in to Yahoo!   BBC – Homepage   http://mail.google.com/   Google Sites

Browse by category
There are countless themes available and you can browse and select favourites from the featured, top-rated, Google or artists categories

View themes on the New Tab page
The best way to view a theme that you have just installed is to navigate to the New Tab page. To do this, click the 'File' menu and select 'New Tab' from the top of the menu

Add style and flair
Themes allow you to add an individualised look to your browser. A new theme replaces the default and adds an alternative skin to the window and tabs

Customise your Chrome browser

The best way to add style and flair to your browser is to install one of the many themes available

Minimisation of the user interface has been a trademark of Google Chrome ever since the beta was first released in September 2008, and the last four years have seen the browser go from strength to strength. In fact, it's testament to its popularity that Chrome has now gained a 20 per cent share of the global browser market, and this is in part due to the interface being secure, uncluttered and intuitive.

A prominent feature is the ability to be able to customise Chrome to suit your personal browsing preferences. For example, you can quickly and easily install a new theme at any time. In short, themes change the skin (or backdrop) of Google Chrome and give the browser an enhanced look and feel. There are hundreds of themes available, and you can find special themes developed and created by Google and artists from around the world in the Chrome Web Store's Themes Gallery. And when you find one you like? Simply install it and try it out.

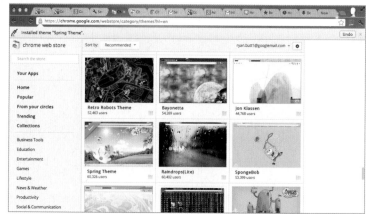

Google Chrome | Customise Chrome with new themes

  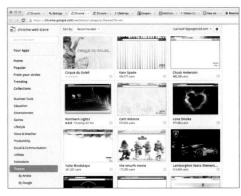

1: Getting started with themes
The easiest way to install a new theme is by going to Chrome's Preferences page. Do this by clicking on the 'Chrome' menu and then choosing the option.

2: Personalise your browser
Now scroll down and, under the 'Appearance' section, click on the 'Get themes' link to start shopping for a whole-new look.

3: Chrome Web Store
You will now see an online marketplace called the Chrome Web Store. This is the gateway to myriad themes, so have a look through them.

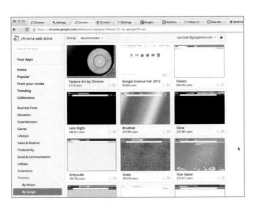  

4: Explore Google themes
On the left-hand side of the screen you will see categories that include Apps, Extensions and Themes. Scroll to Themes and click 'By Google'.

5: Theme Gallery
Browse the thumbnails, and when you find a theme you like, click it for more info. You will now see the theme in more detail and any reviews it has.

6: Check the ratings
This one is called Grass and the ratings look okay. Click 'Choose Theme', and then click on 'Add' on the box that appears.

7: Top-rated themes
Return to the main Chrome Web Store page, browse the thumbnails and select another theme to install. This time, browse them 'By Artists'.

8: Waterway Theme
This skin is called Johnny Cash. Whatever your preferences, there will without doubt be themes that appeal to you.

9: Themes by artists
Return to the Theme Gallery and, without selecting one of the two linked pages, you will be on the 'Featured' page by default. Do have a look around…

Manage your browsing history

Erase your Chrome browsing history in four simple steps

Google Chrome sports a variety of easy-to-use but very impressive features. For example, the stealth Incognito mode lets you browse sites without a record of your browsing history being retained. However, for much of the time you will be browsing in 'standard' mode and managing your history will soon become second nature courtesy of Chrome's History page. From here you can perform a range of tasks, including navigating a list of all sites visited in the last ten weeks.

You can also clear selected items from the History page or choose to erase your entire browsing history. Evidence of your history is not just limited to the History page, though. The New Tab page shows a list of your most frequently visited sites and there are times when you might want to erase the thumbnails on view.

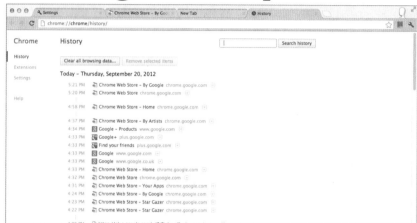

Google Chrome | Effectively manage your browsing history

1: View your browsing history
You can quickly view a list of all websites visited over the last ten weeks. To do this, click the spanner icon on the browser toolbar and select History from the menu that appears.

2: Erase selected items
You will now see the History page. Search for pages visited by keyword or clear selected items by checking the boxes next to the items you wish to remove and then clicking 'Remove selected items'.

3: Clear entire history
Alternatively, you can clear your entire browsing history by clicking 'Edit items' and then the 'Clear all browsing data' button. When the dialog box appears, select how much you want to erase and click 'Clear browsing data'.

4: New Tab thumbnails
The New Tab page shows a list of frequently visited sites. To remove a specific thumbnail, hover over it with your mouse and click the X that appears in the top-right corner. To reset the page, clear your entire browsing history.

Use Chrome's tabbed browsing

One of Chrome's most innovative features is its development of dynamic tabs

Although simplicity is a key attribute of Google Chrome, the browser sports myriad features that are designed to promote ease of use. Nowhere is this more obvious than in the combined search and address bar and support for tabbed browsing. Tabs ensure that Chrome enhances the online browsing experience, and once you get used to tabbed browsing you will find that searching the web is both effortless and rewarding.

The tabs are easy to use and, like other popular browsers, you can arrange and re-arrange tabs, create new ones, close those that are no longer required and even transfer tabs from one window to another. However, Google Chrome takes tabbed browsing a step further and, in doing so, it raises the bar a little higher.

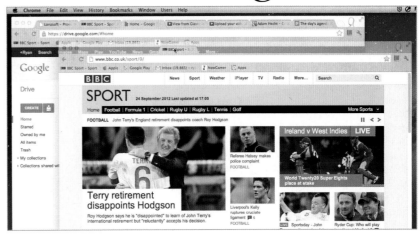

Google Chrome | An introduction to tabbed browsing

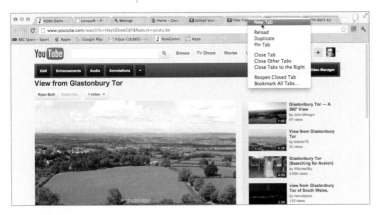

1: Create new tabs
Creating tabs is easy – just right-click on a tab and choose 'New Tab', click on the spanner icon in the top-right corner or press command + T.

2: Rearrange tabs
To relocate a tab, click, hold and then drag it to the left or right. To close a tab, click the 'X' icon.

3: Dynamic tabs
A neat touch is the ability to drag a tab from the browser and create a new window. Try it to see what we mean!

4: Simplified browsing
When you create a tab from an existing tab, the new tab's placed next to the original. This makes it easier to keep related tabs organised.

Create and manage bookmarks

Google Chrome promotes effective management of your web favourites

Bookmarks provide you with single-click access to your favourite webpages and, like all good browsers, Google Chrome enables you to create and manage your bookmarks so you don't have to type long URLs in the address bar. There are several ways to bookmark an interesting page that you come across, but the easiest way is to click the Star icon. The bookmarks bar contains all the bookmarks and bookmark folders created in Google Chrome, and a neat touch is the ability to be able to dock the bar directly below the address bar at the top of the browser window for easy access.

It's worth getting familiar with Chrome's bookmark manager as it's instrumental in organising your bookmarks and folders.

Google Chrome | Get to grips with Chrome bookmarks

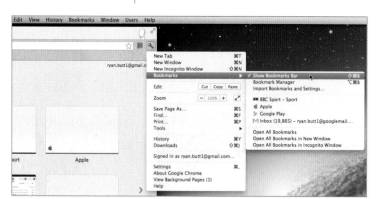

1: Dock the Bookmarks bar
Dock the Bookmarks bar under the address bar so you have easy access to your favourites. Click the spanner icon on the browser toolbar, select 'Bookmarks' and then choose 'Show Bookmarks Bar'.

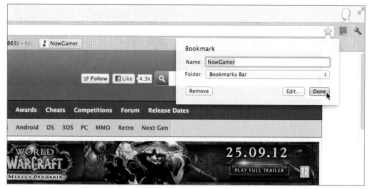

2: Customise bookmark settings
Navigate to a page that you want to bookmark and click the star icon to save it as a favourite. Edit the bookmark name so it's instantly recognisable to you in the future. The bookmark will be created in the most recently used bookmark folder.

3: Bookmark manager
Now click the wrench icon and select 'Bookmark Manager'. This lets you add or delete a bookmark or folder, search bookmarks or edit the name of a bookmark or folder. You can also drag and drop bookmarks and folders to move them.

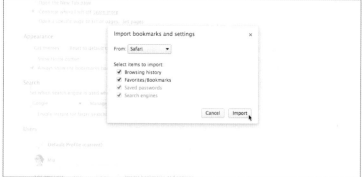

4: Import existing bookmarks
You may well have a number of pre-existing bookmarks in Internet Explorer or Firefox. To import them to Chrome, select 'Options', 'Personal Stuff' and then 'Import data from another browser'.

Manage your downloads in Chrome

The ability to download files and manage them is essential in any good browser

Your browser must fulfil a number of functions – one of which is the ability to download files from the internet as and when required. Chrome simplifies the task and puts security at the forefront of the process.

For example, if you are downloading an executable file (those that have a .exe, .bat or .dll extension), you are advised to first confirm that you have agreed to the download by clicking Save on the downloads bar at the bottom of the browser window. This action helps minimise the risk of a malware attack, because if the download URL is recorded on a list of malicious sites, a warning will appear. You can then choose to abandon the download by clicking Discard.

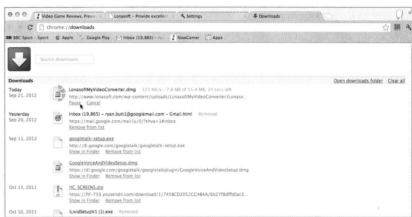

Google Chrome | An introduction to managing downloads

1: Download multiple files simultaneously
Download a file in Chrome and you can keep a watchful eye on the progress in the inconspicuous download manager at the bottom of the browser window.

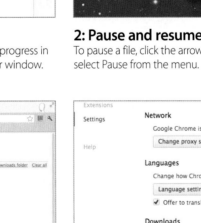

2: Pause and resume
To pause a file, click the arrow on its button in the Download Manager bar and select Pause from the menu.

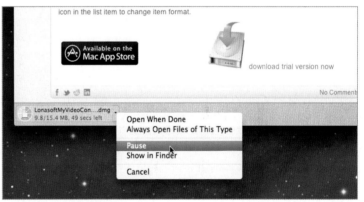

3: Downloads page
Click the spanner icon and select Downloads from the menu that appears. From here you can search them by typing a keyword or term in the search box.

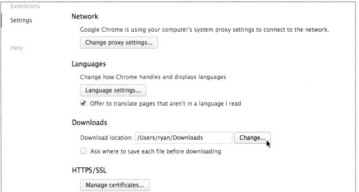

4: Change default download location
Click the spanner icon, select Settings and then 'Show advanced settings' at the bottom of the page. Scroll to the Downloads section and click Change.

Understanding Google Reader

Why trawl for content when Google Reader can do it?

News websites are obviously updated regularly throughout the day, but what about other sites that you visit regularly – like pages dedicated to your favourite bands? Visiting them all to check for new content can be time-consuming and, in some cases, fruitless, which is where Google Reader comes in.

Google Reader is an RSS feed reader that lets you conveniently view and manage your feeds, label them and share them with friends at the click of a button. The service constantly checks your favourite news sites and blogs for updated content to ensure you never miss a thing. What's more, the service pulls all of your favourite site feeds together in one convenient place, acting like your own personalised inbox that covers the entire web.

This service is free – all you need is a free Google account – and requires no software to install, and you can start subscribing to various sites and get a constant stream of news feeds delivered to your page in seconds.

> "The service checks your favourite news sites for updated content to ensure you never miss a thing"

○ Search bar
A search engine enables you to find items you've read, liked or shared, plus you can find notes you have added to feeds

○ Subscribe
Subscriptions can be added by clicking on the link in the top-left corner

○ Subscriptions
The existing subscriptions you have can be viewed here, with the number of new posts shown in brackets

○ Recommended
If you want to save time on searching for sites to subscribe to, click on 'Recommended sources' to get RSS providers based on your personal tastes

○ Time and date
If you hover your cursor over the date that accompanies each feed you can see the time it was first published and the time it appeared on your page

Adding a personal touch

How to apply personal opinion to your feeds

Google Reader offers a feed-sharing feature to enable you to pass interesting feeds on to your friends and family, but Google has given you the space to add your point of view to the feed you're sharing.

You will find the 'Share' button at the bottom of each post in your reader; that allows you to post the story on Google+. You'll also find the 'Email' option, and selecting this brings up a ready-made email. You can then select the recipients you wish to send it to, as well as adding notes to apply it to the story you wish to share. Of course, if you're

signed up to Google+, sharing a post on there will allow you to send it to specific circles, add extra recipients, add your own comment and send an email to your circles on top of all that.

You can also search for people who are sharing publicly by using Reader's people search. To search for someone, click the 'Browse for stuff' link in your left-hand sidebar. Next, click the 'Search' tab near the top of the page and then enter a person's name, email address, or topic of interest into the 'Search People' box.

Key features

Add subscriptions

Subscribing to a new source to add news feeds to your Google Reader is easy. Start by clicking on the 'Add a subscription' link in the top-left-hand corner and then type in keywords before hitting 'Add'. You will then be presented with a list of news sources. To add new ones to your main page hit 'Subscribe'.

View your items

The feeds from your subscribed-to sites can be accessed by clicking on the 'All Items' link in your Home panel. This will present all of the feeds in one easy-to-view list that you can manage by marking as read or selecting how they're displayed.

Manage your stuff

Google Reader provides plenty of freedom for you to share your feeds with friends, post on Google+, and get a complete rundown of your site statistics, including how often you use the service, total number of items read, shared, etc.

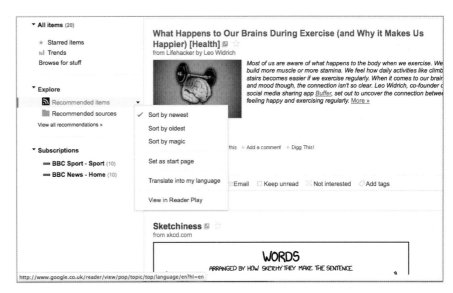

Recommended items

Knowing full well that you probably don't have time to trawl the web extensively for quirky stuff, Google Reader will lovingly deliver cute and outlandish stories to amuse you and lift your mood. Simply click on 'Recommended items' and you'll be presented with a list of interesting, slightly quirky stories to digest and share with your friends.

> "Google Reader will deliver outlandish stories to amuse you"

Why read when you can play?

Another feature that is integrated into Google Reader is Google Reader Play, a fast, fun way to browse interesting stuff on the web. Utilising the same technology as the 'Recommended Items' feed in Reader to identify and aggregate the most interesting stuff on the internet, Reader Play is a great way to quickly catch what's hot based on items similar to things you have previously liked, starred or shared.

A guide to Google Calendar

A powerful web application that lets you keep track of time

Google Calendar is a powerful but easy-to-use internet calendar, and there are several good reasons why you should choose this feature-packed time-management solution to organise your schedule. For example, you can create multiple colour-coded calendars (handy if you want to separate personal and business schedules) and choose to share events with co-workers, friends or family. Customisable reminders help you stay on schedule, and you can choose to have reminders delivered by email or SMS text message.

You can also opt to sync your schedule with desktop personal information manager (PIM) solutions such as Microsoft Outlook or Apple's iCal. And if you own a smartphone, you can use it to access your agenda while away from the desktop. On a final note, although Google Calendar is a web application, support for offline access means that you can view a read-only version of your schedule even if you have no network coverage.

> "You can create multiple colour-coded calendars and share events with co-workers and friends"

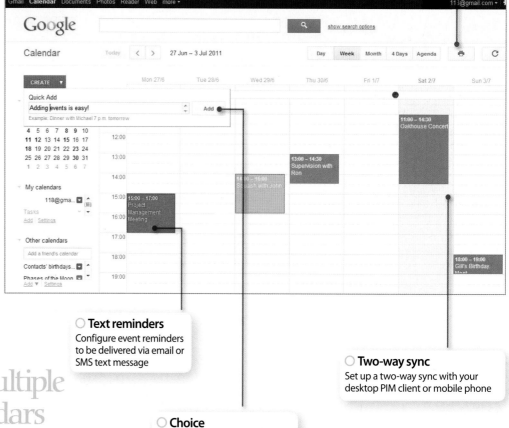

Print
Share or show off your calendar with co-workers, friends and family

Text reminders
Configure event reminders to be delivered via email or SMS text message

Choice
There are several ways to quickly and easily create new events

Two-way sync
Set up a two-way sync with your desktop PIM client or mobile phone

Make Calendar work for you
Customise the settings to suit your personal preferences

One of the real benefits of Google Calendar is ease of use. Create a new calendar and you can immediately start using it to manage a busy schedule. However, to get the most from this fully functional time-management tool, our advice is to spend a few moments configuring the settings to meet your individual requirements. To access the settings, click the gear (Options) icon at the top-right of your Calendar and select 'Calendar Settings'.

Click the 'General' tab, select your time zone and then choose your preferred date/time format and default meeting length. A neat

touch is the Speedy Meetings feature. Check this box and it encourages meeting efficiency and gets you to your next meeting on time. 30-minute meetings end five minutes early and 1-hour meetings end ten minutes early.

Scroll down and you'll see you can also configure the first day of the week as Sunday or Monday. Make your choice and then click the 'Calendars' tab. From here you can see which calendars you can view and modify. Click 'Browse Interesting Calendars' and you'll see a range of calendars, including ones with phases of the moon and week numbers.

Key features

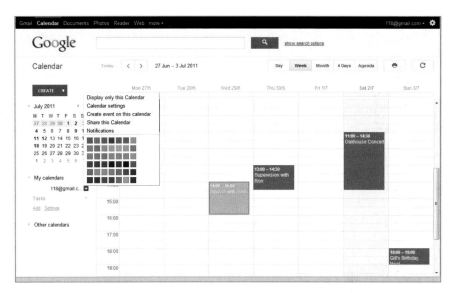

Set reminders

One the best features is support for event reminders, which is very convenient if you're a bit forgetful! You can set different reminders for different events, and notifications can be delivered by desktop alert, email and/or SMS. You can even choose to have your agenda sent to you via email every morning!

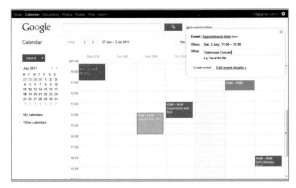

Adding events

Adding an entry is easy. Click the day where you would like to make the appointment and if the event spans more than an hour, click and drag. Type the title and event time in the box and click 'Create Event'.

Viewing options

Google Calendar makes it easy to organise and manage a busy schedule. You can quickly and easily switch between calendar views and choose to check or examine your schedule by the day, week, month, or next four days.

Share calendars

Not only does this feature-rich web application let you create colour-coded calendars, it lets you share them with co-workers, friends or family. And you'll be pleased to learn that you can also view schedules that others have shared with you. As an aside, you can invite others to an event that you've created in your calendar simply by typing their email address in the Guests field.

Sync calendars

One of the strongest features is support for calendar synchronisation. Download and install Google Calendar Sync and you can configure either a one-way or two-way sync with your desktop PIM application. You can also choose to set up two-way syncing with your mobile phone's built-in calendar or the mobile version of Google Calendar. Do this and you are not tied to the desktop as you can view, organise and manage your agenda wherever you are.

Share your schedule with others

Google Calendar lets you know when everyone is free or busy

Organising your schedule shouldn't be a burden, and with Google Calendar it's easy to keep track of your agenda and important events in one handy and easily accessible place. One of Google Calendar's most notable features is its ability to be able to share your schedule with friends, family or colleagues at work. Not only can you grant permission for named individuals to have limited or unlimited access to your calendar, but you can also view the schedules that others have opted to share with you.

You can share your calendar in several different ways. For example, you can grant access to specific Google Calendar users or even share it with the whole world if you choose to make your agenda public.

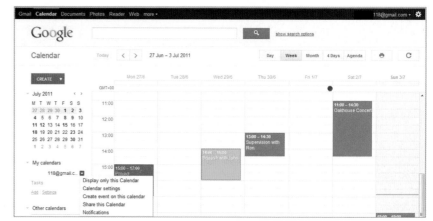

Google Calendar | Learn how to share your schedule

1: Make your calendar public
If you want to make your calendar public, click the down arrow in the calendar list and select 'Share this Calendar'. Now check 'Make this calendar public'.

2: Share with contacts
To share your schedule, click 'Share this Calendar' and enter you contact's email address. Select the level of permission that you wish to grant from the menu.

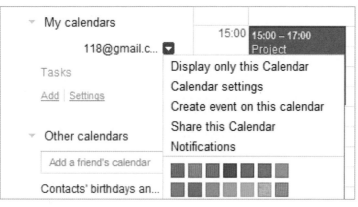

3: Share with non-Calendars contacts
To share your schedule with a contact who doesn't use Calendars, you must use its address in HTML format. Click the down arrow and select 'Calendar Settings'.

4: Share the URL
Scroll to the 'Calendar Address section', click the HTML icon and you'll see a pop-up window with your calendar's URL. You can now email this information.

Customise your Calendar reminders

You will never again miss an important appointment or anniversary

One of the benefits of Google Calendar is the fact that it keeps track of your own events and then lets you share them with others. However, one of the problems with an internet calendar is that it's on the web and not always accessible. That's not the case with Google Calendar, as not only can you view a read-only version offline, but you can also create event reminders in the form of desktop alerts, email or SMS text messages.

You can choose to receive notifications for new meeting requests, amended or cancelled invitations, invitation replies and event reminders. You can even create a repeating event, which is handy if, for example, you have to attend a recurring weekly project management meeting.

Google Calendar | Configure custom event notification reminders

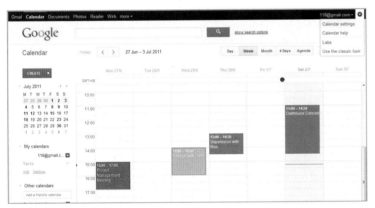

1: Notification types
Click the gear icon at the top-right of the screen and select Calendar Settings>Calendar tab. You can now set notifications for new invitations.

2: Email or SMS?
You may opt to receive reminders by email for all the invitation types, but request that you are notified of any changes or cancellations via SMS as well.

3: Personalise your notifications
The next step is to personalise the notification reminders. In the 'Event Reminders' field, select how much notice you wish to be given.

4: Daily schedule
If you have to adhere to a hectic schedule, our advice is to consider receiving a daily reminder notification for all the day's appointments and other events.

Invite guests using Calendar

Your internet calendar lets you invite guests to events created in your schedule

Google Calendar brings a whole raft of features to the time-management table. For example, your calendar need not exclusively be yours as you can choose to make it public or share it with just a few named and trusted contacts.

Even if you don't want to share a calendar, the good news is that you can send invitations, and even if potential invitees do not use Google Calendar, you can still track their responses. In turn, they can invite more guests, comment on your event and make changes to the event details (if you have given them permission to do so). Google Calendar currently enables you to invite 500 guests to each event, and we reckon that this should fulfil the needs of most users.

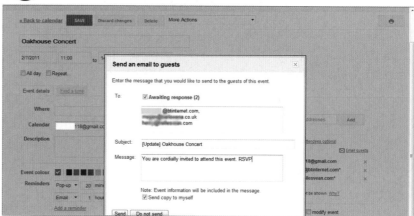

Google Calendar | Send out invitations to guests

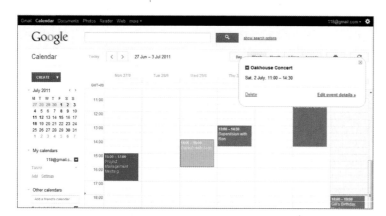

1: Event details
Your calendar lets you create invitations for events. To invite a guest to an event, click the event (or create a new event) and select 'Event Details'.

2: Create guest list
In the 'Add Guests' section, enter an invitee's email address and click Add. You can invite up to 500 guests per event. Each guest will appear in the list below.

3: Select permissions
Now select the appropriate permission options in the 'Guests can' section. When you have added the invitees, click 'Email Guests' to send out the invites.

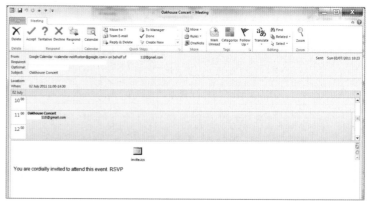

4: iCalendar attachment
Your time management tool supports the iCalendar format, so a guest can use the file attached to the invitation to display the event in their own calendar app.

Sync events with the desktop

Here's how to set up and configure Google Calendar to sync popular personal information managers

Google Calendar does a great job of helping you keep track of and manage a busy schedule, and this functional time management solution has a number of useful features. One of our favourites is the ability to be able to sync events and appointments with some of the most popular desktop personal information managers (PIMs). The benefits of this are obvious and once configured, you will be able to access your calendar anywhere at any time. As a bonus, setting up the sync options is straightforward and takes just a matter of minutes.

PC users will need to download and install Google Calendar Sync. Once enabled, this handy app lets you automatically sync events between Google Calendar and Microsoft Outlook's calendar. Several configuration options are available and you can determine the direction of information flow as well as the sync frequency. There are three types of sync options available and if you opt for the two-way sync, all events in your main Google Calendar will be synchronised with your default Microsoft Outlook calendar.

Google Calendar | Configure the desktop sync options

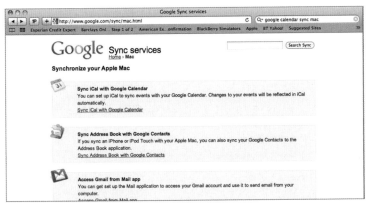

1: Check compatibility
The first step is to check that you're using a compatible PIM client. Google Calendar will sync your schedule with Outlook, Apple iCal or Mozilla Sunbird.

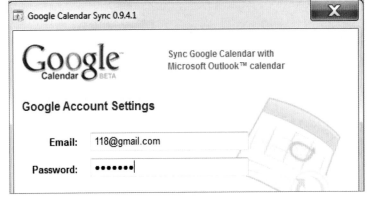

2: Google Calendar Sync
If you are a Windows user, you will need to download Google Calendar Sync. When that's done, log in to your Google account.

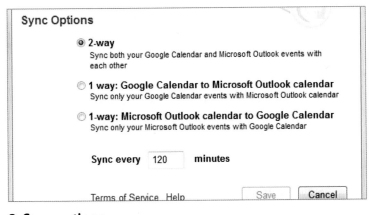

3: Sync options
Now configure the sync options to suit your personal preferences. Set the sync frequency and then choose one of the three sync options available.

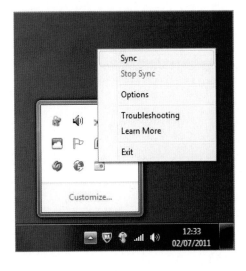

4: Access settings
Alternatively, you can opt to enable one of the 1-way sync options and choose to sync only Google Calendar events with Outlook or vice versa. Finally, you can access and change the settings or force a sync at any time by right-clicking the Google Calendar Sync icon in the taskbar and selecting the appropriate option from the menu.

Create & share with Google Drive

This new storage facility offers a fantastic range of services

It may have been a long time coming, but Google Drive has finally arrived. While the likes of Dropbox, SkyDrive and iCloud have cemented their place as fully functioning cloud-storage options, Drive has been developed to work seamlessly with Google's other applications, and although a little late to the party, Drive is likely to become the default option for many people.

Offering 5GB of free storage, and the option to purchase more if needed, all you need to get up and running is a Google username and password. The service is packed full of features, with everything you'd expect on offer. You can upload files and images, create new documents, share your work with others, set viewing and editing permissions, and organise and search your files. If you already have a Google Docs account, all your existing files will be waiting for you the first time you log in to Drive.

On these pages we'll introduce you to some of Drive's essential features. But as the service continues to expand and improve there's no question that Drive will be a major player in the cloud-storage market in time to come.

"With 5GB of free storage, the service is everything you'd expect"

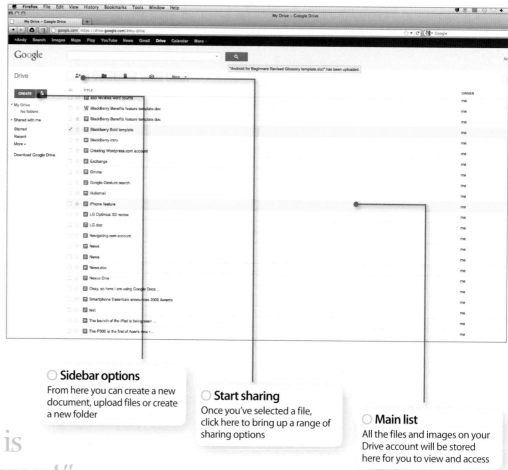

○ **Sidebar options**
From here you can create a new document, upload files or create a new folder

○ **Start sharing**
Once you've selected a file, click here to bring up a range of sharing options

○ **Main list**
All the files and images on your Drive account will be stored here for you to view and access

Advanced scan and search

Find the documents you want in no time at all

Being a storage service, it makes sense that Google Drive offers you the ability to search your files. Being able to type in the file name, or search by the date it was uploaded or modified will make it easier to find what you are looking for.

Google Drive takes this one step further with a feature that even allows you to search for specific words on documents that are scanned. So say you've made a scan of your receipts to claim them back as expenses from work. Once you've uploaded them to your Drive account, using optical character recognition (OCR), the search facility will be able to recognise words from the scanned document and find and display the exact scan that you'e been looking for.

Google even claims that its search function will allow you to upload pictures onto your Drive account. Its image recognition software will be able to find images of locations based upon what you type into the search field.

Though still in its infancy, this is an exciting feature that will certainly help Google Drive stand out from the crowd, especially if it continues to improve over time.

Key features

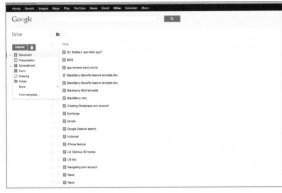

Create documents

Within Google Drive you have the ability to create your own documents. This function integrates seamlessly with Google Docs, and clicking the 'Create' button will bring up options to open up a new blank document, spreadsheet and more.

Changing views and sorting

If the list view isn't working for you, can you display your files in a grid layout by clicking the option in the top-right corner. Selecting 'Sort' will also allow you to arrange your documents in an order that best suits your needs.

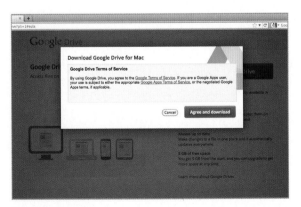

Desktop app

In similar vein to Dropbox, you can download the Google Drive app to your desktop, which will allow you to simply drag files into the Drive folder on your desktop home screen.

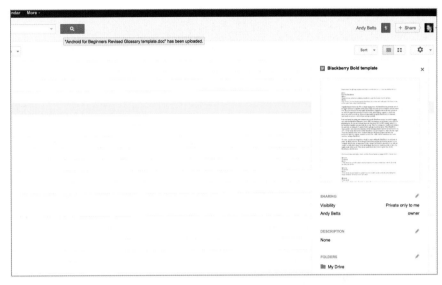

Preview files

The Preview option is a handy feature that allows you to get a quick look at a document, and see who you've shared it with and what folder it's in. In this way, you'll always be able to easily track what you're looking for, as well as your past actions, quickly and conveniently.

"You can display your files in the list or grid layout and sort them as per your convenience"

Organise your documents

You have the ability to create new folders and select where each file or image should be stored using the 'Organise' tab from the top menu. Simply create a new folder by clicking the 'Create' button at the top left of your Google Drive and name it. To group files into folders, select the files by checking the boxes beside their title. Click the folder icon above your list of items and select the folder where you would like to group your files into. Click 'Apply changes'.

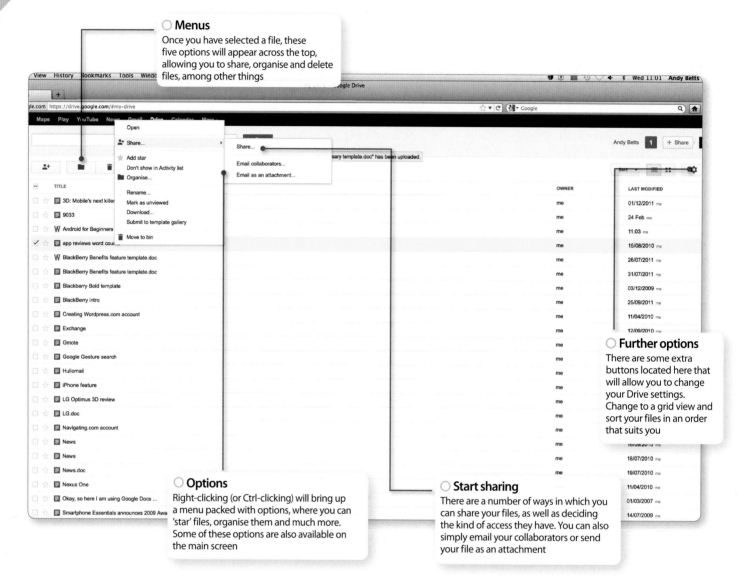

○ **Menus**
Once you have selected a file, these five options will appear across the top, allowing you to share, organise and delete files, among other things

Open
Share...
Add star
Don't show in Activity list
Organise...
Rename...
Mark as unviewed
Download...
Submit to template gallery
Move to bin

Share...
Email collaborators...
Email as an attachment...

TITLE

3D: Mobile's next killer
9033
Android for Beginners
app reviews word cou...
BlackBerry Benefits feature template.doc
BlackBerry Benefits feature template.doc
Blackberry Bold template
BlackBerry intro
Creating Wordpress.com account
Exchange
Gmote
Google Gesture search
Hullomail
iPhone feature
LG Optimus 3D review
LG.doc
Navigating.com account
News
News
News.doc
Nexus One
Okay, so here I am using Google Docs ...
Smartphone Essentials announces 2009 Awa

OWNER / LAST MODIFIED
me 01/12/2011 me
me 24 Feb me
me 11:03 me
me 15/08/2010 me
me 26/07/2011 me
me 31/07/2011 me
me 03/12/2009 me
me 25/09/2011 me
me 11/04/2010 me
me 12/09/2010 me
me
me
me
me
me
me
me
me
me 18/07/2010 me
me 19/07/2010 me
me 11/04/2010 me
01/03/2007 me
14/07/2009 me

○ **Further options**
There are some extra buttons located here that will allow you to change your Drive settings. Change to a grid view and sort your files in an order that suits you

○ **Options**
Right-clicking (or Ctrl-clicking) will bring up a menu packed with options, where you can 'star' files, organise them and much more. Some of these options are also available on the main screen

○ **Start sharing**
There are a number of ways in which you can share your files, as well as deciding the kind of access they have. You can also simply email your collaborators or send your file as an attachment

Share and upload files on Drive

Google's new cloud-storage solution makes creating, editing and sharing easier than ever

As is the case with most cloud-based storage options, Google Drive is an ideal way for you to store and share your documents and images. Being linked to your Google account, it means logging in and getting access to your files is easy, whether you're on a desktop or mobile device.

The functionality on offer with Drive is impressive, and you can upload files and share them with anyone around the world with just a few clicks. Its integration with Google Docs also means that you can create files from within the Drive interface itself. With 5GB of free storage, this is a service that is likely to appeal to many.

In this tutorial we'll walk you through uploading a file onto Google Drive, explaining the settings and options that present themselves in the process. You can then learn how to share your file and grant collaborators permission to edit your work, all from one efficient interface.

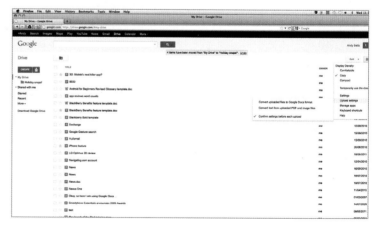

Google Drive | Upload and share files

1: Sign in
Head to the Google Drive site at **https://drive. google.com/**. Sign in using your Google account by clicking the button on the top-right of the screen.

2: The main screen
Once you've entered your details you'll be taken to the main Drive screen. Here you'll see all your files and a range of options along the left sidebar.

3: Upload a file
To upload a file, click the red upload symbol next to the 'Create' button. From here you can select a file on your computer to upload to your Drive account.

4: Upload settings
Afetr selecting your file, you can choose how you wish to convert it, eg into the corresponding Google Docs format. Click 'Start Upload'.

5: Upload complete
When your file has finished uploading, a pop-up will appear. You can now close the box if you've finished with the document, or select the 'Share' option.

6: Share your file
Click 'Share' and a screen will appear showing you who has access to the file. If you wish to share the document with someone, enter their email address.

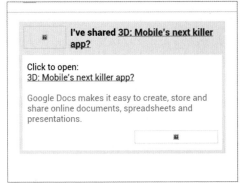

7: Set permissions
From this screen you can choose whether the recipient can just view the document, make comments, or edit it. Click 'Share & save'.

8: Receiving files
The recipient will be able to access the document on their Google Drive account. They'll also receive a message in Gmail, from where they can open the file.

9: Access on Android
If you have an Android phone, you'll be able to access the file you've been sent on your mobile through the Google Drive app.

○ Hover description
If you hover your mouse over an icon or function, it will eventually bring up a pop-up showcasing what the selected option will do. In some cases it will also show you a keyboard shortcut, which when pressed will perform the same action as a mouse select

○ Add comments
You can click on the Comments button (top right) to add comments about the document. If others have been allowed access to the file, this option can be useful for explaining what the document is about

Google desktop
After downloading the Google Drive software for PC or Mac, you get a folder on your desktop which can be used to drag and drop documents (including Microsoft Office ones) inside. Documents will then get converted to the Google Doc format and any changes that you make are then synced between the browser and your PC automatically.

○ Automatic saving
Every time you change anything on the document, Google Drive will automatically save the changes as you type. When you next log in, it will inform you when the last change was made

○ Revised changes
Changes that are made will be saved separately and you can access these for up to 30 days by clicking on the 'All changes saved' option. Then you can select the revisions in the box to the far right of the screen

Create a Google Drive document

In this tutorial we show how to create a document within the Google Drive cloud storage service

Google Drive is a cloud storage solution which incorporates a lot of the Google software under one roof, including Google Docs. All of your files (documents, photos, videos, etc) reside in the cloud and can be synced/accessed to a variety of platforms, including desktop web browsers, tablets and smartphones.

In this tutorial we'll be focusing on document creation using Google's Chrome browser (though you can use whatever browser you prefer). We will show how to create a document, format it, add images, look back at previous revisions (as Google Drive keeps them from the past 30 days) and how to share documents with others.

Firstly, however, since this is the first of the Google Drive tutorials in the book, we will briefly cover how to create a free 5GB Google Drive account and download the desktop software. Note that you will need a Google account to complete the tutorial, which is covered briefly in step 1.

Google Drive | Create a Google Drive document

1: Sign in/up to Google Drive
Go to https://drive.google.com. Click 'Sign in' and enter your existing Google account details and click 'Sign in'. Or choose 'Sign up' to create an account.

2: Create a document
After logging in, view the video overview or skip it by selecting 'Try Google Drive'. Now click on the 'Create' button on the left and choose 'Document'.

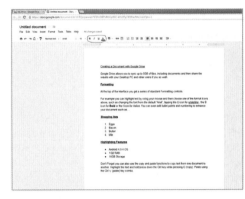

3: Formatting
Enter some text. Highlight text by holding your left mouse button and dragging across it. Add formatting, eg bold, by clicking on the icons above.

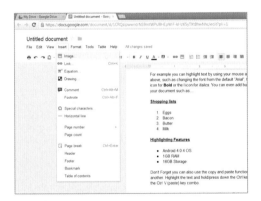

4: How to insert images
Select a blank area, then Insert>Image. Click on 'Choose an image to upload' to browse/insert one. Select it and then resize by dragging the corners.

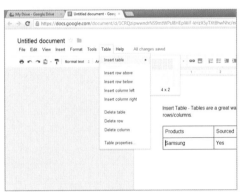

5: How to insert tables
Select a blank area, then Table>Insert Table. Drag across to choose the number of columns/rows, then left-click to select. Click inside the table cell to type.

6: Mistakes and spelling
If you make a mistake, click on the undo or redo icon (top left). For misspelt words, right-click on the word, then select the correct spelling from the list.

7: Rename and save
Select 'Untitled document' (top left). Next, type in your document's name and then click 'OK'. Google Drive will automatically save the changes.

8: Revised editions
Click on 'All changes saved' (top) and you can select multiple revisions of your document. To go back to the revision you want, select 'Restore this revision'.

9: Share a document
Close the revisions box, then click 'Share'. Under 'Add people', enter an email address and choose the person's level of access. Now click on 'Share & save'.

Add extra formatting

By selecting cells or highlighting a row of cells, you can apply additional formatting not covered in the tutorial, such as adding borders to the cells so that they stand out more

Share your spreadsheet

You can share your spreadsheet with others by using the 'Share' button at the top of the screen. This could come in handy if you need others to view your calculations

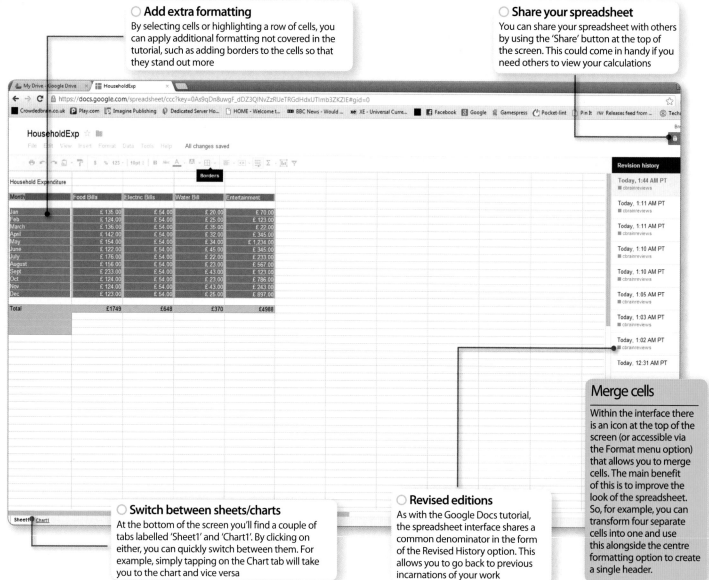

Merge cells

Within the interface there is an icon at the top of the screen (or accessible via the Format menu option) that allows you to merge cells. The main benefit of this is to improve the look of the spreadsheet. So, for example, you can transform four separate cells into one and use this alongside the centre formatting option to create a single header.

Switch between sheets/charts

At the bottom of the screen you'll find a couple of tabs labelled 'Sheet1' and 'Chart1'. By clicking on either, you can quickly switch between them. For example, simply tapping on the Chart tab will take you to the chart and vice versa

Revised editions

As with the Google Docs tutorial, the spreadsheet interface shares a common denominator in the form of the Revised History option. This allows you to go back to previous incarnations of your work

Use spreadsheets in Google Drive

Manage your finances by creating a new spreadsheet using Google Drive

So far in our Google Drive tutorials, we have looked at how to create a new document. While the Spreadsheet element is different, it does share similarities in the form of basic formatting, such as adding bold. However, the main advantage of a spreadsheet can be found in organising everyday tasks. For example, if you need to keep track of your current expenditure or if you want to organise your workload, a spreadsheet is an excellent tool.

Another powerful element of a spreadsheet is the ability to create formulas which can be used to add up rows/columns or individual cells. You can then display the results in a graph format (eg bar or pie charts) to enhance the visual aspect.

We will be covering all of the above in the tutorial. Once again, we have used Google's Chrome web browser, but the steps should be similar whichever browser you elect to use.

Google Drive | **Create a household expenditure spreadsheet**

1: Login & create
Go to https://drive.google.com and log in using your Google account. Now click on the 'Create' button on the left and choose 'Spreadsheet'.

2: Rename your spreadsheet
Click on Untitled spreadsheet (far left), then type a name for the spreadsheet (eg 'HouseholdExp'). Now click 'OK'. The spreadsheet will automatically save.

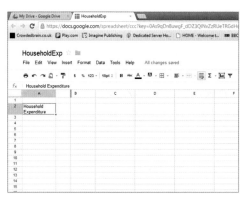

3: Enter content and resize
Click on a cell and type a title. Press Enter, then move the pointer between columns A and B. Hold the left mouse button and drag to resize the cell.

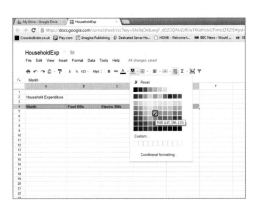

4: Adding colour
Enter six headings. Select the first, hold the left mouse button and drag to highlight them all. Click 'Text Background Color' to change the row colour.

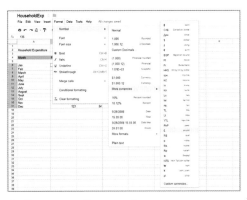

5: Currency formatting
Enter your household expenditure figures into each cell. Then highlight all the numbers. Click the Format menu option and choose the desired currency.

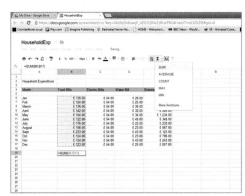

6: SUM formula
Select a cell under the second column, then click Function>SUM. Click on the topmost number and drag down to highlight the column. Press Enter.

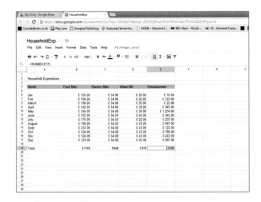

7: Copy cells
Select the calculated cell and press Ctrl/Cmd+C. Select the next cell across and press Ctrl/Cmd+V. The formula will be copied, but the total will differ.

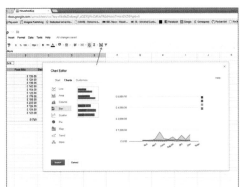

8: Insert chart
Drag to highlight all the cells. Click the 'Insert chart' icon. You can now use the chart wizard. In this example choose 'Bar chart' and click 'Insert'.

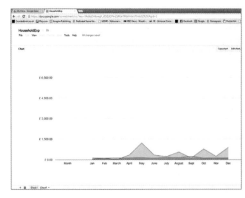

9: Move to sheet
From the chart's right drop-down menu, choose 'Move to own sheet'. You can switch between your sheet and chart by clicking on the bottom tabs.

Switch between slides
As you create slides, they'll automatically appear on the left side. You can select a slide thumbnail to quickly jump to a slide or you can rearrange the slides using the drag-and-drop method

YouTube videos
As well as images, you can insert YouTube videos into your document. All you have to do is select the video option from the 'Insert' menu and then type in what video you want to search for. A long list will appear, from which you can select and then embed the video within your presentation.

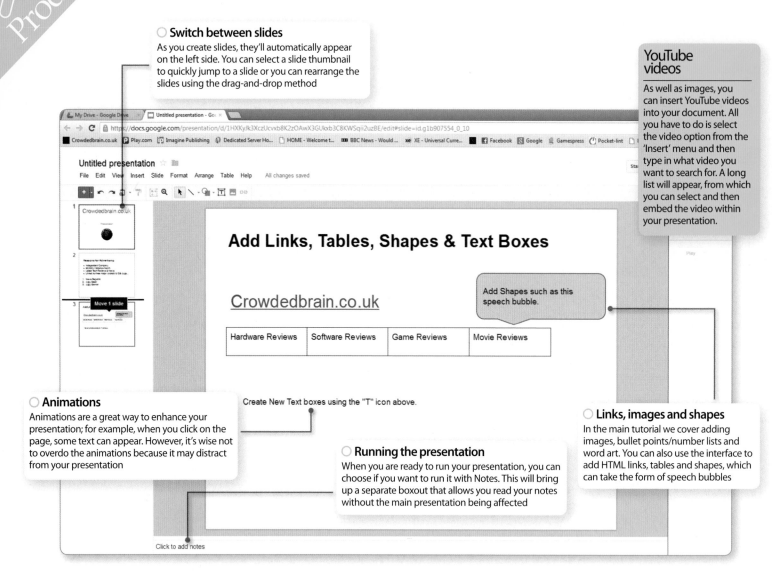

Animations
Animations are a great way to enhance your presentation; for example, when you click on the page, some text can appear. However, it's wise not to overdo the animations because it may distract from your presentation

Running the presentation
When you are ready to run your presentation, you can choose if you want to run it with Notes. This will bring up a separate boxout that allows you read your notes without the main presentation being affected

Links, images and shapes
In the main tutorial we cover adding images, bullet points/number lists and word art. You can also use the interface to add HTML links, tables and shapes, which can take the form of speech bubbles

Design an eye-catching presentation in Google Drive

Presentations are a great business tool for engaging and informing your audience about a product

The Presentation element of Google Drive once again uses a similar interface to the previous applications we've covered, but it does add a more creative balance because you can add animations, images and video clips to create a visual delight for your target audience.

With this tutorial we will guide you on the path by using a technology website as an example. The company is aiming to sell advertising space to a group of investors. Therefore you will get to add the aforementioned content to ensure that the presentation is as eye-catching as possible.

This is the key with any presentation; however, you need to ensure that the presentation has a balance. Too much visual input can be damaging, so bullet points and numbers can be used as well to get your message across. Again, we showcase this in the tutorial.

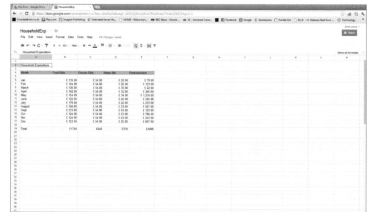

1: Log in and create
Log in at https://drive.google.com, click on 'Create' and select 'Presentation'. Choose 'Get Started', pick the 'Simple Light' theme and click 'OK'.

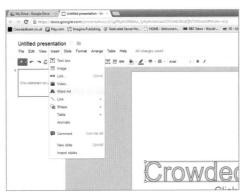

2: Add word art
Click the top of the first box to highlight it, then press Delete. Select Insert>Word Art. In the dialog box, type your company name and press Enter.

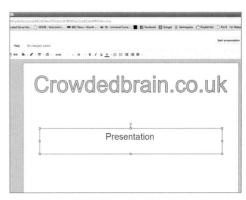

3: Reposition and add subtitle
Reposition the company name by selecting the box (left button) and dragging it up the screen. Select the box below and add an appropriate subtitle.

4: Change colour of font
Highlight the subtitle text and click on the Change Colour icon (to right of underline). Choose a new colour to brighten up the text and presentation.

5: Add animation
With the subtitle text still selected, select Insert> Animate. From the dialog (right), you can choose how the text animates. Click on Play to preview.

6: Insert an image
Select Insert>Image. Click on 'Choose an image to upload'. Browse and select the image you want. Next, resize/reposition the image on the page.

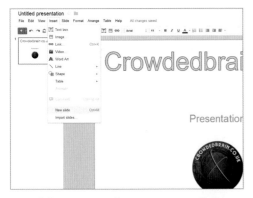

7: Add notes and create new slide
At the bottom, click on the field box to add notes about the particular slide. Once you have done that, select Insert>New Slide.

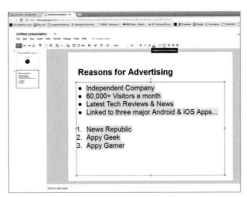

8: Add bullet points or number lists
Add a heading in the top box, then enter a list of points in the box below. Highlight the text and choose the bullet point or number list icon.

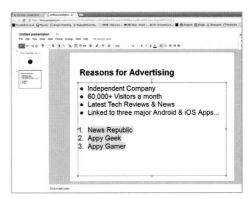

9: Start presentation
When ready, click on 'Start presentation' (top right). Alternatively, click the drop-down menu next to the icon to select how the presentation will start.

Change your themes
After your questionnaire has been completed, you can click on the Themes button to change how your questionnaire will be viewed by others. There is quite a comprehensive list of themes to pick from

Paragraphs and embedded links
Another useful option to add to the form is paragraph text. A user can then type in a longer response to a question, eg 'What things do you like about the site?'. Also, instead of emailing the form, you can click on the 'More actions' option (at the top right) to get embedded iframe code that you can place on your own website.

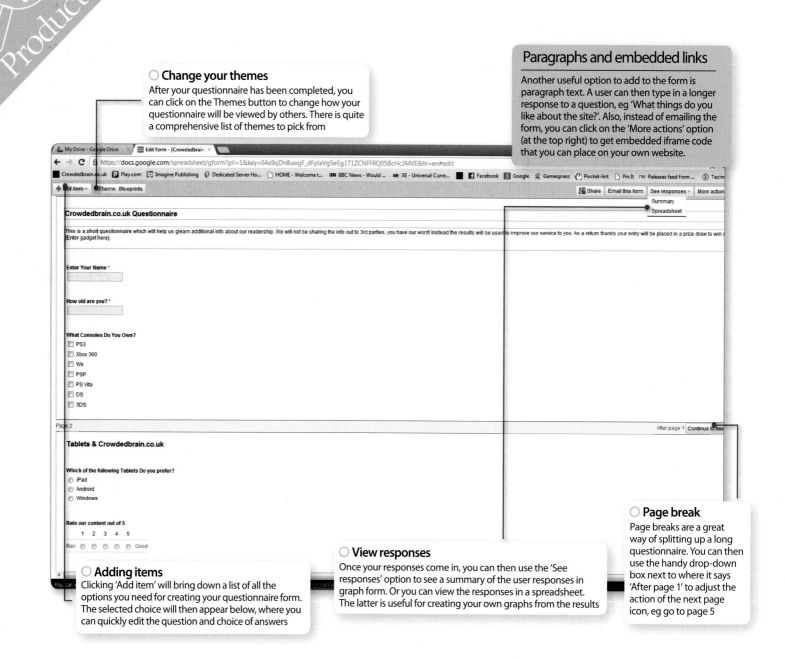

Adding items
Clicking 'Add item' will bring down a list of all the options you need for creating your questionnaire form. The selected choice will then appear below, where you can quickly edit the question and choice of answers

View responses
Once your responses come in, you can then use the 'See responses' option to see a summary of the user responses in graph form. Or you can view the responses in a spreadsheet. The latter is useful for creating your own graphs from the results

Page break
Page breaks are a great way of splitting up a long questionnaire. You can then use the handy drop-down box next to where it says 'After page 1' to adjust the action of the next page icon, eg go to page 5

Construct a digital form in Drive

With Google Drive Form, you can create a series of digital questionnaires with a variety of formats

Most people will have had to fill in a form of some description during their lifetime. The software in Google Drive allows you to create digital/online forms that can be emailed to others or embedded within a website. The form creation software is quite intuitive and by using a series of steps, we can guide you through creating a form filled with rating scales, lists, text-based answers and multiple-choice questions.

In the tutorial we will create a scenario where we are an online website wishing to get more feedback from its target audience. While this may not represent your own primary goal, it will give you an idea of what is possible.

Once again, we used Google Chrome as our primary web browser, but you should be able to complete the tutorial using any browser of your choice – just note that the screens may differ slightly.

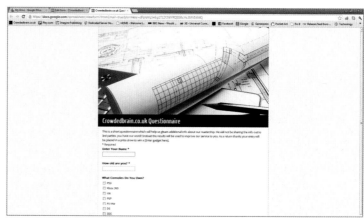

Google Drive | **Create a questionnaire form**

1: Main title and description

Log in at https://drive.google.com and choose Create>Form. Click on 'Untitled form' and enter a name. Select the box below and add a description.

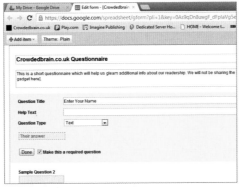

2: Text question

Select the 'Question title' field and enter 'How old are you?'. Ensure the drop-down box is set to 'Text' and tick the 'Make this a required question' box.

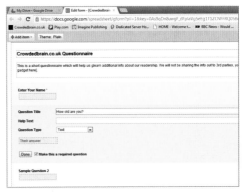

3: Duplicate icon

Click the middle icon (far right) to copy the original question. You can now edit this by selecting the text and replacing it. Click Done to finish.

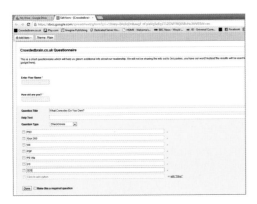

4: Checkbox selection

Select the pencil icon. Replace the text with 'What consoles do you own' and select Question type> Checkboxes'. Fill in a list of choices and click Done.

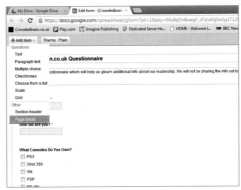

5: Insert page break

Select 'Add item' (top) and choose 'Page break' from the list. Next, give the page a new title, eg 'Tablets & Crowdedbrain.co.uk' and then select Done.

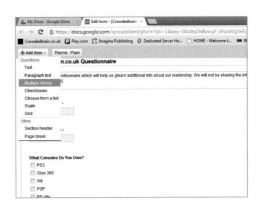

6: Add multiple choice

Select 'Add item', then 'Multiple choice'. Type in a question, eg 'Which of these tablets do you prefer?', then enter your choices beneath. Click Done.

7: Add a scale

Select 'Add item', then 'Scale'. Enter a question title, eg 'Rate our content out of 5'. Now enter your responses below and click Done to finish.

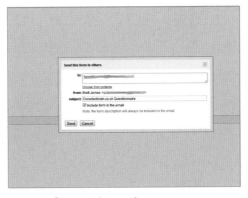

8: Email questionnaire

With the form complete, you can email it to others. Click 'Email this form' (top right), then enter the recipient's email address. Click on Send to finish.

9: View responses

Select 'See responses>Summary'. You can now see a series of graphs and results for your questionnaire. Note: Click 'Back to editing' to return to the form.

Lines and shapes

The Insert menu at the top of the screen contains most of your tools, with the lines and shapes being the method for adding arrows and shapes using a standard mouse drag-and-release process

Publish to the web

Instead of saving the file as a PDF or JPEG, you can also use the File menu option 'Publish to the web'. What the software will do is create a link which others can use to view your drawing. Of course, depending on permissions, they might not be able to edit the drawing. However, it's a great method of getting your work out there to test the water.

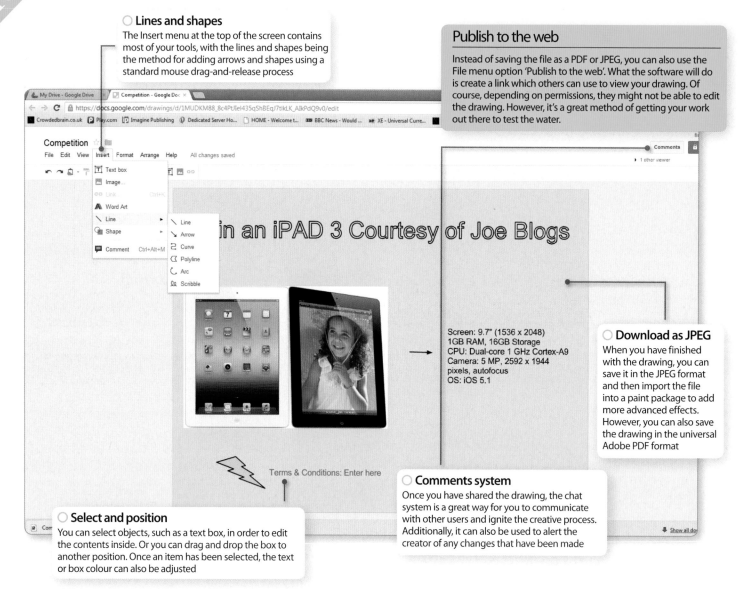

Download as JPEG

When you have finished with the drawing, you can save it in the JPEG format and then import the file into a paint package to add more advanced effects. However, you can also save the drawing in the universal Adobe PDF format

Comments system

Once you have shared the drawing, the chat system is a great way for you to communicate with other users and ignite the creative process. Additionally, it can also be used to alert the creator of any changes that have been made

Select and position

You can select objects, such as a text box, in order to edit the contents inside. Or you can drag and drop the box to another position. Once an item has been selected, the text or box colour can also be adjusted

Create a drawing using Google Drive

While creating a drawing in Google Drive, you can even collaborate on it with other people in real-time

In some ways Google Drive's Draw software is very similar to the Presentation aspect of the package. For example, it has the same shape and line creation functions, along with the ability to add images.

However, the Draw software is more ideal for one-off flyer/posters or for brainstorming sessions, because one of the best ways to use the program is to share the drawing with others and get them to collaborate on your ideas in real-time.

We will be showing the above steps in our tutorial, which will also cover the basic elements of creating a drawing from scratch, adding the images, chatting with collaborators and reviewing any changes that they make.

Additionally, we will briefly showcase how to save the document as a JPEG file, which could be useful for importing the image into a dedicated paint package for subsequent fine-tuning.

Google Drive | Create a flyer with Google Draw

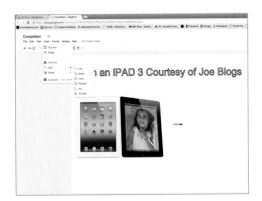

1: Log in and rename

Log in at https://drive.google.com. Select Create>Drawing. Now click on the 'Untitled drawing' field and rename it. Click OK to finish.

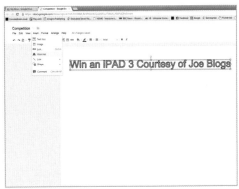

2: Insert word art

Select Insert>Word Art, then type in your text in the box. Now press Enter and position/resize the box on the page to meet your exact requirements.

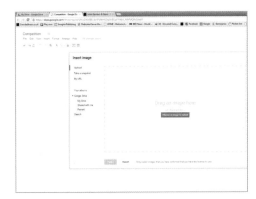

3: Insert an image

Select Insert>Image. Click 'Choose an image to upload'. Select an image. Resize and then reposition the image to the left side of the page.

4: Insert an arrow

Select Insert>Line>Arrow. Click to the right of the image and then drag the line across. Release the mouse button to reveal the arrow.

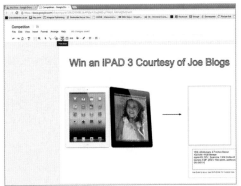

5: Enter text box and bullet points

Click the 'T' icon. Drag across/down (within the main body) to create a box. Add text to it (press Shift+Enter to add more lines). Press the Enter key.

6: Share and collaborate

Click 'Share' (top right), then click the 'Add people' field and enter an email address. Click 'Can Edit', then 'Share & save'. Hit Done when finished.

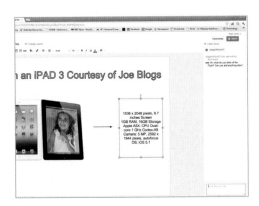

7: Chat with others

Once the user has accepted your invitation, click on '1 other viewer'. You can chat to them by typing in the box at the bottom and pressing Enter to send.

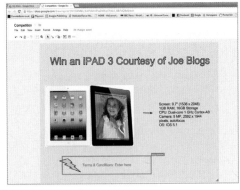

8: Review changes

Changes made by others are highlighted in another colour. You can select the box and press Delete to remove it or change the contents.

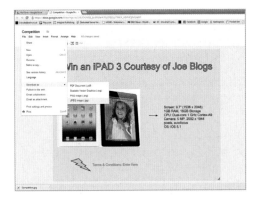

9: Save as JPEG

Select File>Download as. and choose JPEG. Your browser will now download the file as an image. You can then open this in a paint package.

Using Cloud Connect

Free your data with Google's Cloud Connect service

Cloud Connect is a very handy web application indeed. It enables you to create a word-processed document via Microsoft Word, a presentation file via PowerPoint, or a spreadsheet via Excel. Utilising these popular PC-based Microsoft Office programs, it not only enables you to edit them but lets others edit them too, simultaneously and remotely.

So each assigned collaborator will have the ability to edit one of these files while sitting at a PC or Mac in their office or at home, or even with a laptop when sitting in the park or with a smartphone when in a cafe.

In operation, you will be able to change your file and sync it to your computer, whereupon your colleagues will then receive an email notifying them of the changes. They will then be able to click on the link to see and edit the file itself. They can then send the modified data back to the group where everyone can then examine the new updates.

> "Each collaborator will have the ability to edit files while sitting at home"

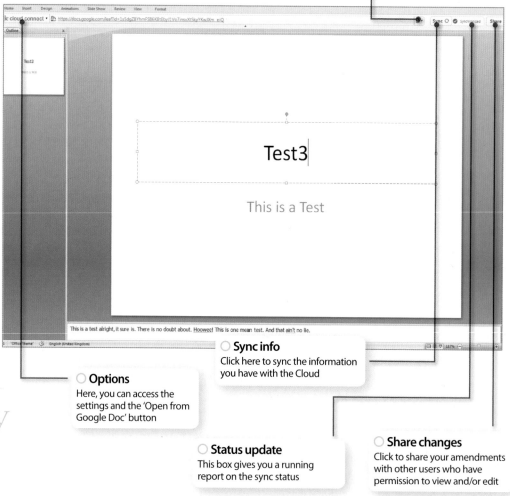

○ **History**
Click here to access the revision history of the file amendments

○ **Sync info**
Click here to sync the information you have with the Cloud

○ **Options**
Here, you can access the settings and the 'Open from Google Doc' button

○ **Status update**
This box gives you a running report on the sync status

○ **Share changes**
Click to share your amendments with other users who have permission to view and/or edit

---

Sync with Google Docs

You can sync your data to other apps in the Google family

When using Google Cloud Connect, you may wish to sync your file with Google Docs (now part of Google Drive). To do this, click 'Document Settings' on the Cloud Connect toolbar. Here, you can select the sync settings for the file you're editing. Clicking on the button will open two choices.

Select 'Automatic Sync', which will allow your file to sync with Google Docs every time you save the file. Alternatively, it will sync to Docs every time someone else edits and saves the document. If you decide to

select the 'Manual Sync' button, though, then syncing will not get underway until you click on the 'Sync' button on the toolbar. This is useful if you only want particular versions of a document to be synced. It's ideal if you want to experiment on a file before others see it.

The Sync indicator will also give you a helping nudge if it sees that you have edited without syncing. Once you have synced, the information you see on your screen at that moment will match what others will see when they open the file.

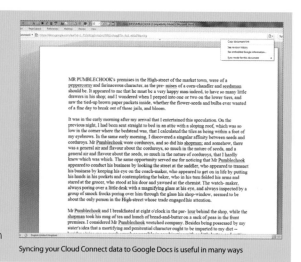

Syncing your Cloud Connect data to Google Docs is useful in many ways

Cloud features

Edit together

One of the most useful features of Google Cloud Connect is being able to allow many people to edit the same data file at the same time. To do this, just add another user with the status of editor. That person will then be emailed with a link. Clicking on this link will enable the new editor to view the file. If they then decide to download it, they will be able to edit the file.

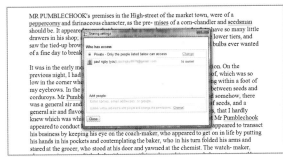

Share and share alike

You can share your file information with whoever you wish, and you can also decide what level of access each of those people should have. To change this access just click the 'Share' button, then type in the email addresses of the people you wish to share with, then click on the 'Change' link to set visibility settings. Once you've done that, click Share and you're done.

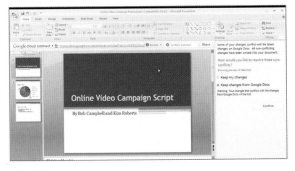

Clash!

One of the problems of multiple people editing the same file is that more than one person may edit the same part of a file. In this case, Cloud Connect tells you that an overlapping edit has occurred. From here, you can view both changes that have occurred and decide which one of those you would like to keep.

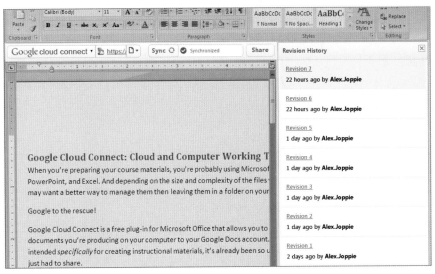

Do your revision

To speed up the creative process, Google Cloud Connect enables a range of people to work on a single document, spreadsheet or PowerPoint presentation. You can see the progress of each new version of your file. So, in Word for example, by clicking on the 'Document Settings' icon, you can then choose 'See Revision History', which will then enable you to see an earlier version of the document for comparative purposes.

> "Even if you're away from an internet connection, you can still edit the file but sync it later"

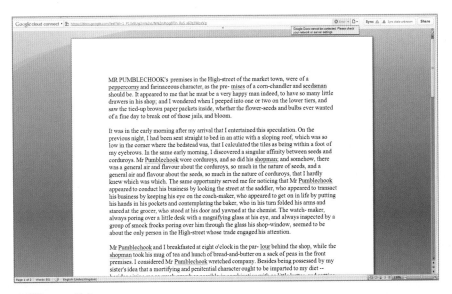

Offline editing

Yes, you can edit changes to your file while you're online, but you can also perform this task while you're offline. This means that, even if you're away from an internet connection or are in your car in the middle of nowhere and away from a Wi-Fi or mobile signal, you can still edit the file but sync it later. A sync error will tell you if there is a connection problem.

Sync Office files with Cloud Connect

Aimed at Microsoft Office users, this service allows many people to edit a single file

With Google Cloud Connect you are able to share and also edit popular Microsoft Office files such as Word, PowerPoint and Excel with a range of friends and colleagues. Connect also encourages you to sync those files from any location. After you have synced your files, the data is then backed up on a regular basis as well as given a web address all of its own. This means that those people you allow to share the file can access and update it from a PC in their office, at home, on a train or in a coffee shop.

So, if you are writing a document, any changes you make are synced so that those changes can be viewed by the other collaborators. If you make changes to a document then your colleagues will receive an email with a link to the changed version.

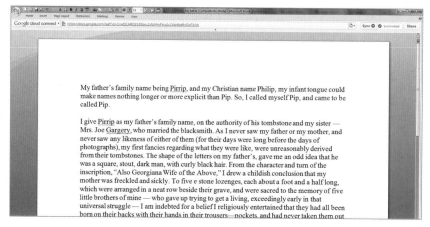

Google Cloud Connect | Sync your Office documents

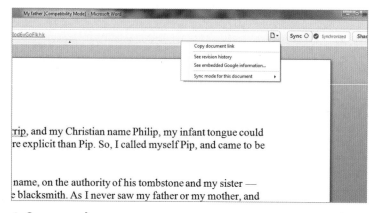

1: Sync mode
To begin, click on the Document icon on the right of the toolbar. A menu will drop down. Select the 'Sync mode for this document' option.

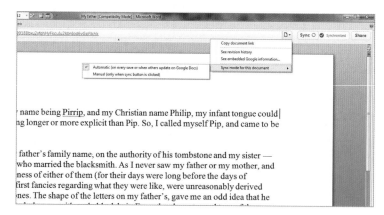

2: Automatic
Two options will appear: Automatic or Manual. If you select Automatic, the document you're working on will sync to Google Docs without any help.

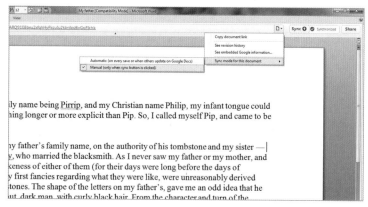

3: Manual
Manual syncing via the Sync button gives you control over when you sync your documents. This can be useful if you want to experiment with the file.

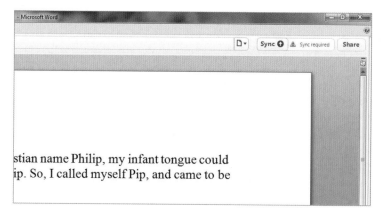

4: Sync State
Check the Sync state indicator. An up arrow means you need to sync up to Google Docs. A down arrow means you need to sync from Google Docs.

Share Office files using Cloud Connect

Now you can share and edit files with a wide group of users all over the world

Sharing a document file is made easier because it is assigned a unique web address. From the moment you create it, you have the power to give access to that file to other people. If you give another person that web address, they can then either view it or edit it, becoming a collaborative member for its creation.

You can keep your document as a private file, of course. There are many times when this would be desirable, like for a diary or a wedding list. If you decide to give someone the web link to that document then it's almost like extending a personal invitation. A bit like having a private forum on the internet or offering an unlisted phone number. It's great if you're a teacher and you want to provide access for a particular document to your pupils.

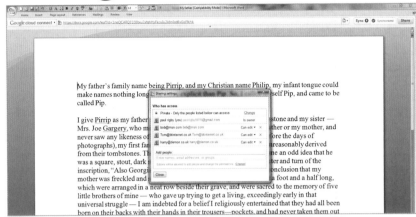

Google Cloud Connect | Share your Office documents

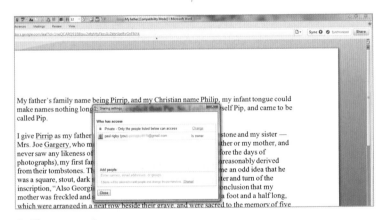

1: Share settings
To implement Cloud Connect's sharing power, click the 'Share' button situated on the top right-hand portion of the Cloud Connect toolbar.

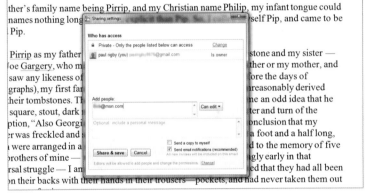

2: Email Addresses
You can type the details of the people who you want to have access to the document. Type in the email addresses of each and click 'Share & Save'.

3: Visibility
You can restrict access to a select list of friends and colleagues, but you can expand that list too. Click the 'Change' button at the top of the 'Share' box.

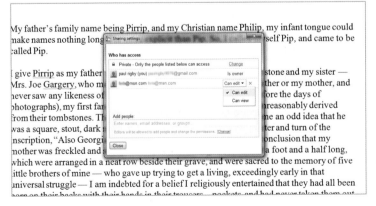

4: Edit or View?
Now you can decide if they can edit the document or if they are restricted to viewing it. Click the option at the end of each address to select a privacy state.

Get to grips with Google Finance

Google Finance will help you invest your money in the city…

Google Finance is a free, easy-to-use investment tool that is useful for all investors. For day traders, there are technical charts that display up-to-the-minute market data. For long-term investors, the service provides detailed financial statements so that it is easy to ascertain if the companies you're looking to invest in are likely to reap you financial rewards. Google Finance also allows you to put together a portfolio of companies so that you can track their performances and get company-specific news stories filtered through so that you can accurately gauge how they affect the market.

The information used on the site is accumulated from thousands of different sources. Financial news is pulled from respected sites such as Bloomberg, The Wall Street Journal and the Financial Times. Additionally, the presence of analyses and opinions from top financial blogs provide a well-rounded reflection of the market. The real beauty of this service, though, is that anyone can benefit from using it.

> "The real beauty of this service is that anyone can benefit from using it"

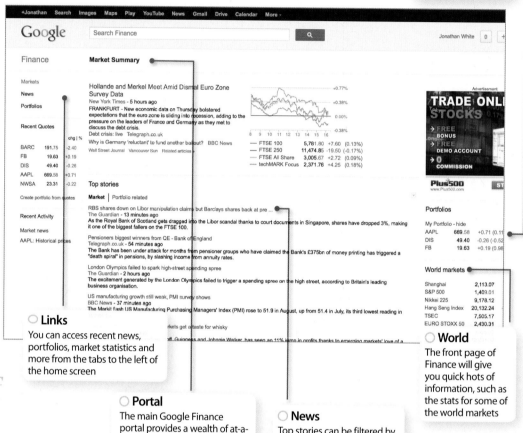

Portfolio
Information that relates to your portfolio of chosen companies is provided on the side of the page for easy reference

Links
You can access recent news, portfolios, market statistics and more from the tabs to the left of the home screen

Portal
The main Google Finance portal provides a wealth of at-a-glance info, such as a 'Market Summary' that relays the most important developments

News
Top stories can be filtered by the market in general, or more specifically to your portfolio

World
The front page of Finance will give you quick hots of information, such as the stats for some of the world markets

Google Finance power tips

Here are a few quick tips to help you get the most out of this service

To delve deeper into the stock information, click on a company to bring up its latest share performance, and you will notice a 'Compare' tab at the top of the table. This can be used to track the performance of several different stocks at one time, or to give you a better idea of how different stocks are doing. Click on the tab, and enter in the stock symbol for an at-a-glance view.

Google Finance also allows you to look ahead by offering after-hours stock quotes for several different companies. Go to 'Settings'

and click on 'Extended Hours', and you will be provided with a figure prior to the market opening and after the market closing. On a related note, don't be afraid to look back. Google Finance provides 40 years of archived stock data to trawl through, which can be incredibly useful if you need to research a particular company. To access this, enter your stock symbol, and when the data loads, click on the timescale next to 'Zoom', select the number of years you wish to go back, and the graph will be amended accordingly.

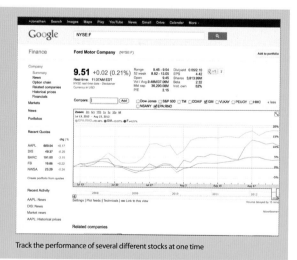

Track the performance of several different stocks at one time

How Finance works

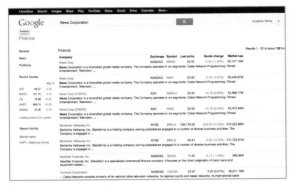

Company search

Using Google Finance's in-built search engine, you can search for stocks, mutual funds and public and private companies using both company names and ticker symbols. These symbols can then be entered in the 'Add symbol' window in the 'My Portfolio' section to add specific companies to your portfolio.

News updates

Google Finance incorporates the Google News service, which gathers and pulls stories from more than 4,500 sources worldwide. Stories are grouped together by topic, so you can read different opinions on a single subject.

Sector summary

On the Google Finance homepage, you can see how major sectors are performing. Scrolling over the bar charts will show you more detailed information for a given sector. To learn more about a sector, click on its name.

Interactive charts

Google Finance charts correlate market data with news stories from corresponding time periods to help you determine if there are links between them. For example, you can see how news stories that relate to a certain company on a specific day have affected the respective company's stock performance for that week. You can also click and drag the charts to see different time periods, and zoom in for more detailed information.

Get company low-downs

The wealth of information that Google Finance delivers on any given company is quite staggering. As well as the news and market performances, including how they compare against other companies in the same market, you get a full rundown of the company history and a list of the people involved. If you hover your cursor over the names in the list, you are also provided with photographs, bios, and other information such as compensation deals and trading activity.

See the world with Google Maps

Get a sense of direction with Google's powerful map toolkit

It may not seem like it, but Google Maps is changing lives for the better. We're better connected, better informed and always get where we want to be thanks to the service. Using Google Maps is intuitive and fluid, letting you look at accurate maps of almost everywhere in the world, plan journeys and find previously unearthed tourist treasures and places of interest with ease.

Getting lost – particularly in dense cities – is common and quite easy to do, but if you have a street name and a postcode then Google Maps will ensure you never get lost in a big city again – and the best part is that it's completely free to use. Even driving is enhanced with Google Maps, as it can give you up-to-the-minute traffic reports based on your location, as well as deliver a great alternative to satellite navigation systems. Built around convenience and delivering it with both accuracy and speed, Google Maps is simply a revelation.

> "Built around convenience and delivering it with accuracy, Google Maps is simply a revelation"

Location
When you search for a specific location, a pin will appear on the map to show you where it is

My Places
This new feature lets you add tags to locations and rate them

Traffic monitor
Simply hover over this pane to get traffic reports

Zoom slider
Moving this slider zooms into the map, while moving it down zooms out

Map
Hit this button to switch between map and satellite views

© 2012 Google, DigitalGlobe, Infoterra Ltd & Bluesky, GeoEye, Getmapping plc, Bluesky, The GeoInformation Group, Tele Atlas

Get directions
Plan routes via Google Maps

While Google Maps is an impressive piece of map-fetching technology, it is perhaps the route planning tool that impresses most. Just under the map search bar you will find a link that reads 'Get Directions'. Simply hit the link then input where you are currently, then where you want to go. Execute the search and Google Maps will automatically trace a route from point A to point B on the map so you can see clearly which way you have to go to get there.

Also, on the left of the screen, Google Maps will relay detailed instructions for how to drive to between destinations, estimate fuel costs and even give you the option to save the route for future use.

You can also switch to the on-foot guide, giving you detailed walking instructions and, in some cases, known bus routes for coach and inner city public transport routes. If your travelling companions want to relay these instructions to you as you drive, simply print the map and guide off by hitting the printer link in the top right of the page. For more detailed routes, you can add multiple stops, rather than a straight A-B route.

The Google Maps route finder is one of the best around

© 2012 Google, TerraMetrics

Maps' core features

Get connected

While you don't need a Google account to access Maps, it does come with many benefits, such as placing custom tags on locations. Either way, visit **google.com** and hit the 'Maps' tab at the top of the screen. The next page will always rest on your country, but where you go from there is entirely up to you.

Start searching

From the first page, you can start searching for a location of interest, or if you already know the address you're looking for, simply type it into the search bar and hit Enter. Google Maps will then locate the place you're looking for.

Search results

After searching, the map view will refresh and a marker will rest over your chosen location. When only one possible location exists, the red marker will read 'A'. If you are less specific, the search will throw back multiple entries listed 'A' to 'Z'.

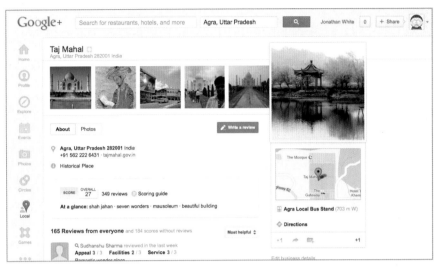

Further reading

If you search for a specific location and in the info pane on the left-hand side you see the option to click on a review, this is where you're taken. Linking in with Google+, you'll be able to access user reviews to see whether it's worth a visit, along with photos and other details. If it's a place you have already visited, you can write your own review and submit it for others to see.

> "Click the name of the venue you searched to read reviews, look at photos of the location and more"

Scrutinise in style

If you're looking to learn more about a location – especially if you're going there on holiday – it sometimes pays to get an even better look at an area to help you get your bearings. In the top-right corner of the map, you can click the 'satellite' icon to change the view to photographic, giving you an accurate view of the area as viewed from above. It's a great way to familiarise yourself with a new place.

Monitor the traffic with Google Maps

More than just a location search tool, Google Maps lets you keep one step ahead

The best way to get started with Google Maps traffic reports is to select a broad geographical location at first, then whittle it down to a more specific area. You need to think about how you are going to approach the city or region you are driving to first, then zoom in for a closer look at detailed routes. Locate the city you're driving to using the Google Maps search bar, then hover over the traffic pane and click Traffic and then Labels to hide or show place names.

This will then show a traffic report. Green roads are not experiencing any known traffic problems, yellow have slight congestion, red areas are slow, and black and red roads are experiencing gridlock.

© 2012 Google, TerraMetrics

Google Maps | Customise your traffic search

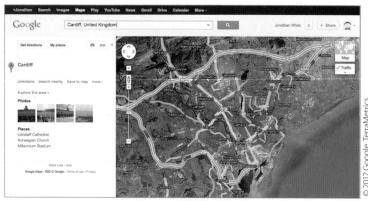

© 2012 Google, TerraMetrics

1: Start searching
Once you can see your target destination, hover your cursor over the Traffic pane to expand it and reveal further options. Hit the Traffic option.

© 2012 Google, TerraMetrics

2: Tweak your report
A 'Live Traffic' pane is now to the bottom-left of the map view. By clicking Change you can adjust how congestion information is displayed.

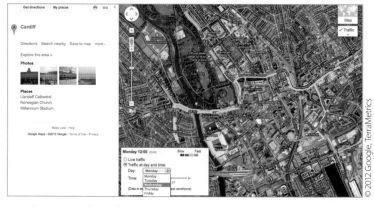

© 2012 Google, TerraMetrics

3: Planning ahead
You can view traffic reports by hovering over the 'Live Traffic' pane and selecting 'Traffic at day and time'. It'll display a projected traffic report for your chosen time.

© 2012 Google, TBluesky, Infoterra Ltd & COWI A/S, DigitalGlobe, GeoEye, Getmapping plc, Infoterra Ltd & Bluesky, The GeoInformation Group

4: A clearer view
If you're finding it difficult to get a decent overview, you can change the way Google Maps displays info. Simply hit the Labels tab to give you a clearer view.

Use the Google Maps webcam

Google Maps also provides streamed webcam feeds of locations across the world

Webcams are a great way of viewing areas of interest across the world in real-time, and if you keep your ear to the ground you will find that there is a large calendar of global events that can be watched online too. Most webcam feeds are owned by companies and tourist boards, but there are a number of personal public feeds too. Some of these are hosted by third-party sites, but you can trust them if they appear on Google Maps.

The bulk of streamed content on Google Maps is hosted by Google's very own Webcams.travel service, which is in beta as you read this. From this site (www.webcams.travel) you can search for any location in the world to see if Google has listed feeds there, or you can go to Google Maps and search for the location you're interested in.

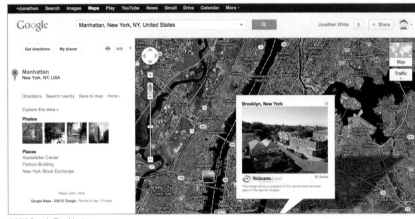

© 2012 Google, TerraMetrics

Google Maps | Locate and view a feed

1: Search for a location
Head over to Google Maps and search for a location, then hover over the 'Traffic' pane. Select 'Webcams' from the available options, you may need to click the drop-down options to expand the menu if you don't see the Webcam option.

2: Webcam locations
Once Webcams is ticked, you'll noticed small black squares appear on the map. These are the available webcams that you can select. The number of available webcams differ depending on the location you're looking at.

3: Watch the feed
Click on one of the black boxes and a preview image will appear, allowing you to see the most recent view from the webcam.

4: Explore some more
Click on the preview image and you'll be taken to the host's website. From here you can view the webcam, and discover others nearby.

Geotag videos in Google Maps

Google Maps delivers a massive library of video content, as well as images

If you want to gain a greater insight into a geographical location or venue, you can browse through an expansive collection of video clips uploaded to YouTube by the Google community. Viewing videos couldn't be easier, as it follows much the same process as looking at images. First, search for the location you're interested in and, once the map has loaded, hover your mouse cursor over the 'Traffic' pane on the top-right of the map.

The pane will then expand. Next, click on video and Google Maps will then pull in all geotagged videos, laying them over the map. From this point you can click on videos to watch them, rate your favourite clips, and even click through to the author's YouTube channel to see their other videos.

© 2011 Google, DigitalGlobe, Infoterra Ltd & Bluesky, GeoEye, Getmapping plc, Bluesky, The GeoInformation Group, Tele Atlas

Google Maps | Geotag a new video

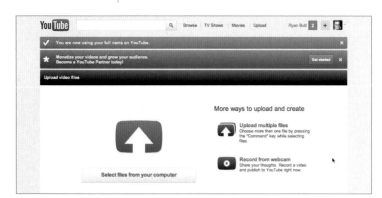

1: Upload to YouTube
First, log in to YouTube and go to the 'upload' link in the top right of the screen. Locate the video on your computer, drag it into the upload box and wait for it to transfer. Once done, you can name and tag it.

2: Copy embed code
Next, view your video on YouTube. Under the player, select the Share button, then Embed. An HTML code for your video will then appear in the box below. Copy this code, as you will need it when going back to Google Maps.

3: Find your location
In Google Maps, click 'My Places' in the top left of the page. You can then create your own map overlay, complete with title and description. Next, click the 'Add a placemark' button and put the icon where you want the video to go.

4: Tag the placemark
Once you drop the placemark onto the map, you can then edit the marker. Click 'Edit HTML' and paste the YouTube code in the box that appears. Save and then your video will be added to the map for either public or private viewing.

Geotag photos in Google Maps

Get a bigger picture of a location via Google Maps and Panoramio

Finding pictures of a location is as simple as searching for the place you want in the Google Maps search bar. Once you have located the area you desire, simply hover over the 'Traffic' pane and select photos. You will then see a series of images placed across the map. You can then hover over the image for a quick description, or click on it to see the full-size image and author name. You can then go one step further and view the image on **Panoramio.com** by clicking the branded link.

Viewing images in Panoramio shows you precisely where the image was tagged, as well as giving you the name of the person who took the snap with links to their full photo gallery. Panoramio is Google's very own photo service linked to Google Maps, Google Street View and Google Earth.

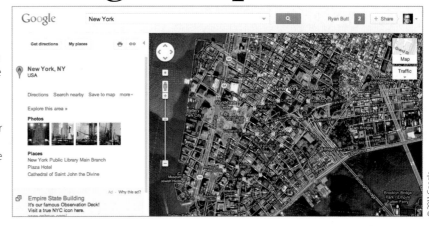

Google Maps | Create and geotag images

1: Join Panoramio
Head over to www.panoramio.com and sign up for a free account. If you already have a Google account, you can use your Gmail address to log in. Once signed up, you can start uploading photos right away.

2: Upload an image
Click 'Upload Your Images' and locate the photo you want to host. After clicking Upload you will be prompted to add in a title, tags and personal comments. Hit Save when you are done and you'll then be ready to add location data.

3: Geotagging the image
Click on 'Your photos' then select the image you want to tag. Next, click on 'Map this photo' and you will be prompted for a city or place name. You don't need to be 100 per cent accurate at this stage, as you can fine-tune later.

4: Mark the location
After searching for the desired location, you will be presented with a map of the area. You can then drag the red pin to the precise spot of your image. Save the position and you will be able to see the image on Google Maps.

Google Earth explained

Get a global perspective on the Google Maps template

Although it was released way back in 2005, Google Earth has existed as a technically impressive tool that has become increasingly powerful over the years. It encompasses all of the map functionality of Google Maps, except it offers so much more than that. It gives you an atlas view of the globe that can be spun on either axis, and zoomed from space all the way down to ground level.

You can view geotagged images of locations uploaded by the Google community, project the weather, gain an insight into the environmental status of regions and even go back in time and view old maps of certain cities as far back as 1937.

As an educational tool, Google Earth is also rich in features, delivering a worldwide insight into our planet, and amazingly, the same functionality exists for both the Moon and Mars – which is perfect for the space boffins out there. If you're curious about our planet, you should check it out.

> "You can even go back in time and view old maps of certain cities as far back as 1937"

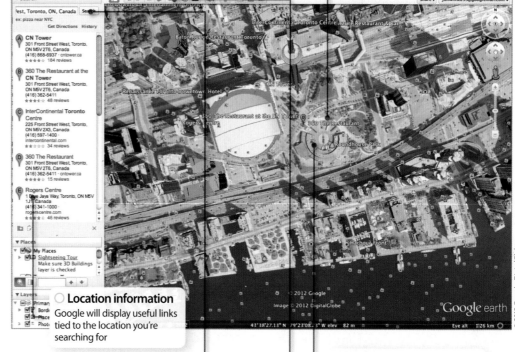

Wikipedia
Click a place name to learn more about it via Wikipedia

Location information
Google will display useful links tied to the location you're searching for

Photos
Click photo names to see the image, and the author's albums

Search
Enter the name of a building or location in the search box and you'll be taken there

Record
Click this icon to have Google Earth record your browsing and create personal tours

Get an insight

We've already touched on how Google Earth can give you a wealth of information on places of interest around the world, but there are myriad features included in the program to help educate you on the wonders of the world. To start, simply search for a place you're keen to learn about and Google Earth will automatically zoom in to the place or landmark in question.

Next, click the name of the place and you will be presented with a pop-up that shows a snippet of Wikipedia's entry on the location. In the left-hand pane, you can also see a star

How to boost your knowledge

rating based on user reviews. You may wish to find out what people thought about this place or landmark, and clicking on the reviews link will take you to a Google+ page.

Here, you can view a range of information about the place you searched for. Along with photos and a Map, you'll be able to read the full reviews from everyone who has posted them on Google+. If you happen to have been to the location, you can even write your own review if you have a Google account. Once you're done, simply click the 'Back to Google Earth' button at the top of the page.

Google Earth expertly combines both history and geography

Inside Google Earth

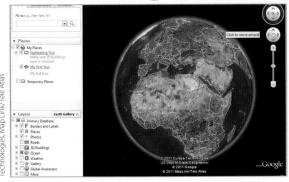

Move around

From the opening view of the world, you can drag the mouse cursor to spin the globe around freely or move the globe around on each axis for a precise view. Once satisfied, you can use the slider below the rotation tools to zoom in and out. Pull the slider all the way down to zoom right back out again.

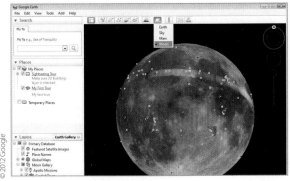

Intergalactic, planetary

Fed up of Earth? Then click the Planets icon at the top of the main window to select Google Earth views of the Moon, Mars and the sky. The controls are the same, and you can even click on charted landmarks to learn more about them.

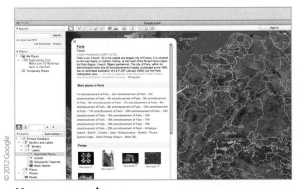

Know your planet

By zooming in slightly, you can learn about countries by clicking place names overlaid on the map. This brings up a brief overview of the country, complete with tagged images uploaded by the Google community on Panoramio.

Viewing images

When you zoom down to ground level on a monument such as the Eiffel Tower, there are a number of ways for you to view related images. Clicking on one of the photo icons brings up a selection of images, and allows you to view images on Google. Double-clicking on the landmark brings up an option to view images in Panoramio. This is a community-based site where you can view images of nearby locations, and share pictures.

"You can zoom down to ground-level landmarks such as the Eiffel Tower or Golden Gate Bridge"

Pop up

In the bottom-right of the Google Earth window you will find a pane called Layers. Here, you can check or uncheck several visual filters, such as hiding place names, showing sunlight, displaying environmental data and more. One of the neatest functions is the ability to make some buildings and landmarks 3D by clicking the '3D Buildings' box. Now, once you zoom into ground level, you will see some buildings standing up in 3D.

Create your own Google Earth Tour

Taking a journey across the globe with Google Earth is insightful, enjoyable and educational

Google Earth is something of a revelation in that not only does it give you the most accurate geographical information, it also has an impressive range of tools and options that give you a rich overview of the world. Because it's so powerful, you must first download the Google Earth application, rather than using it in-browser like Google Maps or Street View.

Head over to **earth.google.co.uk**, download the program and install it. Once installed, open Google Earth and the first thing you will see at start-up is a view of the planet from space. From here you can click and drag to rotate the globe, or use the zoom slider to start your descent down to ground level. You can record your entire session by selecting the 'Record a Tour' button at the top of the Earth view. From that point on, every move you make on the map will be recorded, and it can also be saved for viewing later.

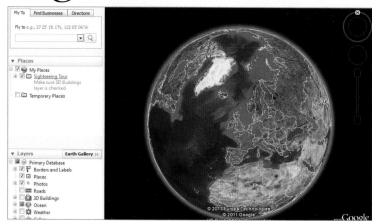

© 2011 Google, Europa Technologies, US Dept of State Geographer, Map Link/Tele Atlas

Google Earth | Record a Google Earth Tour

1: Get Google Earth
First, you will need to download the application. Go to **earth.google.co.uk**. From here you can download the installer or read about Google Earth.

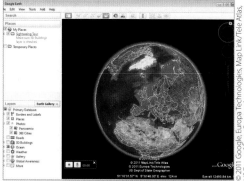

2: Install and start
Locate the Google Earth icon on your desktop, and double-click to get started. First, you will see a view of the world from space.

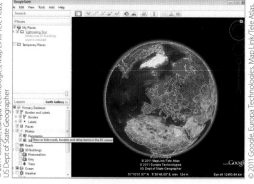

3: Know the basics
Before you record a tour, familiarise yourself with the Layers pane. Check or uncheck the boxes of filters you want to appear on your tour.

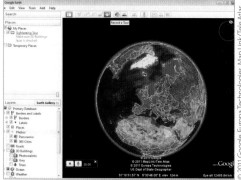

4: Start the show
Above the Google Earth view, you will see a rack of icons. Sixth from the left is a camcorder icon. Click this to bring up the recording control panel.

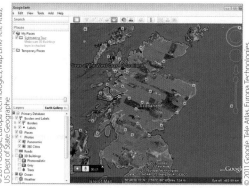

5: Get rolling
Click Record to start capturing your actions. Also, hit the microphone icon if you want to record a voiceover, just like a guided tour presentation.

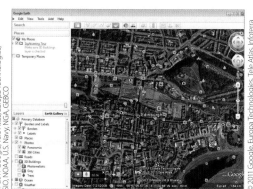

6: Start exploring
Now what you do is your choice. Zoom into places of interest, talk the viewer through them, or simply browse photos other users have geotagged.

Google Earth

How to navigate this incredible application

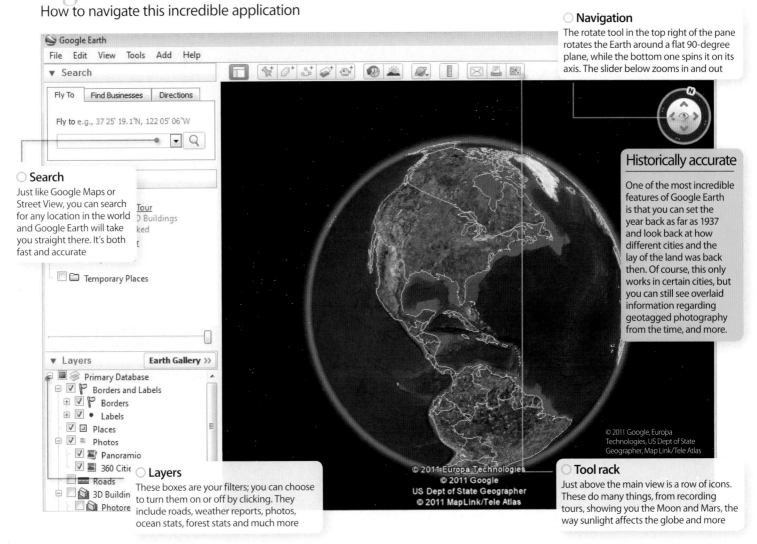

○ **Navigation**
The rotate tool in the top right of the pane rotates the Earth around a flat 90-degree plane, while the bottom one spins it on its axis. The slider below zooms in and out

○ **Search**
Just like Google Maps or Street View, you can search for any location in the world and Google Earth will take you straight there. It's both fast and accurate

Historically accurate
One of the most incredible features of Google Earth is that you can set the year back as far as 1937 and look back at how different cities and the lay of the land was back then. Of course, this only works in certain cities, but you can still see overlaid information regarding geotagged photography from the time, and more.

○ **Layers**
These boxes are your filters; you can choose to turn them on or off by clicking. They include roads, weather reports, photos, ocean stats, forest stats and much more

○ **Tool rack**
Just above the main view is a row of icons. These do many things, from recording tours, showing you the Moon and Mars, the way sunlight affects the globe and more

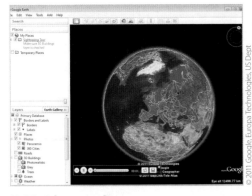

7: Finish recording
When you're done, hit Record again to stop filming. Google Earth will then quickly zoom back out into space, and your recorded tour will start to play.

8: Save the clip
If you want to save the recorded tour and watch it again, click the disc icon on the playback control bar. You can also name it and tag it.

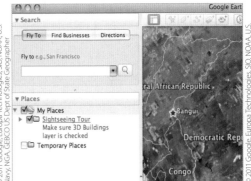

9: Watch it again
Once saved, your tour will appear in the Places pane under 'My Places'. Click your clip and it will preload, then press Play to get rolling all over again.

Model with SketchUp

How one free application can transform you into an architect

Intuitive, fun and free for anyone to use, Google SketchUp gives you the freedom to model just about anything you can imagine. Whether you want to redecorate your home and need to recreate a 3D version of your living room to plan out the refurbishment, want to design a new piece of furniture or model your town for Google Earth, there's really no limit to what you can create with SketchUp.

Using this powerful software is easy. A set of intuitive tools helps you build any structure you want from scratch, but you can download elements you need to complete your build thanks to a kind network of users who share what they have made online.

There are also dozens of helpful tutorial videos on hand to guide you through the process, plus an extensive Help Center and worldwide user community mean that anyone who wants to create 3D models with SketchUp now can.

"There are dozens of helpful tutorial videos to guide you through the process"

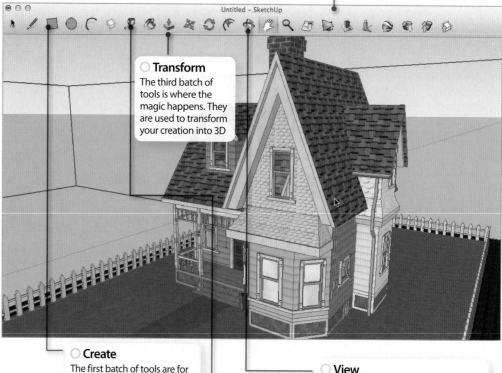

Untitled – SketchUp

Share
The final batch of tools allow you to add models, and share various components of your build

Transform
The third batch of tools is where the magic happens. They are used to transform your creation into 3D

Create
The first batch of tools are for basic creation, ie drawing lines and creating shapes

Measure
The second batch of tools is for adding components, taking measurements and applying textures

View
As your creation is coming together, you can use these tools to orbit, pan and zoom in on your build

How to preview Build with Google Earth

SketchUp and Google Earth are of course part of the same product family, and as such are linked in a very clever way – you can exchange information between them easily. For example, if you need a building site for your build project, then you can import a scaled aerial photograph, including topography, directly from Google Earth with the click of a button. You can then see your SketchUp model in context in Google Earth.

To do this, open up both of the applications, and, in Google Earth, ensure that you have 'Terrain' turned on (this is done via the left-hand column on a Windows-based PC or in Preferences on a Mac). Now, in Google Earth, set the exaggeration to '1' and find the point where you wish to preview your SketchUp creation. Make sure you are zoomed in as far as you can and then press 'R' on your keyboard to ensure that you are viewing from a top-down perspective.

Now make sure that the '3D Buildings' layer in the left-hand column is turned off and switch to SketchUp. Simply click on the 'Preview Model in Google Earth' icon and the app will do the rest.

SketchUp's Google Earth integration is incredible, especially considering they're both free

Key features

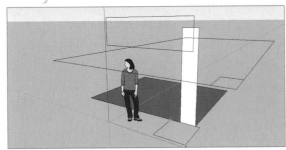

Creating edges and faces

Every model that is created in SketchUp consists of edges and faces. Edges are the straight lines that make up a structure and faces are the 2D shapes that are created when several edges form a flat loop. For example, a rectangular face is bound by four edges that are connected together at right angles. The Pen tool enables you to start creating edges and faces. Simply draw lines to create edges and link up the points to create faces.

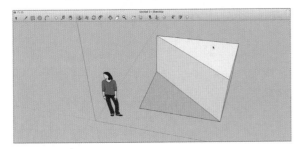

Making it 3D

Any 2D faces that you create in Google SketchUp can be instantly transformed into 3D by using the Push/Pull tool. Simply select the tool, click on the face you wish to extrude and then move your mouse to create the effect. Using this tool you can push and pull rectangular shapes into boxes, pull the outline of a staircase into 3D and create windows and other intricate effects. The ease of use is the key here.

Bring structures to life

A wide range of colours and textures can be added to your build to make it look more authentic. You can paint it with colours chosen from a spectrum, apply a wide range of textures from brickwork, roofing, blinds, water, and many more. Plus, if you are basing your build on an existing building then you can sample textures and colour schemes from photos of the original building. The freedom to create is staggering.

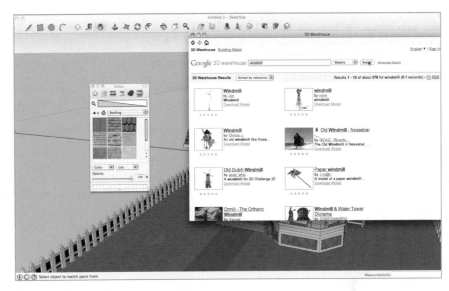

Borrow from the community

There are so many creations uploaded to the internet that you can always find good base models or components for your builds to prevent you from having to start from scratch. If you click on the 'Get Models' tool then a separate window will appear that enables you to input key words into a search engine to find the creations you want. When you find one you like, click 'Download Model' and it will be added to your current project.

"A range of colours and textures can be added to your build to make it look more authentic"

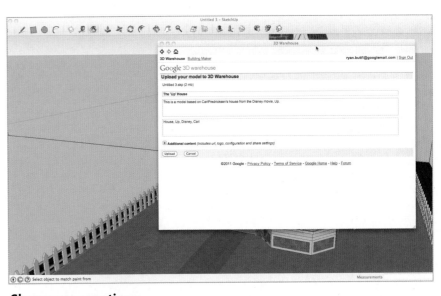

Share your creations

Google SketchUp is all about give and take. By all means use the work of other people to help you learn the ropes and act as a starting point prior to your own applications and modifications to make the build your own, but also be prepared to give something back to the community by uploading your creation for others to explore, admire and use as a template for their own work.

Learn about 3D Warehouse

Now that you have mastered SketchUp, it's time to see how your builds can make a mark on the world

Google 3D Warehouse is a free online repository where you can find, share, store and collaborate on 3D models created using Google SketchUp and Google Building Maker. Using this service you can browse or search thousands of 3D models for just about anything you can imagine, upload your own creations to feature in Google Earth (by selecting the 'Google Earth Ready' checkbox on the 3D Warehouse upload form and waiting for acceptance) and discuss matters of 3D modelling and geolocated buildings with a thriving online community.

Using 3D Warehouse is a great way to gain inspiration from other people's work, collect tips and tricks of the trade from fellow users and acquire free models, items and people to use in your own projects. Here we explore the many great features that this service has to offer.

> "You can browse or search thousands of 3D models for just about anything"

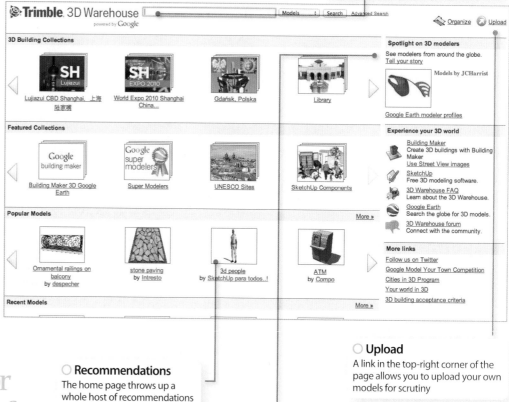

○ Search bar
A built-in search engine enables you to find models and collections with ease

○ Recommendations
The home page throws up a whole host of recommendations across a wide range of categories

○ Spotlight
You can learn about other modellers or tell your own story using the 'Spotlight on 3D modellers' feature

○ Upload
A link in the top-right corner of the page allows you to upload your own models for scrutiny

Earn badges How to get fun rewards

Without doubt, contributors to 3D Warehouse do some amazing work, and as a small reward for their accomplishments, Google has set up a series of badges that users can earn through various feats, similar to Achievements earned in videogames. These badges are then displayed alongside your profile to inform others of your achievements and show off the fact that you mean business and are a big player within the 3D Warehouse community.

Basic badges are earned through uploading models constructed through SketchUp and BuildingMaker to the 3D Warehouse and other, more prestigious badges are acquired through attending specific conferences, of which one has so far been staged in Singapore this year. Extra badges are also earned through submitting 3D models to Google Earth (for which badges are awarded for submitting a certain amount up to 1,000) and fun activities such as geo-modelling April Fool's Day.

To see the badges that you have earned, click the 'My Warehouse' link in the top-right corner of any 3D Warehouse page and then choose 'My models'. The badges earned by fellow builders are also displayed alongside their profile data. Kudos to all!

3D Warehouse's badges are similar to Achievement systems found in videogames

Inside 3D Warehouse

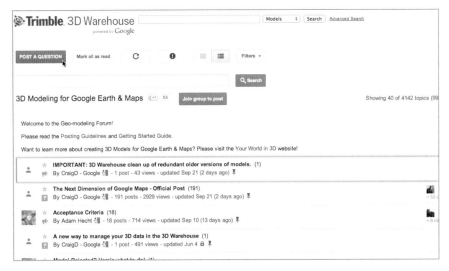

Search for buildings

Using the built-in search engine, users can search through thousands of models that cover a wide range of objects, from famous buildings through to sports cars and furniture to adorn your own creation. Simply enter in keywords, click 'Search' and you'll be presented will all items that meet your criteria. You can then view and examine these for inspiration for your own builds or even download and import them into your own project.

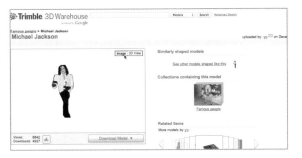

Populate your models

As well as buildings, objects and assorted objects to use in your project, you can also search for collections of people to populate them, including famous celebrities. Like before, enter keywords into the search engine to locate individuals or use the menu next to the search engine to locate 'Collections' of folk to import. As you can see, the results can be quite interesting!

Make contact with like-minded builders

If you want to ask questions, get tips, share experiences or just complain about the difficulties you're having, then there is a thriving online 3D Warehouse community forum where you can do just that. From the home page, cast your eyes over the 'Experience your 3D world' section in the column over to the right and then click on the link that reads 'Google 3D Warehouse forum'. From there you will be taken to the community forum page that usually makes for an entertaining and informative read.

> "You can also search for collections of people to populate your builds, including famous celebrities"

Upload buildings to Google Earth

Users can select the option when uploading their models to verify that it is 'Google Earth Ready'. This checkbox should be checked if the building is a real, current and correctly located model of the building. When a model is submitted via this process, the model will be reviewed by Google staff who will check the model's qualifications under certain criteria.

Cities In 3D

As more than 350 million internet users have turned to Google Earth to better understand and navigate their world, local governments have been quick to realise the importance of the app as a means of showcasing their own towns and cities. With the Cities In 3D program, essential information such as 3D data, aerial imagery and vector data can be uploaded to Google Earth to help users consider real-estate investment, plan travel itineraries and view their community in its best possible light.

Mobile

Learn how to use Google's amazing apps while on the move with these expert hints and tips

> "With the Android platform, Google's apps have a place to shine"

190

176

162

"Google's apps are just as effective to use when you're out and about"

Apps suitable for Android and iOS

Understanding Google Sync

Share the love and your data with Google's sync options

If you're just getting started with your Android phone, you'll be forced to set up a Google Gmail account. Use it – don't neglect it. It might seem a little unreasonable to have to use a new email address just to use your phone, but trust us – it's easier than the other options. First up, open a Gmail account and sync everything you can with it.

You'll want to sync your contacts, your calendar and whatever else you can to your new account. Google's flurry of services – Maps, Google+, Blogger and more – all tie seamlessly with Android's interface, so using them all with a single account from your phone makes your Android experience much richer.

Syncing basically shares user-inputted data between each app and service so you don't have to copy one set of data manually to another. Hence, syncing your email client with your calendar will provide you with detailed appointment information.

"Google's flurry of services all tie in with Android's interface"

○ **Details**
Your own personal email address details will be placed here

○ **Syncing**
The circular rotate icon appears when a particular module is undergoing syncing

○ **Modules**
Each module that can be successfully synced is listed here

○ **Sync checkbox**
Click on the tickbox to decide to sync or not

○ **Begin syncing**
Click here to initiate syncing or to remove your email account

---

The computer sync
Sync with your desktop

Although their primary use will always be to make calls, mobile phones have become much more than simple communication devices. Using a single handset, you can take pictures, shoot videos, organise your contacts and daily calendar, send and receive messages, and play music. But managing those extra features can be a challenge.

For example, after you take a photo with your cameraphone, it doesn't do a whole lot of good until you can get it off your phone and onto your computer. Of course, you can always send multimedia messages through your carrier's data service, but that can be

expensive if you're a shutterbug. On the flip side, while using your phone's organiser won't cost money, inputting your information on a standard phone keypad is time-consuming and tedious. With mobile phone-syncing software, you become the master of all that's on your phone by syncing your mobile directly to your PC. You can transfer pictures, messages, contacts and ring tones from your phone to your computer, edit them on your PC using the software, then transfer them back. And best of all, you don't have to buy the software – it will be provided for you by your handset manufacturer.

You can get a detailed breakdown of how much sync space you have left

Key features

Syncing on Android

Unlike other phones, the action of syncing your data between varying modules, apps and services on an Android phone is easy to set up. In fact, you don't really have to, because the syncing feature is wrapped up neatly within the phone's operating system. Here, you can see the status on this new phone, which has yet to undergo a syncing operation (hence the lack of synchronisation records).

Sync when you're winning

Before you can contemplate syncing your data among the varied apps that you may feature on your phone, there are one or two preliminaries to address first. For example, you will need to set up a primary Gmail or Google apps account on your phone. Once you have done that, you can then begin to think about syncing the data on it.

New account

Once you've finished setting up your email account, you can view it by clicking on the Gmail icon in your apps page. This will launch the email client. A new screen appears showing your current inbox and any new emails that may have arrived. At the top of the screen, you will see your email address highlighted within an embossed box. Click on it to trigger the account screen.

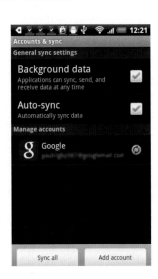

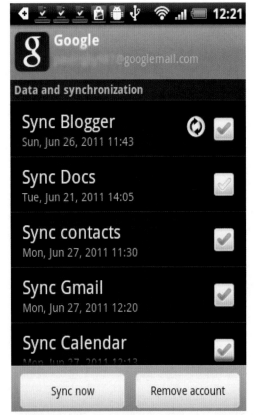

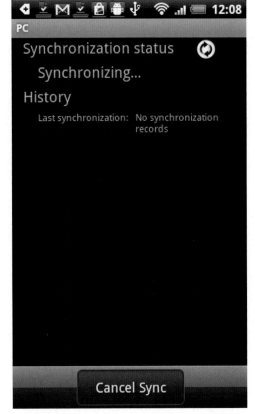

Menu key

Once pressed, the screen changes again to show the list of email accounts that you currently hold and the number of unread messages attached that are sitting in their respective inboxes. Here, you can just see the one account. The next stage is to press the Menu key on your phone, up pops a menu where you can press the Settings option, a new screen will appear showing your account and the sync options.

> "Before you can contemplate syncing your data, there are one or two preliminaries you need to address first"

Syncing modules

There are a variety of modules that you can assign to sync. When you decide to sync your phone, the operation is simple and clear. Just click on the button at the base of the screen. This triggers the selected modules to sync and the data is shared among the relevant areas on your phone. A notification will appear on screen with the sync operation is underway while a rotating icon will swing into action.

An overview of the Google Play Store

Find your way around the re-branded Android Market

Remoulded and renamed, Google Play has replaced the old Android Market as the new hub for Android users to download apps from. But crucially, the Google Play Store has much wider reach than the Android Market as it now allows users to download books, music and rent movies. This means there are likely to be far more reasons for you to visit the store. Having this central hub means all your entertainment needs will be serviced in one place.

On the home page, you can see banners for the most popular current downloads on Google Play, and then individual sections for apps, books and movies. Movies can be rented and viewed in HD on your smartphone, something that is bound to impress anyone looking over your shoulder on the train. You can also keep track of all your downloads in the My Apps section, which lists everything you've downloaded from the Store and also gives you update information to ensure you always have the latest version. You can link different Google accounts to the Play Store and view your downloads on each as well as open or launch an app directly. The Settings section also allows you adjust the download setup, changing whether or not you would like widgets created on your home screen for your downloads.

Play Store | **Find your way around**

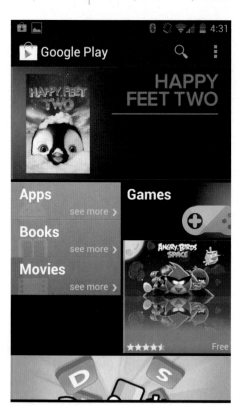

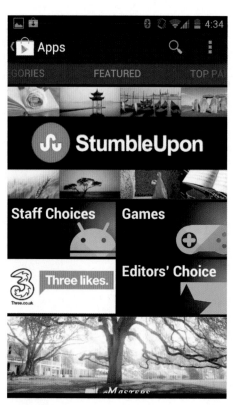

1: Home Page
The Play Store home page has banners advertising the most popular downloads. Scroll to see what's on offer, or Search to find something.

2: Apps
Hit the Apps button to head to the app-dedicated section of the Play Store. Here you'll find Staff Choices, games and more.

3: Books
Head back to the home page and then tap Books to see all of the downloadable books available. Swipe left and you can view books by category.

The App Page

The key parts of the download page

○ Description

Get a more detailed description of what the app's about here. This will help you decide whether you want to splash the cash and purchase the app

○ Share

If you find something you think others might like, you can share it by tapping the Share icon and choosing one of the options, such as Google+ and Gmail

○ Buy

The price of an app appears in blue in the header at the top of the screen. Tap it to start a purchase by opening the terms and conditions screen

○ Reviews

Scroll down the page to read reviews from other users who have downloaded the app. Each will provide a star rating and an overall summary of opinion is shown in graph form at the top of the review section

A complete record

The All screen lists everything you've ever downloaded and installed, all tied to your Google account. If you ever reset your phone, or buy a new one, you will find your favourite apps here.

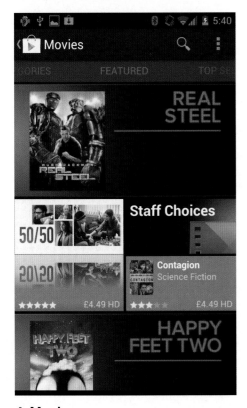

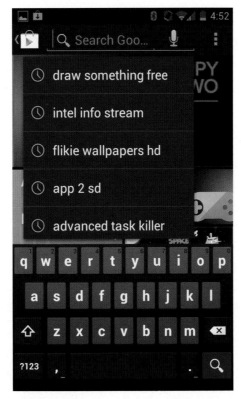

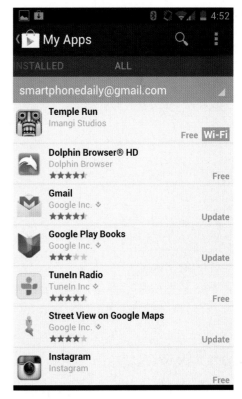

4: Movies

The Movies section looks a little like Apps and Books, and features interactive banners. There are plenty of films available for users to enjoy in HD.

5: Search

Tapping the Search icon allows you to be specific in your browsing, and as a useful additional feature, all your previous searches are saved.

6: My Apps

Next to the Search icon is 'My Apps'. This gives you a list of all your downloads, as well as telling you if any updates are available.

Purchasing an app

How to get the most out of Android's growing app market, starting with your very first app download

The expanding range of utilities, games and other fun stuff on the Play Store is making the platform extremely competitive in the world of smartphones. It is something you should get stuck into as soon as possible in order to get the most out of your Android handset.

There are a couple of provisos before you begin, however. First and foremost, you will need to set up a Google Mail account in order to use the Play Store. Simply point your phone's browser to http://mail.google.com and follow the simple set-up instructions, and you're all set. Having your Android phone linked to a Gmail account will help you in all sorts of other ways, too – it even lets you back up your entire phone contacts book to your email account in case your phone is lost or stolen.

The other thing to think about is exactly how safe and high quality the content on the Store is for you and your phone. Unlike Apple's App Store, the Play Store is a relatively unmonitored environment. This means that while there is often a greater range of choice in what you can download – at very cheap prices – rogue applications will sometimes appear that won't offer you much in the way of value, or may not even work with your unique handset.

It's best to check out reviews from other users first (shown on the download page for each app), or download a demo if one is available. That said, the Play Store is a burgeoning and vibrant shopping experience, so join us now as we demonstrate how to start purchasing apps.

Play Store | Shopping on the Store

1: Go to the Store
Access the Play Store app which can be found on the home screen and tap on it to open up Google's replacement for the Android Market.

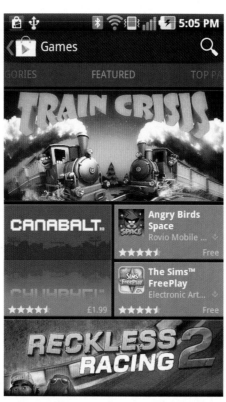

2: Apps or Games?
The Store is split into Apps and Games sections. Here, we'll be hunting down and downloading the game Doodle Jump, so hit the 'Games' tab.

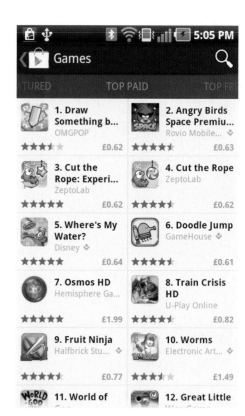

3: Sections
Games are split into sections. 'All games' gives you a list of the most popular games. 'Top paid' and 'Top free' offer the best paid and free games.

Navigating the Store

How to shop quickly and effectively

○ **Featured app**
The main screen features a prominent featured app that regularly changes to tempt you

○ **More options**
Tap the menu button and you'll be able to access information on your account, your apps, as well as getting help and changing the settings

○ **Search**
The search function lets you track down what you want, or even type keywords in to help you locate an app you didn't know existed

○ **Sections**
You can select Staff Choices, Editors' Choice and Games categories from the Play Store home screen

Check for updates

Logging onto Play Store after you've bought apps and games will automatically check them for updates. If there are any available you'll be greeted with a menu which allows you to automatically queue up updates for those that accept it, while ticking off manual updates for any with changed permissions.

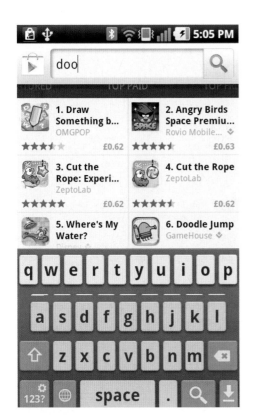

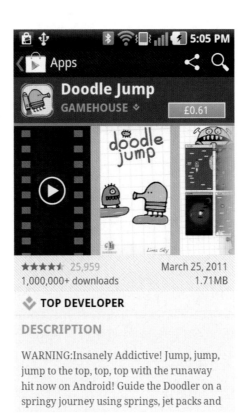

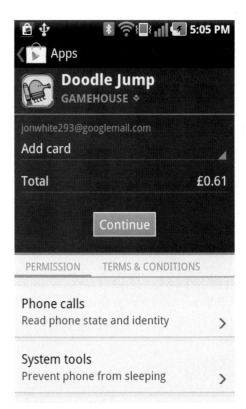

4: Search for success
Simply typing 'doodle' into the search box at the top will bring up a list of selected results. Touch the suggested title that matches your query.

5: Purchase
Select your app and click Buy. After that, the Buy box becomes an 'OK' agreement for the permissions you give the program.

6: Pay and play
Buying an app for the first time, you'll be asked to add a credit card account to Google's secure server. Just follow the on-screen instructions.

Use Play Books while mobile

The new Play Books app is packed with great reads. Here's how to access your downloads over multiple devices

If you're an avid reader, chances are you've got plenty of books stored on your device. If you invest in a new device, it can be extremely tiring and expensive to download each book again. Luckily with the new Play Books app, you'll be able to access your books on any Android device.

The new Play Books app is packed with the latest and greatest reads, as you might expect, but it's also a great example of an app using cloud-based software. As long as you're logged into the same Google account that you originally used to download the book, you'll be able to access it from any other Android device. This saves you the time and effort of having to re-download it again.

For the purpose of this tutorial, we'll be downloading books to our Samsung Galaxy Nexus device and then accessing them on our LG Optimus Black. We'll show you how to find the Play Books app and go through the basics of downloading the book. We'll also show you other possibilities on how you could share your book among all your devices. So follow this tutorial closely and you'll never need to download the same book twice.

Play Books | **Download a book**

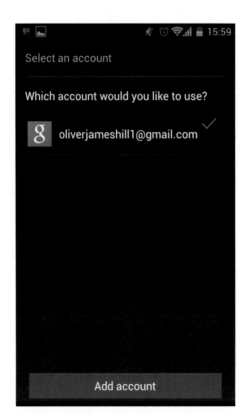

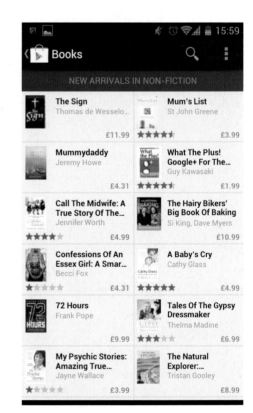

1: Download the app
Find the Play Books app on the Play Store and download it if it isn't already on your device. Once downloaded and installed, open it.

2: Check your account
Press the Options icon at the top right of the app and select Accounts. Ensure you're logged into your primary Google account.

3: Find a book
Start searching for a book to read. If you pay for the book, you won't need to worry about having to pay for it on another device.

Reading a downloaded book

A look at all the options available to you

○ Share

If there's a book that you're enjoying and you wish to let people know what you're reading, hit the Share option and you can either send a link via Bluetooth or Gmail so people can purchase the book, or add a post to Google+

○ Font and brightness

Tapping on this icon will allow you to increase or decrease the size of the font – for easier reading – or increase the brightness, if you have a device that allows it such as the Nexus 7 here

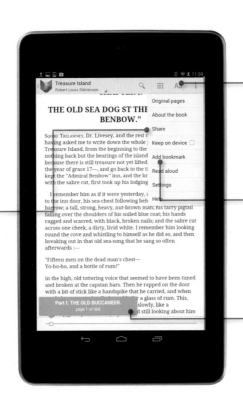

○ Options

The options menu here opens up a whole world of possibilities. You can find out more information about the book, select to keep it on your device, add a bookmark, have the book read aloud and more

○ Scroll through

If you wish to jump to a particular page or chapter of the book, simply drag your finger along this slider to the location you desire

Switching between accounts

Don't worry if you're using different Google accounts on multiple devices. You can easily switch between accounts to get all the books you downloaded on one device. Another option is to create a universal Google account solely for Play Books.

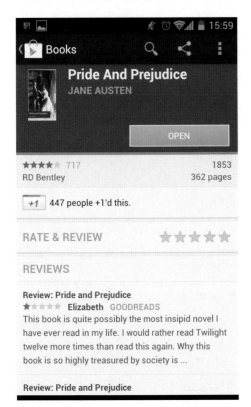

4: Download the book

You can now start downloading the book. It takes a little while, but when on a secondary device, you'll have instant access to it.

5: Is it compatible?

A few books are incompatible with some phones, so ensure that it works. Your secondary device will now be able to download the book for free.

6: Other sharing options

Another way of sharing your downloaded books between different devices is by uploading them to an alternative cloud-based app.

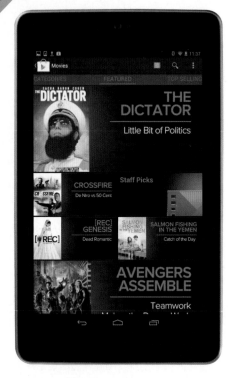

Play movies on your Android device

The rebranded Play Movies section gives you instant access to the latest films. We show how to do this over multiple devices

Some people might be under the impression that sharing movies between devices, over a cloud-based app, is difficult to achieve. Thanks to the recently updated Play Store, the ease of watching movies over different Android devices has been vastly improved, and the renamed Play Movies app has been given a makeover to make it as accessible as possible.

The main principle behind the Play Movies app is the same as before. As long as your Android devices are all connected to the same Google account, you should have no problem in watching movies on them all. If you use the same Google account on your desktop computer, you'll also have full access to your movies, and will even be able to watch them through your YouTube account on your desktop browser.

In this tutorial, we'll show you the basics of renting a movie and how to navigate around the Play Movies app. We'll also show you how to access your movies on a secondary Android device, and give you some tips on things to look out for when trying to share your movies between devices.

Play Store | Download a movie

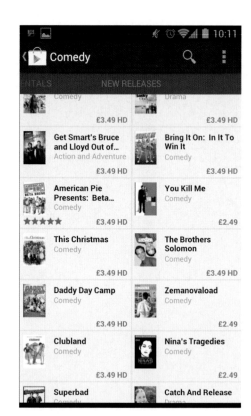

1: Download Play Movies
If it's not already on your device, you may need to download the Google Play app from scratch. Once it's downloaded and installed, open it.

2: Play Movies home
The first tab has all your rentals; the second stores your personal movies. Press on the Google Play symbol to rent a new movie.

3: Select your movie
There's a decent choice of movies available to rent from the store. You can search through movies by their popularity, or by their genre.

Download a film

Enjoy movies while you're mobile

○ **Renting**
With most films nowadays, you'll have the option to either rent the film in HD, or standard definition. Once selected, you'll be told how long you have to watch the movie

Watch your internal storage

Constantly downloading movies might seem like a great idea at the time, but they're massive files that'll soon eat up your device's memory. If you pay for a movie, it's yours to download whenever, so you don't have to keep it on your device.

○ **Tell people about it**
Tapping the 'Share' button will allow you to tell others what you're about to watch. You can either send a link so they can download it too, or post straight to Google+

○ **Trailer**
If you're unsure whether you want to rent the movie, watching the trailer might help make up your mind

○ **Extra information**
In this section you'll find more information about the movie, who stars in it, and what other people thought of it. Google Play will also recommend other movies similar to this

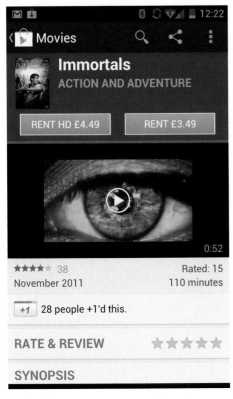

4: Options
Once you've found a film, you can watch a trailer to see if you want to take the next step and rent the movie, or get it in HD.

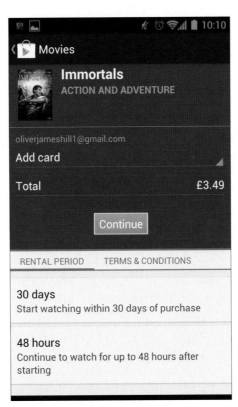

5: Rent the movie
If you decide to rent the movie, you'll have to wait for the film to download, which may take a little while.

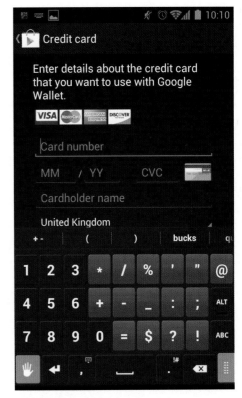

6: Pay for the movie
You'll need to make sure you're using the same credit or debit card on all your accounts. Once you've entered your card details, hit Confirm.

Get searching with Google Mobile

The mobile-specific version of the popular search engine

Google's search engine is by far the most popular search facility of its kind on the internet, but there is another version of the utility that, despite its similarities, stands alone as a tool: the mobile version of the engine, Google Mobile.

This engine is just as easy to use and manipulate on mobile devices, and is optimised to perform on smaller screens. It works just like the desktop version, but tailors the experience for mobile. All the classic features are there, with search dominating the main home screen as always, but you can also search for images, video, keep up-to-date with the news and much more. There's also the option to use your location to ensure that the results you receive are specific to your current whereabouts. So if you use Google on your PC or Mac regularly, you'll be right at home here.

> "The Google search engine is just as easy to use and manipulate on mobile devices"

○ **Tabs**
Click on these tabs to search specific categories

○ **Search**
Click here then enter search text, click on the magnifying glass to search

○ **Extras**
Additional subject-specific location searches can be found here including fast food and petrol stations

○ **Location**
A range of location-related subjects allows you to search for local pubs, cafes and the like

○ **Settings**
Enter the settings screen to modify how you wish to search

My Location

Interact further with local businesses

Yes, you can search for local business information by utilising generic search names like 'pizza' or 'bank', but when you do enter one of these generic names and local information does flag itself, you can do more with that information than merely accessing the basic contact details and distance from your present location.

For example, if you press the local pizza house on a pizza search, it will pull up a new window. On the window will be the full name of the business plus its current star rating. Underneath that will be the business phone number which, upon pressing, will

call there and then. Next will be a link to a full map generated via your GPS system along with an option to generate directions to lead you to the business.

After that is a details button that, when accessed, gives you a mini-map plus its address, opening hours plus attached reviews and phone number. Access those details and you can read full reviews and then have access to other, similar businesses. In this case, restaurants, coffee shops, bars, fast food merchants and more, along with cash machines, petrol stations, shops and other attractions.

Google Search integrates with Maps to provide all the location information you need

Top functions

Location

Google recognises that you need to search for a selection of essential business and other services that are close to you. So when you input an essential word into the search engine, it won't tell you that there is a place to fix your car in Outer Mongolia if you happen to live in Doncaster. Hence, if you type in 'pizza', you will receive a selection of pizza houses that are near to your location.

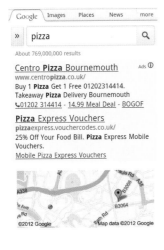

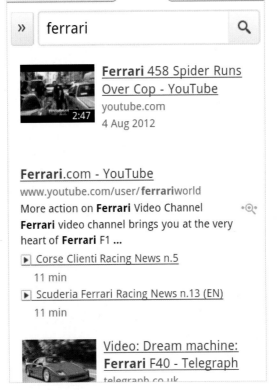

Google Suggest

The search aspect of Google Mobile tries to be comprehensive by responding to your requests in a broad fashion. It does attempt to second guess you, however, by deducing what it thinks you might need judging by the type of request you have made. Let's use the example of Liverpool. If start to enter that name, Google will try and assume what you want to search for, and you can select one of the drop-down options if it's right.

> "It won't tell you there's a place to fix your car in Outer Mongolia if you live in Doncaster"

View images

Another aspect of the Google search engine that helps you to cut down on the time you spend filtering through the information that is presented to you is the viewing images option. If you want to find a picture of a cat, for example, just enter your 'cat' search word and then scroll to the top of the screen accessing the 'images' tab to see a series of clickable thumbnails.

View the news

Accessing the news can be done in exactly the same way as viewing images, but you have a choice of two access methods to get you underway. If you want to find something specific, enter a search word or words and then scroll to the top, click news and any story containing your search words will be presented. Otherwise, keep the search box blank to receive a broad array of news items collected under varying banners.

Watch videos

Many users ignore the treasure trove that is the 'More' option that is present at the top right-hand side of the Google search window. Click here to open up a screen packed with new options. Here, you will find the video option. Click to move the video search to the centre of the Google search home screen. Enter a search parameter and ready-to-view videos will be listed, each accessible via a click.

Search pictorially with Google Goggles

Use your camera to scan objects

Google Goggles is something of a marvel and it's only available on Android. It works pictorially, using image-recognition technology to identify landmarks, art and so much more. It comes in handy as a barcode and QR scanner and it also lets you add contacts from business cards, just by passing your phone's camera over it.

Goggles can also translate between languages. By opening the app and selecting the Snapshot option from the main menu, you can use your camera to point at a word or phrase and the app will translate it for you once you have selected the words that you wish to decipher.

In this tutorial, we're going to look at how you can point your phone at an object and have the app search for the item via Google, bringing up suggestions and showing similar items.

It's one of those apps that every Apple iOS device owner would love to get their hands on because it's so versatile and incredibly useful.

"It comes in handy as a barcode and QR scanner"

○ Landmarks
Google Goggles is an invaluable travel guide. You may not guess a building's use, but using this app you will soon be able to find out as it scans the building and matches it to its vast database

○ Contact info
The text-recognition software built in to the app means you are able to scan a business card and have Google pick up on the words that are printed on it

○ Barcodes
If you see a QR code, use Google Goggles to scan it and be taken to the URL it points to. The site will open in your phone's web browser. This saves a lot of time having to tap in the websites's URL

○ Logos
You can point your phone at a logo you are not sure about and have it scour Google for the image, showing you the correct matches for it. Simply take a photo of the logo and then allow it to use that to find the image

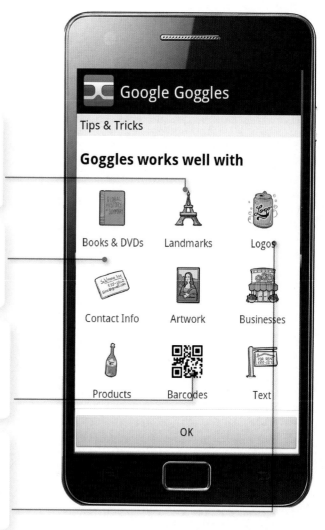

Google Goggles

Tips & Tricks

Goggles works well with

Books & DVDs   Landmarks   Logos

Contact Info   Artwork   Businesses

Products   Barcodes   Text

OK

Google Goggles | Search using images

Snapshot   Continuous

Load Image   History

1: Start your search
Google Goggles allows you to search by using an image rather than text for the query. We're going to take a photo, so tap Snapshot.

2: Take a photo
Line up the object you wish to photograph on your phone and when you have it in place, press the Camera button and a snapshot will be taken.

Similar Images (No objects recognized)

3: See the results
Now a list of the results will appear. If your object is not recognised, Goggles will present a host of similar images, or you can suggest the result.

4: Enable search history

When you suggest a better result, you need to enable the search history that lets you revisit images you have taken, add notes and share results.

5: Add a note

To add a note with your image, tap the pencil icon in the top-right corner when you view your picture. Type your note and tap Save.

6: Pick up on text

If there is any text within your photo, Goggles cleverly detects it and the words will appear at the bottom of the screen.

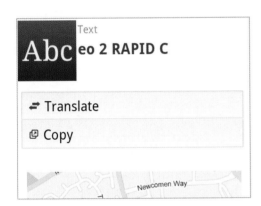

7: Search using the text

You can use this to search Google. It'll bring up any incidences using that word, such as the company of the product which you've taken a picture of.

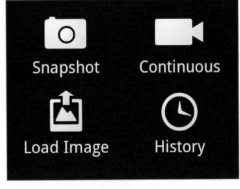

8: Translate printed text

Open up the Goggles app and select the Snapshot option. Point your phone at the word or phrase you want translated.

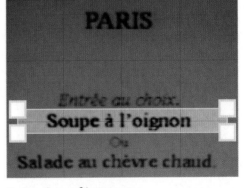

9: Region of interest

In the bottom-right-hand corner is a region of interest button. This will allow you to draw a box around a specific word or phrase.

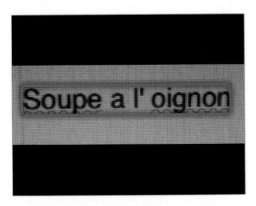

10: Translate the words

The app photographs the text that you have pointed your phone at. It will begin scanning the text before looking for a match.

11: Perform a web search

When you tap on the translated result, not only can you see the translation on a full page but Goggles will perform a web search for entries relating to it.

12: See your history

You can go back to your images at any point by selecting the History option. This will let you see all your saved pictures.

Get started with Google Now

Keep your life in check with Google's new companion feature

Google Now is an intelligent piece of software that monitors certain things about your life, and in return provides you with useful information that you can use to your advantage. This information is shown in a variety of cleverly designed panels.

The longer you allow Google Now to monitor your life, the more information it can provide. For example, after a few days of monitoring your commute to work, Google Now will then begin to notify you of new ways you can reach your work, as well as give you up-to-the-minute information about any potential delays that you may encounter. The range of topics that Google Now covers is pretty impressive, and after a few days of having it, you'll soon see the benefits of using it.

Any new information that Google Now wants to share with you is displayed in the newly designed notification menu, from which you can then select to get further information about each piece of information specifically. Read on to explore some of the basic uses of Google Now, and how you can get the best out of it.

Google Now | Get updates tailored to your lifestyle

1: Home Screen
Now can be accessed from anywhere on your phone. To access it, drag it up from the bottom of the screen to the Google icon that appears.

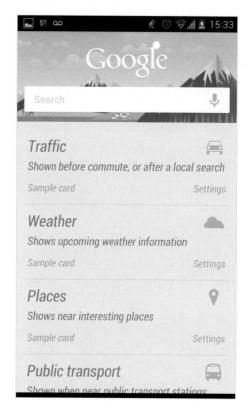

2: The first time
When you open up Now, you'll have to follow the tutorial. You'll be shown the range of cards you can access once you regularly use the feature.

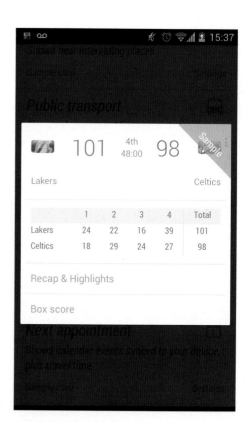

3: View sample cards
After the tutorial you'll be able to take a look at the design of the cards, find out what to expect, and have the chance to disable cards.

Google Now notifications

Find out how to get more from Google Now info cards

○ **Start a voice search**
As well as starting a text-based search using the bar at the top of the screen, you can also press on the microphone symbol to start a voice search using Google's revamped voice recognition system. This might take a few seconds to load

○ **Check your notifications**
The new notifications bar with the Jelly Bean update often displays info related to Google Now, so be sure to check it regularly. It'll also alert you of any changes to your cards, like whether you'll hit traffic on your commute

○ **Link with other apps**
You'll find that certain panels are closely linked to many other Google apps. For example, when you use the commute panel, you'll see your route planned out in Maps

○ **Pinpoint your details**
You won't get the full benefits of Google Now until you've used it for a while. It tracks your movements, and specifically pinpoints places you visit often, so after a few days the info should be more personalised

Smart thinking
Once Google Now has had a chance to get to know your lifestyle, it will start giving you some really useful information. If you search for your favourite sports team, for example, you'll start receiving updates on all of their matches.

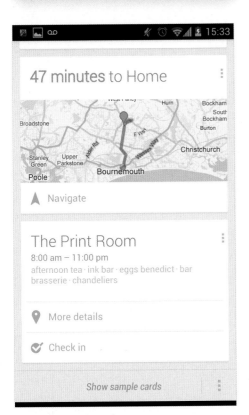

4: After a few days
Now will begin notifying you of new cards based on the data it has collected. If your GPS is enabled, you'll likely receive the weather card.

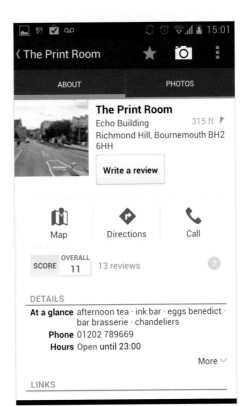

5: Get more info
Each card host a lot more information that can be accessed by pressing on one of the cards. Now can alert you to landmarks, restaurants and more.

6: Pinpoint your cards
If you are receiving too many/little notifications from Google Now, you can change the settings by pressing the options button on the right.

Learn to use Gmail

Interacting with the best email system on the planet

If you're a smartphone user then there's a fair chance you're also a Gmail fan, since Google's email client is a great mobile option. As you may know, Gmail combines the advantages of web/server-based email (spam/virus filtering, backups are down to Google, etc) with lightning-fast search. It means that, for many, Gmail on your mobile phone is a viable alternative to a local desktop app.

Although Google operates a number of mobile-optimised web versions of Gmail, on the Android OS it implemented a native email application. It's utterly focused on accessing your Gmail and providing all the functionality you'd have in the desktop web version, but faster, slicker and completely mobile.

Gmail isn't just available on Android, you can link your account to your iPhone too, and access you emails on the move whenever you like.

> "Provides the functionality you would have in the desktop web version, but faster and slicker"

○ **To and From**
In addition to showing the sender and intended recipient(s), note 'Show details'. This option will reveal their email address

○ **Star**
As featured below, tapping the 'star' icon to add a yellow star to an email containing vital information makes it easy to find

○ **Reply time**
The arrow icon is for replying to the email, perhaps the most common thing you'll do. So the designers made it easy to find!

○ **Show pictures**
With 'rich' emails now more and more common, downloading their content can take a while over a slow data connection

'Star' support — Never lose an important email again

The idea is a simple one, yet it's wonderfully effective. As more and more emails come into your Gmail account, some will naturally contain some rather important information – perhaps they might contain passwords, reference numbers, user names, addresses and a whole host of other essential data you want to keep close at hand. You know you'll want to return to access these pieces of information again in the future but you don't want to go through the hassle of guessing a search string to find a particular one.

Well, there's a very simple and effective solution for this. Simply 'star' any such email, ie mark it as 'important', and then you can bring up just the starred emails later. To do this in Gmail, simply press Menu, then 'Go to labels' and tap on 'Starred'. Just browse through them and then open them up as normal.

If you end up with a lot of starred emails, you may want to go one step further. So here's a huge tip: you can go one better and search within the starred emails by adding "in:Starred" in front of your normal Gmail search keyword. It may be geeky, but it's oh-so-powerful – and that's so often the beauty of Google and its applications.

Starred emails make it easy to source important information

Key features

Your latest Gmail

Part of the charm of
Android and Gmail
is that it 'just works'.
No settings needed
to configure IMAP
addresses, no tweaking
of SSL security or sync
intervals… it's Google's
mail system and your
Google-powered phone
is online, so it 'just
works'. You can set a
shortcut on one of your
home screens or use
the Gmail widget. Either
way, you're one tap away
from your emails.

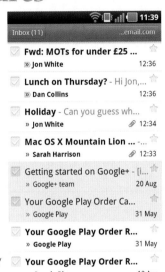

Sending mail

Replying to emails is trivial,
but it's almost as easy
to create an email from
scratch. There are a couple
ways you can do this.
Either tap the Menu button
and select Compose, or
if you wish to reply to an
email, select the arrow
button next to the sender,
and choose if you wish to
reply, reply all, or forward
the email. You can then
compose your email on the
next screen.

Finding something

One of the best features of
Gmail is that it's quicker to
search than it is to organise.
With other email systems,
you spend your whole life
filing messages into folders
and generally organising
emails. Here, tap on the
Search icon and then
just type a word or name
representing what you
want to find again and tap
the magnifying glass icon.
Search matches appear
within a second or so.

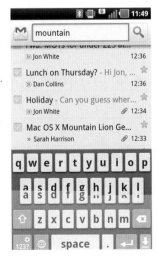

Sensible attachments

As emails come in, they'll be handled
just as they would in your desktop
web browser when accessing your
Gmail. You can send and receive
documents as attachments, which
will be shown as a paperclip icon on
the relevant email. If you receive a
document, you can choose to either
download it to your phone, or get a
quick preview.

> "As emails
> come in,
> they'll be
> handled
> just as they
> would in
> your desktop
> web browser
> when you're
> accessing
> your Gmail"

Images

As smartphone have improved over
time, so have their ability to deal with
images. The bigger memory, faster
processors and larger screens mean
that viewing an image sent as an
attachment is clear and easy. Simply
choose to view the image in the
email, and scroll to the bottom until
you see the image. As you can see
from this screenshot, the image looks
as good on mobile as it does on a
desktop machine.

Sync Gmail across mobile devices

You can now use Gmail in a cloud computing environment

Until recently, doing all your work on a computer meant being frustrated by the same old problems: you couldn't access data while out and about, look up a document from your network if you only had a smartphone, and you couldn't collaborate with colleagues who couldn't access your network. The solution? Shift your data to the cloud. Now, if you have a Google account, you can store your documents in your Google online storage area and, with Gmail, email to the cloud.

Gmail has fast become a popular email client to such an extent that numerous platforms can utilise Gmail, including Android and Apple's iOS. What makes Gmail a powerful option for anyone looking to utilise the program is its ability to sync to a common data space or cloud, transferring data from one platform to another and from one device to another, even if they are running on completely different operating systems. Hence, with Gmail, you can compose an email to a friend or colleague while using your Android phone, and then send it their iPhone without any problems, and without the receiver having to translate it or convert the file in any way.

Gmail | Sync to use Gmail

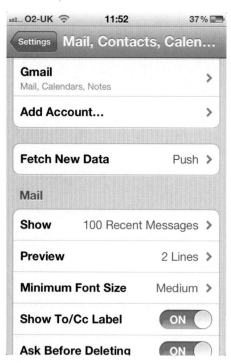

1: Settings
Open the Settings application, then open the Mail, Contacts, Calendars section within. Under the Accounts section, tap Add Account. You will be taken to a list of email account suppliers.

2: Wizard!
Select Gmail to initiate the email wizard to trigger a step-by-step process. First, enter your account information. Under Name, enter your own name. Then enter your full Google email address.

3: Password
The most important part of the process is to include your password, which will be your Google Account password. Be sure to include a mixture of letters, numbers and symbols.

Gmail account information

Decide what information enters the cloud

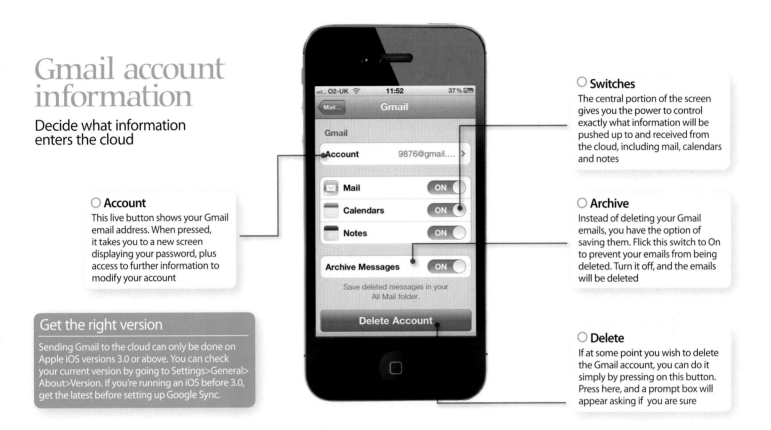

○ **Switches**
The central portion of the screen gives you the power to control exactly what information will be pushed up to and received from the cloud, including mail, calendars and notes

○ **Account**
This live button shows your Gmail email address. When pressed, it takes you to a new screen displaying your password, plus access to further information to modify your account

○ **Archive**
Instead of deleting your Gmail emails, you have the option of saving them. Flick this switch to On to prevent your emails from being deleted. Turn it off, and the emails will be deleted

Get the right version
Sending Gmail to the cloud can only be done on Apple iOS versions 3.0 or above. You can check your current version by going to Settings>General> About>Version. If you're running an iOS before 3.0, get the latest before setting up Google Sync.

○ **Delete**
If at some point you wish to delete the Gmail account, you can do it simply by pressing on this button. Press here, and a prompt box will appear asking if you are sure

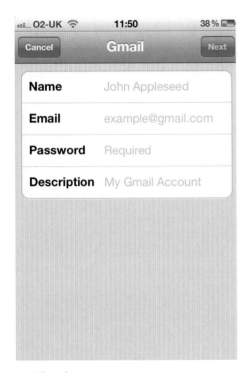

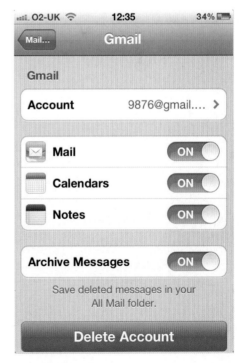

4: Check your account
Once the essential information has been inputted, press the Next button. If everything has been typed in correctly, each line will briefly display a tick mark.

5: In the cloud
A new screen will ask if you wish to switch on email, calendars and notes. Select the Google services you want to sync via the cloud. Once done, press the Save button.

6: In the end
You will be taken back to the Accounts screen. To finish the process, click on the newly created Gmail account, and decide whether to retain Archive messages by switching on this feature.

A guide to Google Calendar

Get your life organised and never miss an appointment

Google Calendar is one of the lesser known and least complex calendar applications, yet the very fact that it syncs instantly and perfectly to the wonder that is Google Calendar on the web makes it a superb way to organise both your life and the lives of those around you.

With Day, Week, Month and Agenda views, it's easy to visualise what your commitments are for the upcoming day, week or month, and to plan ahead. Most usefully of all, you can set one or more reminders for each event or appointment. Once entered (on the phone or on the Google Calendar page in your desktop browser), wherever you are, your phone will remind you just before an event to tell you where you're supposed to be or who you're supposed to call. Your poor memory will never make you late for anything ever again!

> ## "Wherever you are, your phone will remind you of your appointments"

○ Timings
It's easy to change event timings using the spinners. The critical one is the start time ('From'), as that's the one that the reminder alarm is cued from

○ Event title
As you might expect, this is the text that's seen in each Calendar view. Keep it short and accurate

○ Where
This is a text string for you and others to use (eg 'Meeting room three') – there's no Google Maps integration (yet)

○ Description
This may seem redundant, given that you have a descriptive title at the top of the form. But here's where you can add important multi-line meeting notes and extra info

○ Repetition
Events can be automatically repeated, with some wide ranging choices for you, eg 'Monthly (every first Friday)'. This saves you from forgetting to enter future occurrences

Sharing calendars

If you have a partner, or work for a company, or perhaps belong to a club, then why not view multiple calendars, and really be informed?

Although you are unable to create new calendars in the application itself, these are still fully supported. The idea is that you might have one for yourself (the default), plus one for business events (create this in Google Calendar on the web), and you'll probably also appreciate being able to see your partner's calendar too. In the latter's case, get them to log into Google Calendar on the web, and then choose to 'Share' their calendar with you (ie with your email address). Their entries will then show up, colour coded – and bang up to date – in your Calendar on

your phone, which is pretty cool. And yes, you can tweak the colours that are used using a palette picker on the web version.

When creating events in Calendar on your phone, there's a list in the form where you can choose which Calendar the entry should be entered in. If all goes well, as shown here, then you can get a great idea of up-and-coming events from all your calendars by browsing around the various views. You even get appropriately coloured text in the non-graphical Agenda view.

Share calendars, and get an idea of what your friends are up to

Calendar's features

Month at a time

Calendar's default view is arguably one of its least useful functions. With this, you can swipe up and down with your finger in order to move between months (like a traditional calendar), and appointments and other entries are depicted by tiny blue triangles. The size of these is supposed to represent the length of time involved, but in most cases you're going to want to tap on a day to get more details.

The Day view

The Day view in Google Calendar is almost as rudimentary as the Month one, but at least events are shown in full. The biggest drawback is that the fixed time grid means that you'll usually have to scroll up and down a lot to see your appointments. Still, it's easy to tap on the appropriate time slot in Day view and fill in details of a new event. The default duration is an hour, but you can easily change this.

Week and Agenda

Tap on Menu, and you can call up Week view, which also has fixed time slots and requires scrolling, but this does show seven days at a time, and is good for planning ahead. Even better, arguably, is the lesser known Agenda view (again, pick it from the Menu), which has no bothersome time grid, and which simply lists upcoming events in chronological order (ie, a list of what's coming up).

A new appointment

From the Day view, you can tap on the appropriate time slot you need, and the 'Event details' form will appear. Most of it is hidden beneath the virtual keyboard, but don't worry, you can scroll the page up as needed. To adjust a start or finish time, just tap on the time button and a handy 'spinner' will appear. A tip: if the event is all day (eg a conference), it's quicker to just check the 'All day' box, and the times go away.

> "From the Day view, tap on the appropriate time slot you need, and the Event details form will appear"

Reminder times

Setting reminders is crucial, but you may get fed up with changing the default reminder time of 'ten minutes' every time you create a new appointment. This may well be not long enough for you (get dressed, drive somewhere, etc), so tap Menu and then on Settings. Now, scroll right down, and tap on 'Default reminder time'. You'll possibly want to set this at 15 or 30 minutes, but it's up to you.

Stay up to date with Google Calendar

Check your appointments while you are on the move

Life can be rather hectic, especially if you have a busy job, a family and a social life. So it's possible that you may find that you have a work calendar, a personal calendar, a family calendar, a significant others calendar and probably several other calendars you keep an eye on for work and for play. The obvious problem with this set-up is that it can become confusing very quickly, and rather overwhelming to a degree that calendar entries can easily be missed, especially if all of your calendars are spread across multiple platforms. After all, what if you use a phone, tablet and desktop interchangeably, and need everything to sync without having to think about it?

This is why it is necessary to send your Calendar data into a cloud space; the type of data that is based on one single source, but can be viewed on a variety of platforms over a variety of operating systems, being one set of information that is accessed via a range of computing and mobile devices.

Google Calendar is a very popular iteration of the popular utility, and is widely used. So how do you go about moving the data from this utility to other OS platforms and devices?

Google Calendar | Check appointments while mobile

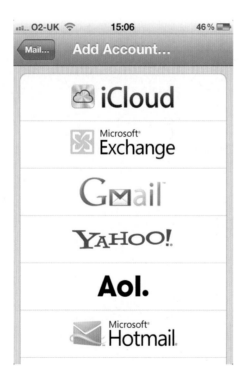

1: Settings
Open the Settings application on the home screen, then open the Mail, Contacts, Calendars section within. Under the Accounts section, press Add Account… You will be taken to a list of popular account suppliers.

2: Exchange
It may appear to be logical to select the Gmail option in order to set up a Google calendar, but in this case do no such thing. Instead, select Microsoft Exchange as your supplier of choice and then carry on with the process.

3: Password
Enter your username with the @gmail.com tag and your password. Make sure your password features a mixture of text, numbers and symbols. Click Next, and a server entry will appear. Use m.google.com as your server.

Calendar information

Decide what information enters the cloud

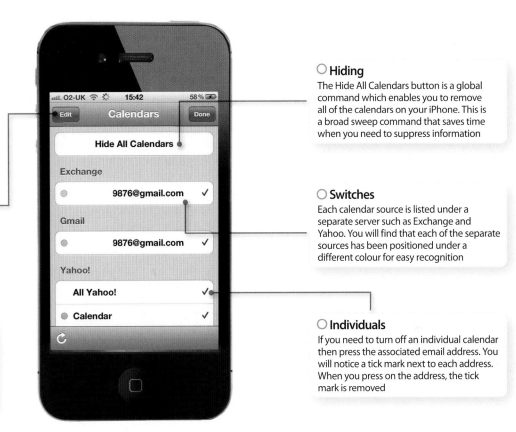

○ Edit
Click the Edit button and click on the calendar of your choice to be taken to a new screen. Here, you can change the colour associated with your server. Choose your colour, and click Done

○ Hiding
The Hide All Calendars button is a global command which enables you to remove all of the calendars on your iPhone. This is a broad sweep command that saves time when you need to suppress information

○ Switches
Each calendar source is listed under a separate server such as Exchange and Yahoo. You will find that each of the separate sources has been positioned under a different colour for easy recognition

○ Individuals
If you need to turn off an individual calendar then press the associated email address. You will notice a tick mark next to each address. When you press on the address, the tick mark is removed

The right one
Syncing Calendar to the cloud can only be done on Apple iOS versions 3.0 or above. You can check your current version by going to Settings>General>About>Version. If you're running an iOS before 3.0, get the latest iOS before setting up Google Sync.

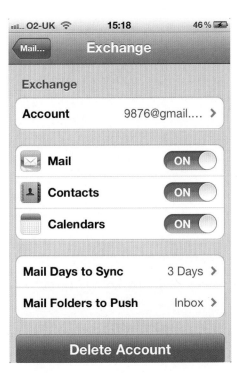

4: Sync
Choose what you want to sync: Mail, Contacts and Calendars. Each option can be switched by flipping the switch to the right of each title. Turn the Calendar syncing option on to allow data in and out of the cloud.

5: View
To view your new calendar, simply tap on the icon. Next, tap the Calendars button to view the other calendars from any other mail account that you have synced to your cloud account, such as Yahoo, for example.

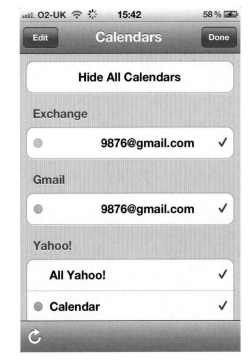

6: Toggle
Each Calendar can be switched on or switched off by pressing on the calendar itself. When pressed, the tick mark will toggle on and off, and allow data in or out of the cloud, so you always have a visual representation of what's going on.

Access the cloud with Google Drive

Upload and even create files with Google's storage system

Cloud-based storage allows users to upload their documents, videos and images and access them over a number of devices. For example, if you upload an image in Dropbox on your Android device, you can log in to the same account on your tablet and then download the same image.

There are plenty of cloud-based servers available for Android users, all trying to entice people to their system by offering tasty free storage. Dropbox, SugarSync and Box all offer storage facilities, and all come with a sizable chunk of free storage to boot. Google's new service – Drive – offers the same functionalities as these other apps, but also has a bit more focus on syncing with other Google apps. New users can download the app from the Google Play store and receive an instant 5GB of space.

In this tutorial we'll show you the basics of navigating Google Drive, as well as show you how to upload files and, ultimately, free up some bytes on your device.

"Download the app and receive an instant 5GB of space"

Google Drive | Store your files in the cloud

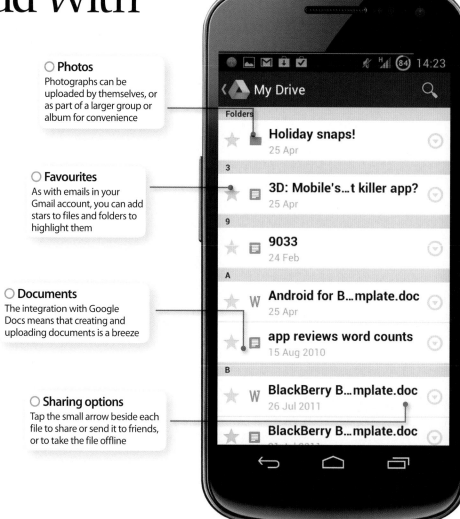

○ Photos
Photographs can be uploaded by themselves, or as part of a larger group or album for convenience

○ Favourites
As with emails in your Gmail account, you can add stars to files and folders to highlight them

○ Documents
The integration with Google Docs means that creating and uploading documents is a breeze

○ Sharing options
Tap the small arrow beside each file to share or send it to friends, or to take the file offline

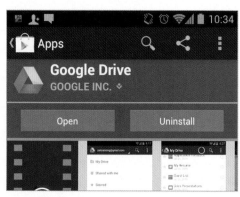

1: Download Google Drive
Go to the Google Play store and use the search bar to quickly find Google Drive. Download, install and load up the free app.

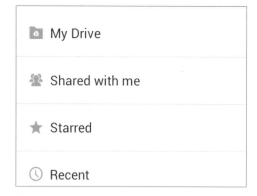

2: Explore the home screen
My Drive lets you see everything you've uploaded. Shared with me shows you files that others have given you access to and Starred are your favourites.

3: Sync with Google Docs
Through Drive you can create new documents and upload them instantaneously. To do this, open the options menu and select New.

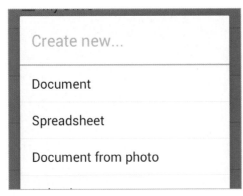

4: Create a new document
The Create new menu will appear and enable you to access Google Docs and prepare items to upload. For this tutorial, select Document.

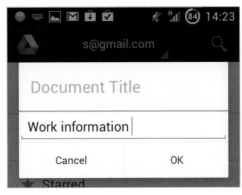

5: Type and save
Type and format the document as normal. When finished, tap the tick in the top-left corner to save the document to Google Drive.

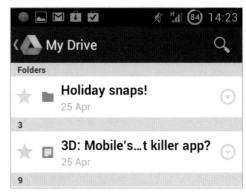

6: Upload a document
Go to the Google Drive home screen and select Documents. Documents you've saved, including your new one, will be listed here.

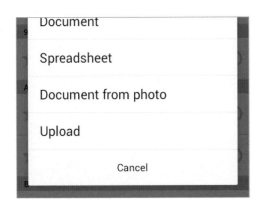

7: Upload a photo
Press the options button on the home screen and select New from the menu. Tap Upload and then Image. Pick a picture to upload then hit OK.

8: Manage your uploads
Files can be edited and changed via the cloud, and you can make some available for offline viewing – handy if you struggle to get a signal.

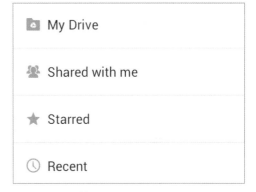

9: Use a different account
To use another account, ensure you're still signed in then make any files you want to add to your secondary account available offline.

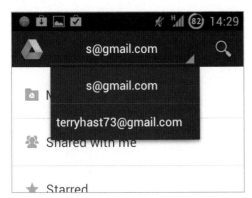

10: Make the switch
On the home screen, tap the bar showing your current Gmail address to see a drop-down menu. Simply tap an account to switch to it.

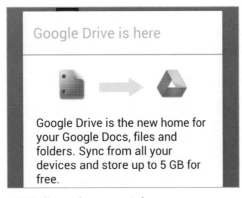

11: Follow the tutorial
If you haven't switched accounts before then the Google Drive tutorial will once again load up, giving you handy step-by-step instructions.

12: Start uploading files
Files can be uploaded and accessed in the same way. You can switch between your various Gmail accounts as often as you like.

Get to grips with Google Maps

Take a look around the only map you'll ever need

Google Maps is easily one of Google's best apps. Bringing the whole world to your smartphone, it's an excellent navigational tool, and a great way to discover what's around you. On a basic level, it will pinpoint your location so you never get lost, and show you where all the major towns and cities are in any given country. It's when you dig a little deeper that you really see everything it has to offer.

If you're trying to find your way to a destination, the app will help you navigate to where you want to go. The different map views allow you to zoom right in to a specific street, and you can spend hours just travelling around the world seeing the sights. There are also plenty of social options, allowing you to find nearby friends and locate restaurants, ATMs, and much more. And if you're trying to avoid the traffic jams, Maps has got you covered.

All in all, Maps is a feature that can really transform the way you use your smartphone, just take a look at what it has to offer.

"You can spend hours travelling around the world seeing the sights"

○ **Layers**
View traffic info or change the map view to satellite, terrain and more

○ **Local**
Find nearby places of interest by tapping this icon

○ **Directions**
Find your way to a point on the map using the directions feature

○ **Search**
Tap this icon to search for specific location in Maps

Navigation Get up and running

Google Maps is much more than just a modern version of the Ordinance Survey map. One of the best features is the ability to get directions to any location you wish to get to. While the Navigation app goes into a little more detail and works almost like a satnav, the directions feature in Maps can be just as useful.

Simply tap the directions option and you'll be able to enter a start and end location. Hit 'Get directions' and the map will load up, showing you the route. This in itself is an excellent tool if you want to discover the best way to get somewhere,

or the places you pass through on your journey. However, it goes even deeper than that.

The main screen will display the expected journey time, and the step-by-step driving directions. You can then scroll through your journey, seeing every turn you need to take, and how long you need to travel along each road. The directions are displayed along the top of the map, and by selecting 'Directions List' you'll bring up a written display of the directions so you can see every turn you need to take, and every road you'll be travelling on.

View your route on the map

Get a closer look at where to go

Use Maps on the move

Search

One of the main features of a map app is the ability to find a place that you're looking for. It's easy to search for a location using Maps, simply tap the magnifying glass and type in your location of choice. The app will give you a list of possible options as you type. Wherever it is in the world you want to have a look at, Google Maps will be able to take you there in next to no time.

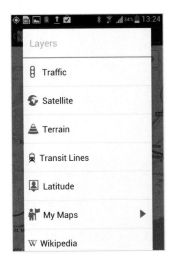

Layers

If you're looking for a little extra detail on your map, Layers is the place to come. Not only can you change the map view, you can also view traffic data (showing you which roads it's best to avoid) and transit lines, if you want to see where the nearest railway line is. The number of features here differs depending on your device.

Your location

One of the best things about owning a smartphone with Google Maps is that you never need to worry about not knowing where you are. By turning GPS and location services on in your Settings, when you open the Maps app and tap the compass icon, the on-screen maps will show you where you are. You can then zoom in and close as you need to make sure you know exactly whereabouts you are.

Map view

The basic map view is often the most useful, however sometimes it can be a little dull if you just wish to explore some of the world's most popular destinations. For example, setting it to Satellite view allows you to view locations in incredible detail, zooming right in to landmarks and buildings with pinpoint accuracy. You can also set the map to Terrain view, to get an idea of the lie of the land.

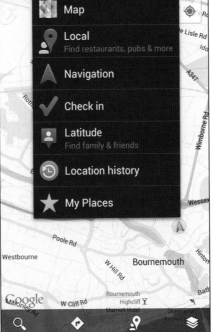

"Maps comes packed with extra options, that will help improve your overall map experience"

Options

Google Maps comes packed with extra options, that will help improve your overall map experience. Firstly, you can tap Local to discover nearby restaurants, banks and more close to your current locations. Latitude will allow you to discover the whereabouts of your friends and give you the chance to meet up, Navigation will take you through to the Google Navigation app. You then have other basic options such as location history and your favourite places.

View Google Latitude

A wide-angle view of Google's Latitude service

A natural extension to the social-networking model and its associated genre of apps, Google Latitude enables your friends to see exactly where you are and, of course, for you to see where they are.

Neatly integrated into the Google Maps app on Android, through Latitude you can also check in with your friends when you arrive at a particular place or location. In fact, you can pre-program Google Latitude to automatically tell your friends that you have arrived at your chosen destination. It's a great program to use for when you have arranged to meet your friends at the local cafe, for example.

Such a program is ideal to prevent those annoying occasions when you just miss someone because they took a different route to reach your location, they were looking at something in the shop next door or they were running a few minutes late and didn't get a chance warn you.

> "You can pre-program Latitude to tell your friends that you've arrived at your chosen destination"

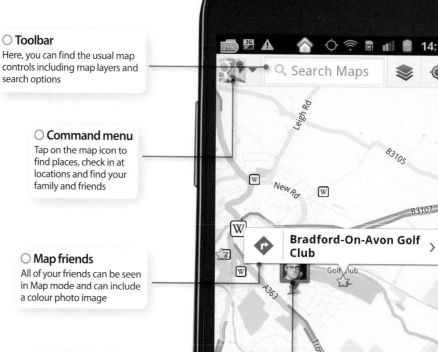

○ **Toolbar**
Here, you can find the usual map controls including map layers and search options

○ **Command menu**
Tap on the map icon to find places, check in at locations and find your family and friends

○ **Map friends**
All of your friends can be seen in Map mode and can include a colour photo image

○ **Friend info**
More information on their location can be found by pressing the face icon

---

Privacy You can control how much is revealed

The more you read about Google Latitude, the scarier it sounds. Everyone knows where you are, you can't put a foot out of place without everyone knowing about it, and what about people you really don't want to meet? You'll be happy to learn that the program does include several privacy options that give you control over what info is released to the public and how much information is visible to the viewer.

Firstly, you will only be available to viewers who you like and trust. Secondly, you can control who sees you and at what level. That means that you can identify, with each and every person who is able to access your location, a general city-level location or, for more specific detail, a street-level location. Alternatively, you can hide your location from your friends.

The location itself can also be varied. So, on the most open level, you can reveal everything about where you are, or, for the rather more cagey user, you can manually set your location on the map. Finally, you can hide your location entirely, if you do not want to be visible. You can also share your location with others on a variety of social-networking sites.

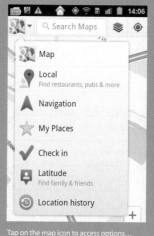

Tap on the map icon to access options…

You control who sees what information…

Key features

Check in

When you're roaming the town and you find that you're ready to declare to your friends that you have arrived at a destination and are ready to meet them, before you reveal yourself to an anxious public you can decide exactly where that place may be. Your phone's GPS will generate a list of possible locations for you to use. Just scroll down the list and select the location of your choice.

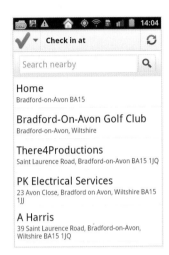

Location information

When you've found your preferred location to utilise as a check-in spot to reveal to your chosen friends, you can pick it from the list. Once selected, this screen appears, giving you information on the location itself. In addition to that, the display offers two primary menu choices. Both provide reassurance on how your privacy is handled because you are able to reveal your presence on your terms.

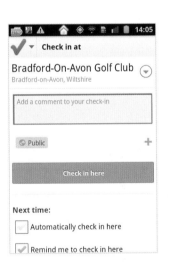

More check in

When you decide to check-in to a location such as a cafe or other meeting place, the program supplies additional options for you to consider. One of which is the automatic selection. This option works closely with your GPS system so that, once you arrive at a location, your phone senses exactly where you are. It then pushes out a signal to your friends, via Latitude, to tell them that you have arrived.

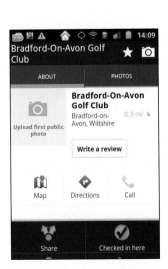

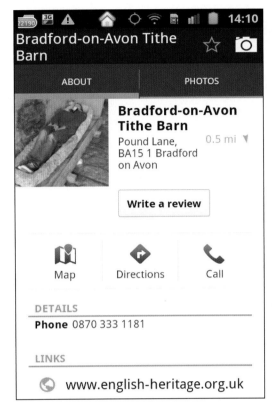

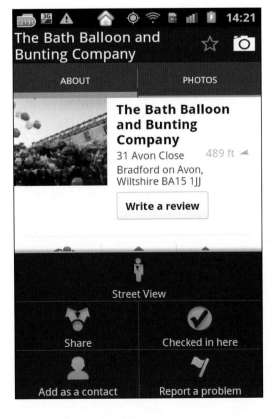

Location details

Accessing the location itself will generate lots of information with many additional options that allows you to interact with it. Apart from being able to call the business location itself, you can generate directions to it from your current position or view it on the map. You can also review it via a text entry and a star rating. More details can be accessed via the internet, while a running distance from the location can be provided on screen.

> "Apart from being able to call the business, you can generate directions to it from your position"

More details

There are further options relating to your current location. When you decide to exit, there's an option to tell your friends that you are leaving by accessing the 'Check out of here' mode. The 'Street View' option provides a street-level map view showing you where you are and what is in the immediate vicinit, and the 'Share this place' option enables you to tell others about the location via social-networking sites and more.

Find your way with Google Navigation

Google's beta version of Navigation in easy steps

It's only in beta at the moment – so it's best to use with a measure of caution – but Navigation is Google's attempt to make all of those drive-type GPS navigation systems **obsolete.** Integrating within its Maps app, Navigation gives you a driving-perspective, internet-connected GPS navigation system with voice guidance.

You can search your location using real English as opposed to the syntax-correct instructions needed in many commercial GPS navigation systems and, when you have sourced your location and are on your way, a Traffic View gives you the traffic status for the journey up ahead. The program also has multiple view options, including a Satellite View to give you a 3D map option, plus a Street View to provide a street-level viewpoint.

The system also enables you to search along your route, so if you need to find a place to eat during your journey, you can plan a suitable stop-off point.

"A driving-perspective navigation system with voice guidance"

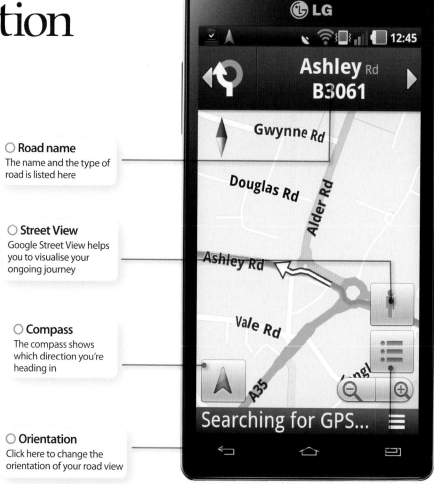

○ **Road name**
The name and the type of road is listed here

○ **Street View**
Google Street View helps you to visualise your ongoing journey

○ **Compass**
The compass shows which direction you're heading in

○ **Orientation**
Click here to change the orientation of your road view

Navigation settings
Get up and running

Initially accessing the Navigation is one of the most difficult parts about using it. Once you are aware how Navigation initiates itself then it's easy to proceed, but if you're a raw beginner you may find yourself throwing up your hands and exclaiming, 'Well, where is it then!?'

To bring the application to a live status, you need to be using Google Maps. Find a location that you want to move towards and access the menu to tell it how to get there. It's at this point that you will find the Navigation option, which will be displayed as a blue arrowhead. Click on that and accept. You will also need to source text-to-speech support from the Play Store if you want to use the voice guidance, but the program takes you directly to the right place to install the correct program. In this case it is an app called

SpeechSynthesis, which is available for free. Downloading it is quick and painless.

Once you've done all that, you're on to the main part of the app. The menu screen allows you to type in your destination of choice, or dictate it if you'd rather just tell your phone where you want to go. You can also get straight into the map view, or select if you want driving directions or walking directions. On top of all this, you can view your recent destinations, click through to your contacts and get directions to their locations, or view any starred destinations you have made.

Navigation really is packed full of fantastic features that will help transform your phone into the ultimate satnav, and you never need to worry about getting lost again!

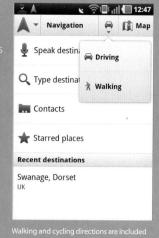

Walking and cycling directions are included

Key features

Text instructions

If you prefer a non-visual alternative to the drive-based navigation instructions and require something rather more detailed, then the text directions option is ideal. Not only does it give you handy turn-by-turn directions, but it also informs you if you have to pay to cross a particular road or bridge. You are also told how long each particular section of the direction lasts in terms of distance, while visual signals help when changing direction.

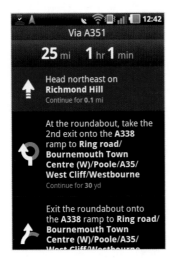

Extra options

There are so many options available in Navigation that it's difficult to list them all here. From the different map views to find alternative routes, everything you should need is covered. There are also a few nice touches including the ability to avoid motorways and toll roads, so you'll never be surprised by any extra costs along the way.

Map View

There are many view options to be had within the Navigation app. This view overlays the driving instructions on a familiar map-like animation. For many drivers, this option may be the most easy to utilise and to follow, principally because it is, for many people, the most familiar, resembling as it does a general paper map. Note that the directions are superimposed onto the roads while voice directions can be toggled on or off.

Street View

If you're using the map view but wish you could get a little closer to the action, then the Street View option will be perfect. Tap the icon of a man and you'll be taken down to ground level, where you can get a much clearer look of what's around you and where you should be heading. The arrow will point you in the correct direction, and this can be a great tool if you want to see exactly where your next turn is.

> "If you prefer an alternative to the drive-based navigation instructions, then the text directions are ideal"

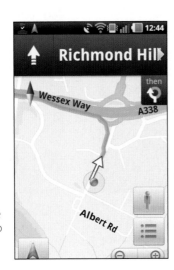

Stop to eat

When you are travelling along your route, it might be a good idea, especially if the journey is a long one, to search for other locations along the way. Navigation enables you to search for any kind of business along your route, or turn on frequently used layers onto the map. These might include essential information such as the location of petrol stations to planned food stops with the locations of restaurants or parking.

Google Earth goes mobile

You've got the whole world in your hands

The Google Earth desktop program first became available back in 2005. It made virtual travel a reality as the entire globe could be viewed through satellite and aerial photography, from the comfort of your desk chair. Now, that same technology has come to your pocket. Google has ported the popular Google Earth program to your Android or iOS phone or tablet. The latest update includes some fun new features like Tour Guides and 3D imagery of popular destinations.

The app is completely free and full of handy little features. By utilising the GPS function on your mobile device, it enables you to easily find your own location and see what's around you. The menu system gives you access to several toggle-able layers like Businesses, Panoramio Photos and Wikipedia entries, so you can discover more information about places.

In addition to this, the latest update of the app includes a 3D buildings feature (only for devices equipped with a dual-core processor). Most major cities worldwide have the 3D building data already completed – including London, Paris, Rome, Madrid, Berlin, New York, Los Angeles, San Francisco, Tokyo and Rio de Janeiro – and the list is ever-growing. This amazing feature allows you to perform virtual fly-through tours of your favourite destinations and see all the sights.

Exploring our globe has never been more convenient or fun. See your childhood home, or visit your holiday destinations ahead of time. Having the entirety of the 'Big Blue Marble' fit into your pocket is truly a world wonder.

Google Earth | A globe on the go!

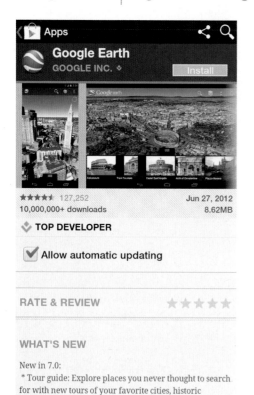

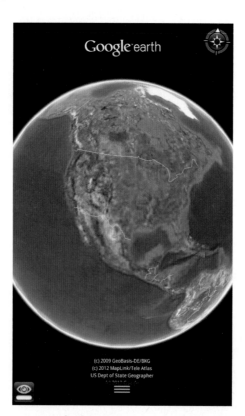

1: Download and install
Download Google Earth from the Play Store or App Store and install it. The app is free, but 3D only works on dual-core devices.

2: Launch the app
When you launch the app for the first time, a brief tutorial will show you how to navigate it. You will begin with a space view of our planet.

3: Check your position
Ensure GPS is enabled on your device. Open the menu and choose 'My Location'. You'll be treated to a dramatic fly-in animation to your location.

Explore your world

Learn how to travel virtually

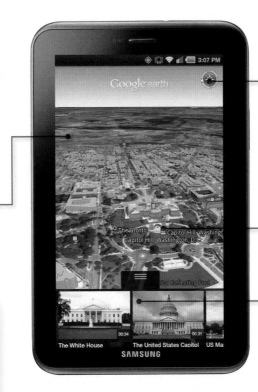

Compass direction
Like a real compass, the top widget always point north. Tapping it will hold your position, but reorient your view so north points to the top of your device

Information icons
Floating icons indicate additional information to explore. The small yellow squares are Place icons and give brief information. The familiar Ws link to Wikipedia entries. These can be turned on or off through the Layers menu

Fly around
The more you explore a location and the more you see, the more there is to discover! The information seems endless and will provide hours of educational entertainment

Fly-around gallery
Slide open the dock on the bottom of the screen to view a gallery of bookmarks and fly-arounds relating to the area. Clicking on one activates the map movement, letting you explore fun new locales

Navigation
The multi-touch navigation of the 3D space of Google Earth can be a bit tricky to master. Swiping is familiar and the view pans as expected. Most touch-screen users also understand the pinch and expand gestures for zooming in and out. There is also the two-finger-twist to rotate the view, and the double finger drag will tilt the view in 3D space.

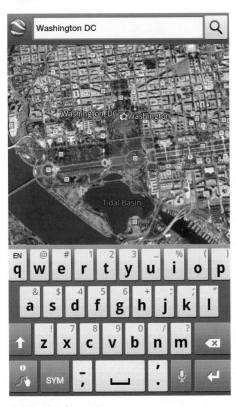

4: Find a location
Open the menu and tap Search. Type in the description of a location, or a street address. Or tap the mic button and speak the location name.

5: Pan and zoom
It supports multi-touch gestures. Swipe to pan the camera around; spread/pinch to zoom in/out. Tap the Look Around icon to easily tilt the view.

6: See more info
Tap any floating icon to see more info on a place. There may be photos, video clips and Wikipedia entries, depending on which Layers are enabled.

Get to know Google Translate

Google Translate is a must-have app if you travel the world

There's no shortage of translation apps on the Google Play Store, but none of them are as comprehensive as Google Translate. The app itself is extremely easy to use and benefits from the stylish design that Google incorporates into all of its apps today.

The app supports over 30 languages and you can translate using any of them, with full support for Google Voice Search and a unique handwriting feature also included.

As you type you'll notice that an instant translation will appear just above what you're typing. However, it's once you've finished entering your text that Google Translate really comes in to its own. There's a voice feature that lets you listen to the translation, along with a sharing option and a full-screen option to see the translation in full.

The Google Translate app is available for both iOS and Android devices, with both platforms supporting corresponding voice features.

"The app supports over 30 languages to translate from or to"

○ **Switch the language**
Press the arrows next to each language to open up a menu, from which you can switch between languages

○ **Get a better view**
Press on the translation to see a full-screen version of it

○ **Copy and paste**
Press on the clipboard icon to copy the translation, from which you can then paste directly into a message

○ **Get some audio**
The microphone icon represents an audio version of the translation that you can listen to, to aid pronunciation

○ **Save a translation**
Use the 'favourite' feature to save certain translations that you can use at a later date

Translate pictures Use your camera

One of the most original features in Google Translate – and one that makes it truly stand out from the other translation apps available on the Google Play Store – is being able to decipher text using the camera on your device.

When in the middle of a translation, you simply need to press on the camera symbol on the bottom of the app to open up your camera. Steadily aim your camera at a passage of text, or just something with a few words on it, and take a picture of it.

Your device will now take you back to the Google Translate app and your picture will be

displayed at the bottom of the app. When you press on the photo, you'll now be asked to highlight the text within the image. Carefully use your finger to follow the outline of the text displayed and then wait for the app to try to decipher the text in the translation box above the picture.

This photo translation feature may seem like a bit of a novelty, but can be a godsend when you're in another country and faced with foreign language signs that you need to translate back to English. So make sure you've got Google Translate installed on your device before going off on your next vacation.

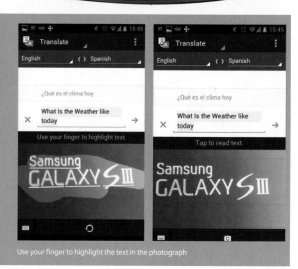
Use your finger to highlight the text in the photograph

Key features

Use your voice
As well as typing phrases to translate, you can use the microphone on your device to speak directly into the app and base the translation on that. Using this feature is a great substitute for having to type out long passages of text, or if you're unsure of the spelling of some words. For the feature to work properly, you need to speak slowly and pronounce all the letters in the words you're saying.

Switch language
Google Translate covers a wide range of languages that you can translate to and from. To choose which ones to use, tap the toolbar at the top of the app and select the languages from the menu. The language you most frequently use will be listed at the very top of the menu, and underneath you'll find the Detect Language, if you're trying to translate from a language you're unfamiliar with.

Translate as you type
As you begin typing, the translation will appear directly above the text you're entering. The app is great at recognising different punctuation marks, so you'll have no trouble translating questions, for example. As you type, you do need to make sure you keep an eye on your spelling of words, as not only can this lead to the app not understanding the word, it can also give you a false translation.

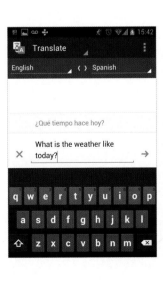

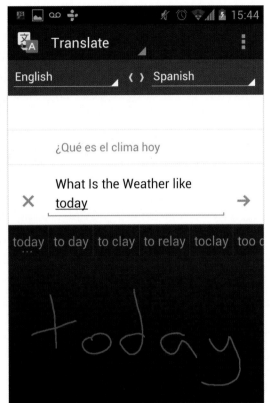

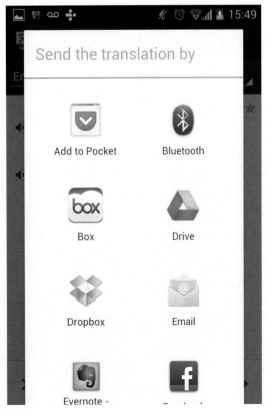

Perfect handwriting
Using the handwriting feature can be a fiddly affair, but if you have clear and legible handwriting, then it can be a nice change from manually typing out text. This feature requires you to use your finger to put words together on the screen, but is best used with a stylus. As you begin writing on the screen, the translation will appear above. It can take a little while to get used to and unless your letters are very clear, the app can have trouble discerning what you've written.

"After translating a phrase, you can share it with a variety of other apps and social media platforms"

Share your translation
After you've translated a phrase, you can share it with a variety of other apps and social media platforms. One of the best uses of this feature is sharing your translation to an email or SMS message, where you can use it within a message you're typing out. If you're translating a large amount of text, send it to Pocket, from which you'll be able to read it at a later date or time that's convenient for you.

Read at any time with Google Reader

Enjoy your favourite content whenever you like with Google Reader

Google Reader is a reading app that lets you keep track of the news and other content that your favourite sites, blogs and publications upload. Whenever new content is added by one of these sites, it'll appear within the app, allowing you to choose when you want to read it. The design of the reading feature is a little basic, but perfect for a bit of light reading on the daily commute. As well as sourcing your own content, the app has a large focus on preloaded content, allowing you to select more content from many other sites, some of which you may not have even heard of. The app also includes a simple but effective filing system where you can manage all the articles you've read, as well as store them in their relative categories. The Google Reader app is exclusively available to Android devices.

"As well as sourcing your own content, the app has a large focus on preloaded content"

○ **Refresh your page**
Press the refresh icon at the top of the app to keep your news feed up to date

○ **Favourite an article**
To 'favourite' an article you've read, press on the star icon next to it

○ **Condense your results**
By pressing on the All Items tab at the top of the app, you can choose the type of content you want to view

○ **Which publication?**
Each piece of news listed includes the source's website or blog name

○ **Delete an item**
Long-press on any one of the entries and select the delete option to remove it from your news feed

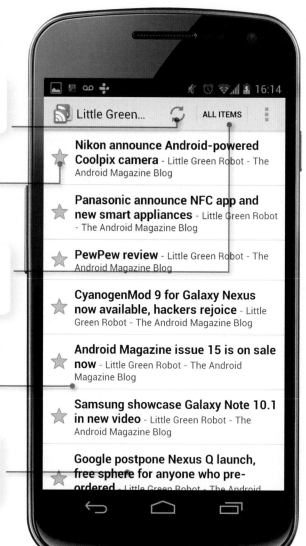

Discover new feeds

Add new content to Reader

By opening the search tab within Google Reader you can start searching for new content by simply entering a few keywords in to a search bar and seeing the results. This feature gets a whole lot deeper, however, even to the extent where you can search for keywords in a specific forum, which can lead to even more content.

Google Reader does a great job of tracking keywords and searches made by other people. It then alerts you to content that it feels you might want to read. But it's important to limit how many keywords you

input in to the app, as it won't take long for Reader to soon fill up your news feed with a wide variety of content.

Another way of searching for content to peruse in Google Reader is through RSS feeds. Don't worry if you aren't familiar with these feeds, as Google Reader has a large selection of preloaded RSS feeds for you to use. When you choose one of these feeds to follow, all the content from that publication or website that's uploaded will automatically appear on your reading list with the other content you've added.

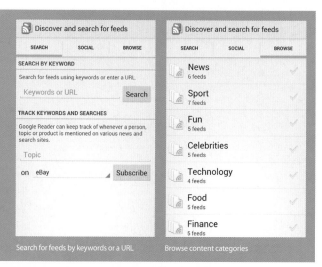

Search for feeds by keywords or a URL   Browse content categories

Key features

Managing accounts

One of the most important aspects of Google Reader is making sure all your various Google accounts are in sync. Having all the accounts in sync will mean that all your content is spread to each of them, even if you aren't currently using them. When you open up Google Reader for the first time, you'll be able to select which account you want to use, but also if you want to sync any other accounts alongside it.

Add some tags

When searching for new content, or looking to appropriately file your current articles, you'll want to make sure you apply some tags to them. These tags will help you search for the content a lot easier, as well as give Google Reader an indication to the type of content that interests you. When searching for new RSS feeds, Google Reader will include these tags as predetermined keywords.

Simplicity of reading

Compared to many news reading apps, including Google's own Currents, the reading section of Google Reader may look a little basic, but it includes all the things you need. Pages can be controlled simply by swiping on your screen, and text can be enlarged, if needed. Once you're done with the article, you can either store it within the app or simply delete it altogether.

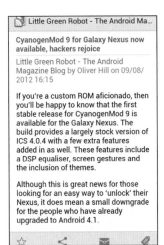

Keeping track of content

When you start sharing your content to the Google Reader app, it can soon fill up, and you might not be able to find specific articles. However, there's a great feature within the app that'll let you keep tabs on all the content you add to it, by automatically putting it into folders. All the content is split into different categories which Google Reader predetermines when you add it.

> "Once you're done with the article, you can either store it within the app or simply delete it"

Audio and video

If you're worried that you won't be able to listen to or watch any audio or video content via the Google Reader app, then there's no need to be, as the app does a good job of catering to multimedia content. Audio has a microphone symbol next to it, allowing you press on the link to listen to it, and any video content will take you to the original source of the video so that you can watch it directly from there.

Shop online with Google Shopper

Need some retail therapy? Try Google Shopper

You know the phrase, 'Shop till you drop'? Well, with a smartphone and Google Shopper there is no need to expend any energy at all because this app enables you to address the shopping experience from a variety of angles.

You can search for actual retailers, find directions to reach them in person or give them a call. You can also search for the product using a voice search module. Once you're there, if you need to dig a little deeper about its available books, CDs, DVDs or other products, you can scan the cover of the product you're interested in and your phone will retrieve an array of information relating to it.

Similarly, rather than scanning an item's cover (especially if you chosen product is big and bulky), you can scan its barcode to find similar information. Detailed product information can also be found along with prices and, if you find a bargain, you can also share this information with your friends.

"Shopper enables you to address shopping from many angles"

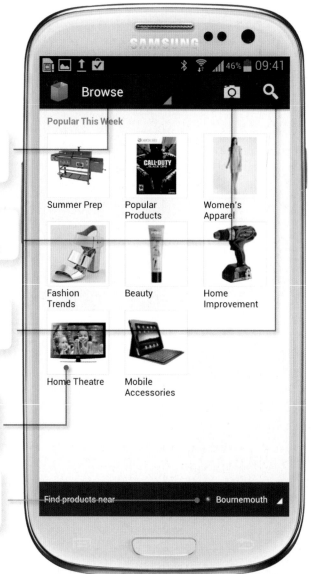

○ **Options**
This menu allows you to browse items, view you lists and more

○ **Camera**
Take a picture of an item, and let Shopper do the searching for you

○ **Search**
Tap the magnifying glass to search for a specific item

○ **Featured items**
This set of images provides handy subjects to help your product search

○ **Nearby offers**
Local offers – which often have a time limit – can be found here

Point and scan

Find information on any product you can see

Finding the right product at the right price is what the shopping experience is all about. Nowadays, walking into a shop on the high street is not always enough. But what if your local shop doesn't stock the item in the first place? Where can you buy it from?

Google Shopper's scanning feature can come into its own for such occasions. The ability to scan the front cover of a book, for example, means that if you're visiting a friend and see a tome that appeals, you just need to point the camera's phone at

the book cover and press the on-screen camera button. The screen of your phone will then shift into Camera mode and you will be able to see an image of the book cover. Once scanned, the screen will change as the book is recognised in the database and the cover will reappear in a rather trim, tidied-up format with the book's full name and if it is a hardback or paperback. You can tag the book with a star to attach it to a priority list, share information with friends, compare prices and even order an eBook version.

Scan the product using the camera…

…and more information appears in the app

Inside Google Shopper

Speak to me

Many people enjoy the shopping experience while others find it excruciating. If you fit into the latter category then the quicker you can find the product for you and closest place to source it, the better. Google Shopper's Voice Search is ideal for this. After tapping the magnifying glass icon to search, tap on the microphone and you can dictate the item you're looking for, and the results will then be displayed.

History

If you're viewing a large number of items, and want to go back to something you saw earlier to compare or purchase, the History option is ideal. This will bring up a clear list of all the recently viewed items, allowing you easy access to something you may have forgotten to add to your Shopping List earlier. It will also show you whether you simply searched for the item, took a picture or scanned a barcode.

Shopping list

If you're on the prowl for a range of different products, then the Shopping List option will be of use to you. By tapping the 'Save to list' option, you can go back and view the items you've saved at a later date. This will allow you to compare items, or return after pay day to the items you like. It is also easy to delete items from your shopping list if you decide you've changed your mind.

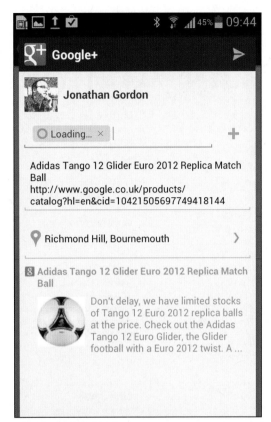

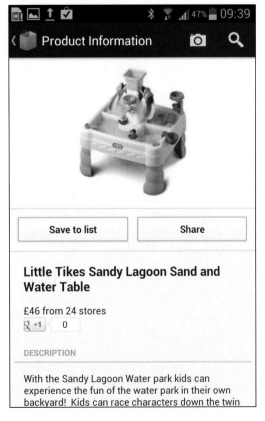

Share your find

If you come across a particular item or deal that you're so impressed with that you feel you need to share it with the world, you can. You're offered a number of options, including via email, in a message, on Facebook, or as shown here, on Google+. Simply select Google+ from the option and a post will be created for you, allowing others to see what you've been shopping for, and purchase the item themselves if they so wish.

"Tap on the microphone and you can dictate what you're looking for, and the results will then be displayed"

Product details

Once you've found an item you like the look of, you're offered up a range of options and information. First off there's a detailed product description, so you know what you'll be getting. You can save the item to a list, or share it, and if you have a Google+ account, you can +1 it. You can then take a look at stores nearby that have the item in stock, and for how much. You can even find the product number if you need it.

Introducing Google Analytics for Android

Check your website stats 24 hours a day, no matter where you are

Google Analytics for Android offers the obvious advantage of being built by the same company that builds the operating system it runs on. It contains many of the major features of its desktop counterpart and will serve as a useful assistant for those who need to keep an eye on their website statistics when away from their desktop computer.

At the time of writing, it is only available for Android devices, but the solution bears all of the hallmarks of its big brother, the most popular web analytics service on the planet.

You can run multiple dashboards detailing everything from unique visitors to average visit duration to goal stats, and the presentation has been perfectly tailored for the smaller mobile screen. Indeed, it is easier to use than the full solution and once you get used to it, the app will be a daily-use solution.

The best analytics service has gone mobile with a bang!

"The best analytics service has gone mobile with a bang"

○ **Multiple dashboards**
You can create multiple dashboards to monitor numerous types of site stats

○ **Real-time stats**
See how many people are visiting your website at this moment with one tap

○ **All about history**
The presentation lends itself well to showing you the true momentum behind your website over a period of time

○ **In the detail**
A simple tap will bring up textual and numeric data within the dashboard itself

○ **Clever alerts**
The automatic alerts show you information about specific areas and are extremely useful

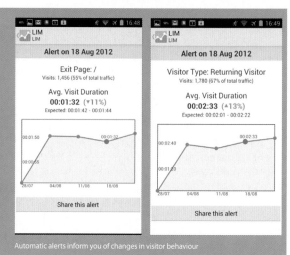

Grow your site
Look back to move forwards

To truly understand the way your website is performing, you need to comprehend how all of the stats detailed within Google Analytics can help you.

When you tap an automatic alert you will be offered a graph showing a historical view of the number pertaining to that particular behaviour. You will be able to see if your visitor duration is increasing and you can then start to understand if they enjoy the content you are creating.

With this information you can then look at the most popular content and work out not only what makes your visitors come to you in the first place but also what makes them stick around to read your work. History is important when trying to build momentum. Throughout Google Analytics you will be given all of the information you need to know if you are on the right track.

The simplicity of the presentation, when married to the complex data, works perfectly when you have a few spare minutes to study exactly what is happening.

Google Analytics is all about data and enabling you to use it to your advantage, so take some time to work with the greatest feature of Analytics for Android.

Automatic alerts inform you of changes in visitor behaviour

Key features

Real-time tracking

The accuracy and timeliness of the tracking within each dashboard is second to none. It'll let you manage your bandwidth allowance and understand how well received your web content is. All of the tracking is available on one screen, which ensures that you can view all of the data you need with minimum fuss. You can set up many different tracking tools which will all work together seamlessly.

Automatic alerts

Alerts can be created to highlight all sorts of targets and to ensure that you are fully aware of what is happening on your website. The level of accuracy shown is detailed yet simple to read and you can share this data via any method that is installed on your Android device. The alerts section is possibly more useful than any other and ensures that you are up to date with every change as it occurs.

Active visitors

At any time you can view the number of active visitors on your site and also see how they got there in the first place. Direct visitors will be shown alongside those who came from other services. The top active pages are also shown, detailing which pages your visitors are reading now. This is an addictive part of Google Analytics. It only takes a couple of taps to see what is happening at any given time.

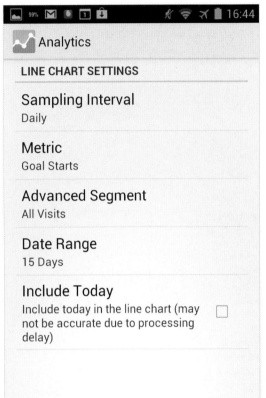

Goals are important

All webmasters should set goals for their websites. With Google Analytics, you have the ability to create multiple goals and to view how well you are succeeding. The type of goal that you set can be tailored perfectly for your type of website. The more goals you create, the more you will understand the way they work and the more you will benefit from the results. It is impossible to grow a site without knowing how successful it already is. Analytics lets you do this.

> "The more goals you create, the more you will understand the way they work and benefit from them"

Ease of use

Ease of use may not appear to be a feature, as such, but when it is built in to the core of a solution it can make all of the difference in daily use. The fact that you can swipe between the main features so easily and that you can tap to gain more information immediately makes Google Analytics much more usable when you are travelling and the data, somehow, feels more immediate.

Introducing Google Currents

Get the news that matters to you with Google Currents

Google Currents is a minimalist news reading app that packs in content from hundreds, if not thousands, of publications all over the world. The app allows users to customise how they want to read the news that matters to them, by offering a variety of categories to explore, and showcasing articles in an easy-to-read and simple layout. A full range of media files are supported, meaning that you can watch, read and listen to the latest news.

Most major newspapers have their very own page within the Currents app, so users can see the latest news feed for each publication without needing to download each and every corresponding app. The app is available for both iPhone and Android users, with Android users benefitting from being able to sync their Currents library with a host of other Google apps that can be downloaded from the Play Store.

> "Google Currents allows users to customise how they want to read the news that matters to them"

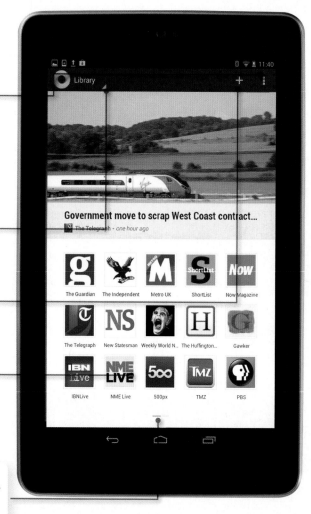

Manage your library
Press the option button at the top right of the app to search through articles and manage your library

Quick shortcuts
The arrow at the top left of the app gives you access to the Trending and Favourites sections

Add a publication
Press on the '+' symbol to see some of the publications you can add to your home screen

Choose a publication
Press on one of the icons to be taken to that publication's dedicated section within the Google Currents app

Select a page
The blue bar at the bottom of the app depicts which page you're currently on. Use your finger to scroll between pages

Adding new publications
Expand your Google Currents library

One of the best things about Google Currents is the variety of articles and publications it caters to. Each publication it showcases has its own dedicated page, and every article is formatted to fit in with the rest of the Currents app. Even though it may look like you have plenty of publications to keep you occupied, by going through a few menus you can expand your library tenfold.

Although many well-known newspapers are already displayed, by accessing the 'Add Publications' page you can choose to add more Currents-supported publications. You'll also uncover many smaller, or independent, publications that have been given the Google Currents treatment, all of which can be found in the same series of menus. While you're deliberating on which publications you want to add to your library, you can also go the other way and remove unwanted publications from the app.

Each publication is classified by its category, and you can go directly to your category of interest to exclusively add new publications from there. With so much on offer, you will be surprised with how much there is to explore.

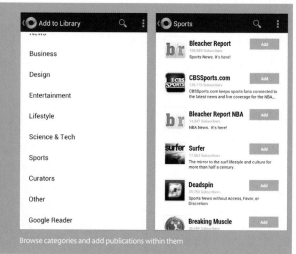

Browse categories and add publications within them

Key features

Trending articles

The Trending section of the app showcases some of the most popular articles in the past 24 hours from a wide range of sources. These articles aren't listed in any particular order, but it gives a great overview of what other people are reading. You can also customise this page so that your trending section will only show articles in the categories that are of interest to you.

Expand media

Google Currents does a great job of displaying a wide range of media files within the app. Videos load up quick and don't tend to buffer for long periods of time. Audio interviews can be opened in a third-party media player, and images can be viewed in both landscape and portrait mode. Just be careful when watching videos when on a 3G network as it uses a lot of data.

Easy to read

Google Currents adopts its own reading layout for articles, regardless of the source. The design is simple and minimalist. Users can skip through the various pages of an article with a swipe of a finger, and load pictures and other media by just pressing on them. While reading, users can also edit the layout of the article to make text bigger for those who are short-sighted.

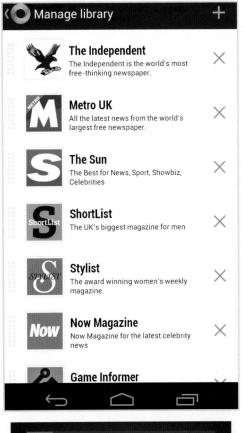

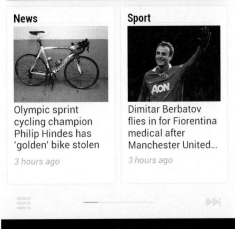

Manage library

When you first start using the Google Currents app, you'll more than likely be overwhelmed by the sheer variety of publications that are available through it, some of which may not be to your interest. By going through the app's settings menu, you can change the preloaded publications that will be displayed whenever you open up the app. This can be particularly helpful if you want to use the app to read articles from just one or two publications.

> "The Trending section of the app showcases some of the most popular articles in the past 24 hours from a wide range of sources"

Publication overview

If you're looking to just catch up with the latest headlines from a few publications, you can individually track each publication's news feed through the app. By opening up a certain publication, you'll be able to see the last couple of articles that were added to Google Currents from the publication. Each article can then be read in full. This feature is a little hard to manage if you have hundreds of different publications enabled within the app.

Get the most out of Blogger

Get your fingers busy with Google's blogging utility

There are many things we love to talk about, and these include ourselves, our interests and hobbies, and the points of view we hold. Blogging is one way to broadcast these feelings. More to the point, blogging enables us to contact like-minded people who can not only sympathise with our views but also increase and enhance that knowledge. Because the internet is such a wide-ranging service, the chances of finding other people out there who share those views are pretty high.

Whether you're talking to fellow fans of a certain football team or people who love to collect shoes, blogs are a great way to keep interests alive. So, if you grow tomatoes and love to blog that interest, chances are that you will draw other tomato growing fans to you along with new information, hints and tips on the subject. Google's Blogger is an ideal tool to get you and your interests online.

"Blogging enables us to contact people who can sympathise with our views"

Manage Blogs
You can manage your blogs here by changing their content and design

Picture
Add a picture and modify your personal profile details

Create
If you wish to create a new post for your blog, simply tap on this icon

Blog updates
If you have joined other blogs, then details will be listed here

A new blog Creating your first blog

Creating a blog is pretty straightforward – if you follow the Google Blogger screens. When you enter the Blogger software just click on the 'Create Blog' button and you will be taken to a new screen which will ask you to type in a name for your new blog. Once done, you will need to give it a web address. Chances are that the address you would want might already be taken, so the software will do its best to find you an alternative that's similar to your desired address.

Once done, you will be taken to a new screen listing a range of templates. These

will offer a range of styles. Examine them carefully because, depending on the style of your blog, one might be more applicable to you and your blog's content than the others.

Now start blogging. A new screen then appears asking you give your first blog a title. A large space underneath is presented for you to type within. Before you post your very first blog, you can give it tags to add the current date and time, and select if users can add comments to it if they so wish. Click 'Post' to post your blog and you're off and running!

You can write and update blogs in-app...   ...as well as add pictures and locations

Blogger's best bits

Instant blog

One of the great things about blogging is the immediacy of the inherent technology. To be able to not only report on events but to constantly update those details means that your readers will be able to interact with you and the changing circumstances of your post. To have and maintain a blog and then combine that with the mobility of a smartphone just adds to the 'live' aspect of your blog.

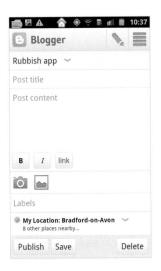

Current location

Part of the power of blogging while you are mobile is sharing – not only your thoughts and views on your journey or relating what you can see, but also giving a sense of the immediacy of your words with a visualisation of your current location. You can trigger a feature within your blog that gives a continuous update on your current location by using your mobile phone's built-in GPS feature to provide a fix.

"To have a blog and then combine that with the mobility of a smartphone just adds to the 'live' aspect of your blog"

Lots of posts

Part of the problem of a successful blog is the potential size. After all, if you have a lot to say, space can be taken up quickly. Add more views and you have the beginning of a great blog but also an insight into how packed with information such a blog might become. This screen gives you an easily accessible list of topics that you can jump to, to either add to or edit.

Pictures

Filling your blogs with text is just one element of what you can provide to your readers. The visual element is a very powerful tool that can provide more explanation and a major impact in the right circumstances. To insert pictures just press the camera icon on the blog page. Then you can include photos in your post by taking a picture with your camera within the Blogger app, or choosing one from your gallery.

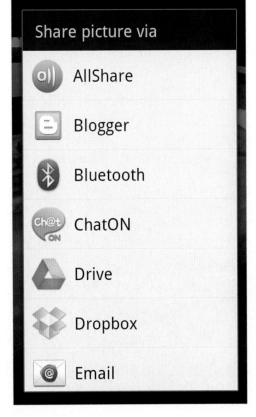

Share

The immediacy that you need your readers to experience when they load up and read your blog is also required by you during its creation, as you fill the blog with text and pictures. If you see a relevant picture that you feel could enhance your blog then you can send photos (and links, for that matter) directly to your blog by selecting Blogger from the Options menus of apps like your web browser and photo gallery.

Upload photos to Picasa

Find out how you can quickly upload photos from your phone to your Picasa account online

The ability to take high-quality photos and share them online instantly is one of the greatest things about a smartphone. Google runs two services that are tightly integrated with Android that enable you to do this. This most well known and established one is Picasa. Originally known as a powerful desktop photo management and editing application, the service subsequently expanded to an online photo album into which you could place all your snaps.

With Google's recent move towards its Google+ social networking service, Picasa is now partly integrated into this as well. This means that when you upload an image from your phone or tablet to Picasa, it will be stored in your Google+ account as well, by default.

The integration of Picasa into Android on mobile devices is quite deep. You don't need any additional software or apps installed on your phone or tablet to use the service, and you won't even need to create a unique Picasa account. Simply use your normal Google account details – the same account you added when you set up your Android device.

It means you can upload and share your images with the world with just a few taps on the screen. This tutorial explains the steps you need to make all the magic happen.

Picasa | Upload photos to Picasa

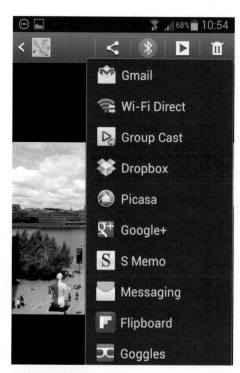

1: Locate your images
On your Android phone, locate the photo(s) to upload. Open the Gallery app and browse to the Camera folder to see the shots you've taken.

2: Pick a picture
Tap a photo to select it, or hold down on one then tap others to choose them. Tap the screen to show the menu bar with sharing options.

3: The Picasa option
Tap the Share icon. You might need to hit 'See all' to see the Picasa option. It will move toward the top of the list of options once you start using it.

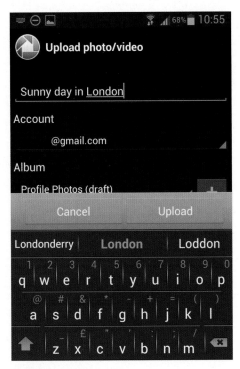

4: Enter a title

Tap on Picasa, then enter a title for your shot. This will help it be identified once it is online. Tap in the box and start typing.

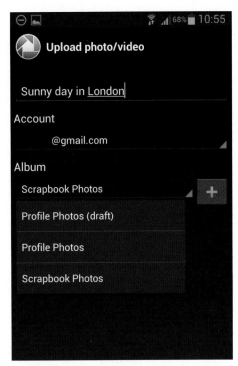

5: Choose an album

You can also select an album to upload the image to. Choose from the predefined albums or tap the green '+' icon to create a new one.

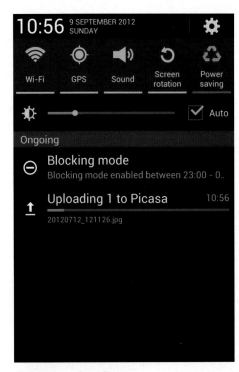

6: Start uploading

Now hit the Upload button and your photo will start uploading to Picasa. Open the notification pane on your phone to see its progress.

7: View on Picasa

You can now view the image in your desktop browser at **picasaweb.google.com**. Log in with your Google account to manage the album.

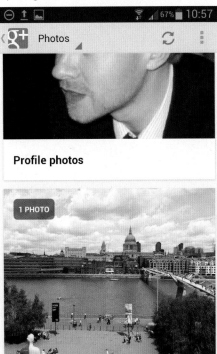

8: And on Google+

The image is also added to your Google+ account. Open the app on your phone to see that it is posted in the relevant album.

9: Add comments

In Google+ you can tap on photos and add comments. Other users can do the same, so adjust your privacy settings if you don't want this.

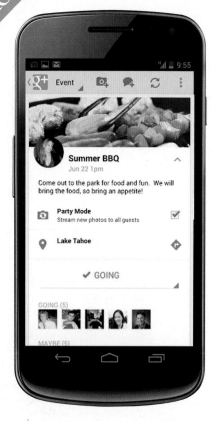

Connect to the Google+ network

Google's social media app has undergone plenty of changes

Google's very own social network, Google+ has seen plenty of updates recently, and its fan base just keeps on growing. A lot of this popularity is due to the social media sites coming as a stock app on most Android phones. It's so simple to connect and share with everyone you know. The way we use messaging has improved, and the overall experience is a whole lot easier to use, especially considering the excellent features it has to offer.

For those who are still new to Google+, the messaging system is rather easy to get to grips with, and a lot of the social media features are explained when you first uncover them. With the Jelly Bean update coming out on more devices all the time, Google+ has seen plenty of new features added to it, as well as some of its older features refined to make them a little easier to use, no matter what device you're using.

In this tutorial, we'll guide you through some of the old features that have been altered as well as show you just how to use all the great new features that have been added.

Google+ | Stay social with Google's revamped service

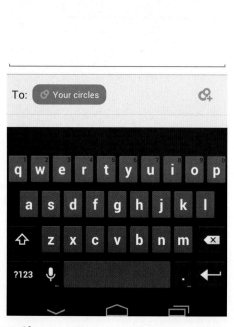

1: Share a post
There are plenty of features to uncover in Google+. Adding new members to your circle can be performed here.

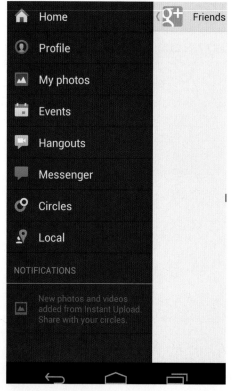

2: Fast new menu
By opening up the side menu you'll notice a few changes have been made. The menu is faster to navigate and new sub menus have been added.

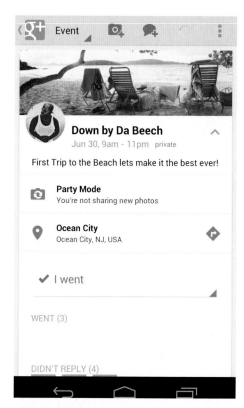

3: Events and parties
The improved events page make creating social events a lot easier. You can invite people on your contact list, or by searching other Google apps.

Inside the Google+ app

Keeping close to your friends and family just got easier

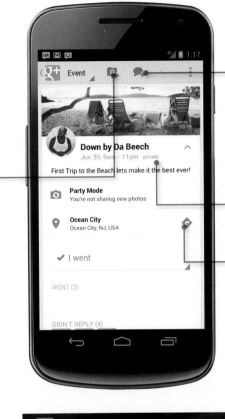

○ **Add new photos**

To showcase some of your photos of your party, press on the camera icon at the top of the app. This will take you directly to the Gallery app where you'll be able to upload photos, or add them from other social media sites

New notifications

Desktop users of Google+ will already be familiar with the '+1' (ie share) button that can be used to send updates to friends about things you've discovered. With the Jelly Bean update, you can now '+1' directly from the new and improved notifications panel.

○ **Invite some friends**

You can invite people to your party, as well as message them at the same time by selecting the speech bubble icon at the top of the list. Confirm everyone you want to add to your party, and press the OK button once done

○ **Public or private**

If you don't want everyone turning up to your private party, then make sure that it isn't set to public. The little blue writing next to the time and date indicates whether the party is public or private to your friends. Pressing it will alternate between the two

○ **Tag your location**

While in Party Mode, you can add a location to your party by selecting the Google Maps symbol halfway down the page. Pressing on this symbol will open up Google Maps, from which you'll be able to select your exact location

4: Improved mass messaging

With the new Jelly Bean update in place, adding people to a conversation is a whole lot easier, and the keyboard doesn't crash as it sometimes did.

5: Mass video chat

Using your front-facing camera, you can start a video chat with someone, and add other people to the conversation too.

6: Easier to navigate photo streams

The photo album app responds a lot quicker than it previously did, meaning that scrolling through large quantities of photos is easier than ever.

Using Messenger in Google+

Similar to IM, the Messenger feature in Google+ is feature packed

Google+ has come on in leaps and bounds in the past year or so, with more people than ever joining up to the social media phenomenon. Google is constantly expanding and exploring a range of new features it can implement into the app – and with Video Hangouts being a fantastic idea, the firm is doing just that. One of the more subtle features implemented by Google is the Messenger feature; although from the outside it looks a little basic, it packs in a whole host of features waiting to be explored.

The Messenger section of G+ works in the same way as most other instant messenger apps work; but with Google's backing, the Messenger service has a few novel tweaks to make it stand out. You can open up a series of conversations with any of the contacts you've made on the social media service, or even send a message to a friend to get them to join. There's even a simple photo-sharing system that many similar apps don't offer.

In this tutorial we'll be taking you through the basics of the G+ Messenger feature, and showing you the features that make this service truly great.

Google+ | Master the Messenger feature

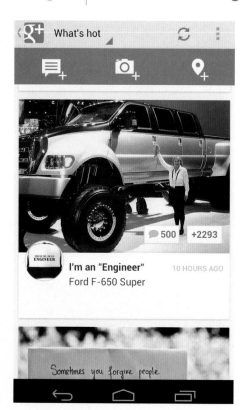

1: Open the app
If it's the first time you've opened the app, you'll need to create an account. If not, the app will launch directly to the home screen.

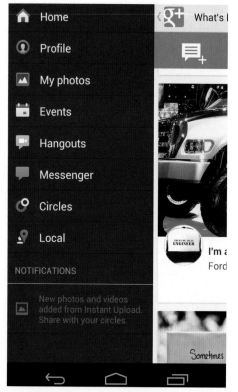

2: Find Messenger section
On the top left, press on the G+ symbol and then select the Messenger option (usually near the bottom, depending on your device).

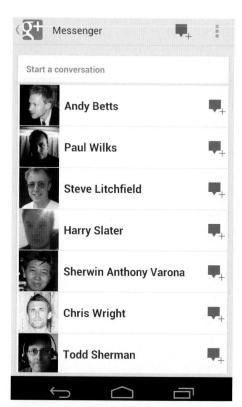

3: Start a conversation
You'll now see a list of the contacts you talk to regularly. To start a conversation, select a contact or search for one using the top toolbar.

Managing your conversations

Start chatting with several people

○ **No multi-chat**
G+ does not include a multi-chat feature within its Messenger system. If you want to chat with multiple people at the same time, you should consider starting a Video Hangout instead

Managing notifications
If you've plenty of conversations open, or other people are contacting you through G+, you'll soon become annoyed with the amount of notifications you're receiving. You can disable or limit them by choosing the option in the G+ settings menu.

○ **Current conversations**
Any conversations you currently have open will be listed at the top of the screen. If you have several conversations open at any one time, you'll receive a notification when someone has responded

○ **Add a new contact**
If you can't find a contact you want to message, or you want to add someone completely new, select the speech bubble icon at the top of the app

○ **Start a conversation**
To start a conversation, simply press on the picture of any contact in the list. Once pressed, a new open conversation bar will appear at the top of the app

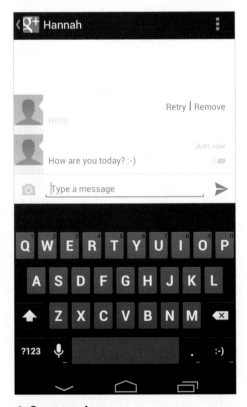

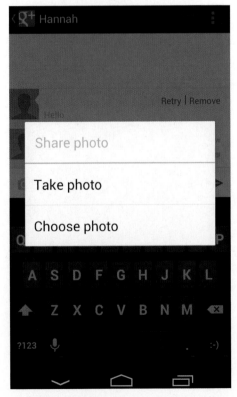

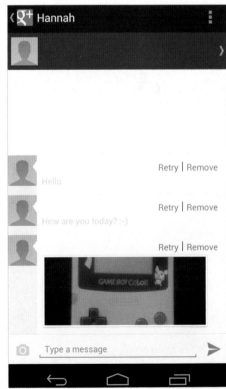

4: Start typing
You can begin typing, as with any other IM app. When you receive a reply, you'll see the profile picture of your correspondent and their message.

5: Adding a photo
Next to the typing bar is a camera icon. Pressing this will let you directly open up the camera on your device and share a photo.

6: Error messages
Sometimes your messages might not send. Press the Retry button next to your failed message, or quit the conversation and start a new one.

Special trial offer

Enjoyed this book?

✔ Gmail ✔ Maps ✔ Chrome ✔ Google Drive ✔ Google+
100% unofficial
Google
Tips & Tricks
Unlock the power of the world's most amazing free apps

Updated for Google Play & Google Drive

500 essential hints and tips inside

Exclusive offer for new

Try 3 issues for just £5*